CONTENTS

ACKNOWLEDGMENTS

Special appreciation goes to David H. Gleaves, Ph.D., whose input has been instrumental in making sure the most current studies and treatments have been included in this book.

In preparing this volume I have reviewed books, journal and mass media articles, Internet sites, monographs and studies by the score to distill current opinion and research findings, and I have carefully tried to give full attribution to authors and researchers whose work I have consulted. Among those who have been especially helpful in sending material, or who have contributed significantly to the literature—and thus indirectly to the success of this book—are Paul E. Garfinkel, M.D.; David M. Garner, Ph.D.; Paul Ernsberger, Ph.D.; George A. Bray, M.D.; D. A. Booth, Ph.D.; Kelly D. Brownell, Ph.D.; Maria P. P. Root, Ph.D.; Patricia Fallon, Ph.D.; William N. Friedrich, Ph.D.; Patricia A. Neuman, Ed.S.; Patricia A. Halvorson, Ph.D.; Janet Polivy, Ph.D.; W. J. Kenneth Rockwell, M.D.; Gerald F. M. Russell, M.D.; the Renfrew Centers; and the National Association to Advance Fat Acceptance, Inc. (NAAFA). I owe much to the Internet Grateful Med search service for making so much material readily accessible to researchers.

I fear there are some whose contributions I have failed to acknowledge. I hope they will forgive me; I am grateful to them all.

—Dana K. Cassell

FOREWORD

Never before in our society has so much attention been paid to what we might call the disorders of eating and/or weight regulation. Not coincidentally, our society is currently preoccupied with thinness, dieting and health, and a great industry has arisen to take advantage of the fear of fatness that has spread through developed nations. No-calorie or low-calorie foods and drinks, sugarless sweeteners and pills sold as appetite suppressants pour onto the market. Writers make fortunes propagating new diets, and health clubs and the markets of exercise machines sell people the presumed benefits of "working out."

The eating disorders category of the current *Diagnostic and Statistical Manual of Mental Disorders (DSM),* published by the American Psychiatric Association, includes the two most well-known eating disorders, anorexia and bulimia nervosa, as well as a residual category called eating disorder not otherwise specified. A provisional diagnostic category called binge eating disorder was added to the most recent version of the *DSM.* Obesity, although technically not an eating disorder, is a much more common problem, affecting at least one-third of the U.S. population; this prevalence has increased from about one-quarter of the population in just the past 20 years.

The literal definition of anorexia nervosa is loss of *appetite* (anorexia) of *nervous,* or *emotional,* origin (nervosa). Bulimia can be literally defined as *hunger with nervosa,* again implying an emotional origin. However both of these terms are probably misnomers because the typical anorexic may *not* experience a loss of appetite (and, in fact, may be preoccupied with food), and for the sufferer of bulimia, the most frustrating part of the disorder may be that he or she binge eats even when not hungry.

In terms of invariable clinical observations with these disorders, both are characterized by gross disturbances in eating behavior and highly characteristic extreme concerns about shape and weight. In both disorders, self-esteem is influenced to a great degree by body weight and shape. These similarities have led some researchers to suggest that the disorders are simply variations on a common theme; however, according to the *DSM,* the disorders are classified as distinct categories, and there are two subtypes of each. With anorexia nervosa, there are the restricting and binge-eating/purging subtypes. With bulimia nervosa, there are purging and nonpurging subtypes.

Binge-eating disorder is characterized by out-of-control binge eating in the absence of any purgative behaviors. Obesity, often minimally defined as being 20 percent above expected weight, is a state rather than a disorder per se, although a sizable proportion of obese individuals may engage in binge eating and may even meet the diagnostic criteria for binge-eating disorder. Conversely, most people with binge-eating disorder are clinically obese.

In addition to the core eating and body image-related psychopathology of the eating disorders and obesity, a variety of additional problems, including depression, anxiety, obsessive-compulsive behavior, post-traumatic stress disorder and substance use, has been described in the related literature. Interpersonal and family problems and personality disorders are also common.

What has happened in our century to bring on all this self-destructive—and family destructive—behavior? Despite earliest attempts to find strictly biological or intrapsychic explanations, our recently developed understanding of the role of cultural factors in the development and maintenance of eating disorders leads one to wonder whether the proper subject for treatment is the individual patient or society as a whole. The most popular etiological explanation of eating disorders and obesity is known as the biopsychosocial model; that is, there is no simplistic single factor explanation. Rather, persons develop eating or weight disorders due to a variety of biological, psychological and social influences, and the degree to which each of these types of influences affects a person may differ depending on the disorder and the individual.

Just as the etiology of eating and weight disorders may be complex and multiply determined, so may the treatment need to be complex and multi-faceted. In other words, most successful treatments integrate features that address both biological (including nutritional) and psychological factors, and even social factors. Again, the degree to which treatment of different biological, psychological or social factors is necessary seems to depend both on the disorder and the individual.

For years, scientific literature on eating disorders and obesity was regrettably separated. The obesity field had been dominated by perspectives from medicine and health risk concerns, whereas the eating disorders field had its roots in the social sciences. As a consequence of this division, persons working in the fields had very few shared interests and had different conceptualization of the etiology, assessment and treatment of these arguably related conditions.

This gap in the literature has fortunately begun to close in recent years. Testaments to this closure include the publication of Brownell and Fairburn's *Eating Disorders and Obesity: A Comprehensive Handbook* (1995); the journal *Eating and Weight Disorders: Studies on Anorexia, Bulimia, and Obesity; The Encyclopedia of Obesity and Eating Disorders, Second Edition* (2000); and *Food for Thought: The Sourcebook for Obesity and Eating Disorders.* This new edition of the latter is meant, then, to further bridge the gap between the literature on obesity and eating disorders. It is also meant to bring an understanding to subjects on which expert researchers both have and have not been able to agree. Under these circumstances it seems that the encyclopedic approach is especially useful, for whereas an encyclopedia cannot give exhaustive information about any subject, it can bring crucial questions about that subject into focus, give the reader a reasonably accurate "bottom line" and list further reading for those who want to know more.

In the past decade, there have been numerous developments in the obesity and eating disorders field; some have been positive, others negative. We have seen the explosion of use of antiobesity medications, only to have them banned due to harmful physical effects. Recent research has questioned the assumed continuity models of eating disorders, shed new light on the biological bases of anorexia and bulimia and increased attention to the treatment of eating disordered individuals with a history of sexual trauma and the controversies associated with doing so. We have also recently gained a much better understanding of which prevention efforts may be successful, which may not and which may actually be harmful. As a testament of the amount of professional knowledge and interest that now exists regarding these disorders, there are now at least five journals devoted exclusively to the study, prevention and/or treatment of eating and/or weight disorders, and several others focused on related problems.

So this sourcebook is timely and valuable. It aims to be especially helpful to students, parents, the eating disorder sufferer in search of knowledge and referral information and the prospective consumer of a vast variety of goods and services that purport to change our eating patterns or transform our bodies (in many cases without changing eating patterns). It will provide insights and accurate resources to those in need. Last but not least, I recommend that readers consult the references included throughout the book and the numerous appendixes.

—David H. Gleaves, Ph.D.
Texas A&M University

PART I

OBESITY AND EATING DISORDERS

CHAPTER 1

AN OVERVIEW OF THE HISTORY OF OBESITY AND EATING DISORDERS

ATTITUDES TOWARD OBESITY AND EATING DISORDERS THROUGHOUT HISTORY

Fashions shift in human beauty as they do in clothes and architecture, a fact pointed out by Anne Scott Beller in her natural history of obesity, *Fat & Thin* (now out of print). Physical proportions strived for and glorified during one era or generation are avoided, even stigmatized, in another.

HILDE BRUCH, one of the U.S.'s earliest and most influential experts in the field, stressed that today's concern about obesity is not new, nor has it always been a negative concern. In her classic book *Eating Disorders,* she noted that the oldest known representation of the human form, the "Venus of Willendorf" (Paleolithic period [20,000 to 30,000 B.C.], found in Willendorf, Austria), is the figure of "an extremely obese woman with large breasts and an enormous abdomen." Other Paleolithic figures represent similar fat women. The idealization of obesity in women continued into the Neolithic period. Prehistoric Greek, Babylonian and Egyptian sculptures also indicate preference or artistic admiration for women with large abdomens and heavy hips and thighs, according to Bruch.

What today's researchers cannot be sure of is whether these archaeological "goddesses" represented women's actual appearances or whether they reflected a cultural ideal. They have usually been taken as symbolic representations of abundance and fertility at a period in human history when famine was an ever-present possibility. But some researchers have surmised that these figures were based on actual models. In any case, Bruch explained, in every age and in every land, people have starved, and typically, during hard times, obesity has emerged as a kind of cultural goal or desirable state.

In very poor societies, where sufficient food is consistently available only to the privileged few, it attains high value and becomes a symbol of wealth and stature. Thus, obesity becomes the prime indicator of the person's prosperity and may become a prestigious and admired characteristic. Research has shown that the southern African's dream was to be fat himself as well as to have a fat wife and children and fat cattle. Bruch discovered during her anthropological research that in some Polynesian cultures it was considered a sign of great distinction to be so well nourished as to become fat. "Malaysian kings were very large and fat; they were treated with special massages and exercises to keep them in good health."

Not only was obesity a condition to be aspired to where hunger was the norm, but gluttony was a common practice during celebrations whenever possible, according to anthropologists. After long periods of not having enough to eat, anticipation of holiday feasting brought forth expressions like: "We shall be glad, we shall eat until we vomit." "We shall eat until our bellies swell out and we can no longer stand."

Bruch adds that ancient travelers reported African cultures in which young girls at puberty were sent to fattening houses to make them ready for marriage. The fatter a girl grew, the more beautiful she was considered, although the men were expected to remain athletic and slim. The king's mother and his wives competed with one another as to who should be the fattest. They took no exercise and were carried in litters when going from place to place.

But the attitude that "fatter is better" did not die out with those primitive societies. Early in the 20th century, when the U.S.'s immigrant masses were struggling to overcome their own hunger and poverty, fat once again became an ideal. These poor immigrant mothers saw fat children as symbols of success. But they did not call their children fat; they bragged that they were "solid" or "husky" or "hefty." Author Harry Golden, who grew up in that environment, relates, "I, too, was a husky kid and when I worried about it, my mother consoled me with the observation, 'In America, the fat man is the boss and the skinny kid is the bookkeeper.'"

Paradoxically, during prosperous times and in affluent societies, obesity is commonly associated with poverty and lower-class status. Today, for example, the American ideal is to be thin, and there is much concern about obesity. The privileged classes of the Western world have been preoccupied since World War II with the problem of staying slim in the midst of all this abundance.

And such was the case during other historical periods of prosperity. The ancient Greeks of the classical age envied their cultural predecessors, the Cretans, for having known of a drug that permitted them to stay slim while eating as much as they wanted. Leaders in Sparta were stern taskmasters in their attitude toward obesity. Young people were examined in the nude once a month, and those who had gained weight were forced to exercise. The Athenians also frowned upon obesity. Socrates is said to have danced every morning in order to keep slim, and Plato was forgiven his fatness only on account of his brilliance. Hippocrates described obesity in great detail and made observations that are still pertinent today.

The Romans disliked obesity as much as the Greeks; ladies of the upper class literally starved to make themselves look slim as reeds. Yet, as with the Greeks, there were also famous Romans who were fat, and exact descriptions of their eating habits have been preserved. It is known that Marius, the defender of Rome, enjoyed enormous quantities of food. Horace, the poet, was famous for the extraordinary variety and elegant preparation of his meals.

During the Middle Ages, also, views on obesity conflicted. On the one hand, gluttony was counted among the venial sins. But obesity was also considered a sign of the grace of God. In Lochner's painting *The Last Judgment,* the sinners being dragged into Hell are stout, and the blessed being led into Paradise are slender.

During the 18th century in England, a law actually existed at one point that women could have a waist size no larger than 16 inches. Then in the early 1900s, the obsession on both sides of the Atlantic grew to the point where women resorted to food deprivation and purging to keep their weight down. Added to that, wire bodices and bustles cinched women's waists to create an hourglass figure, oftentimes to the point of physical injury.

Although the preferred style swung to a more full-figured ideal during the 1940s and 1950s, the 5′6″, 92-pound Twiggy epitomized a return to emaciated models in the 1960s.

A SHORT HISTORY OF ANOREXIA

Although anorexia nervosa has been considered a disease only in relatively modern times, self-starvation has been around throughout history. But our ancestors did not consider it to be a disease. According to Joan Brumberg in *Fasting Girls,* Simone Porta of Genoa, Italy, wrote the first medical account of anorexia in 1500. Very few similar cases were described in medical literature over the next several hundred years.

Although some authors have suggested the generally low standard of living and lack of food during this era as the reason existing cases of anorexia nervosa went undetected, others disagree. Walter Vandereycken and Ron van Deth (*From Fasting Saints to Anorexic Girls*), for example, remind us that physicians in previous centuries were keen observers; they had to rely almost exclusively on clinical examination. Adding to this, they say, the features and complications of severe anorexia are invariably too obvious—almost horrifying—to go unnoticed, even when the majority of people go hungry to some degree. Plus, even in the upper social classes, where people did have plenty to eat and families did call in physicians for health problems and infirmities, possible cases of anorexia nervosa were rarely mentioned.

Extreme fasting has been a practice of many pious Christians throughout history, especially in the late Middle Ages among deeply religious women. Although reports of contemporaries claim that these "saints" sometimes ate nothing but the consecrated host for months, even years, these reports are subject to misinterpretation and exaggeration. Hagiographers (biographers of saints) were more interested in demonstrating that the candidate-saint was indeed holy than they were in refuting that possibility. They were neither historically reliable nor medically precise.

Beginning with the 16th century, first "miraculous maidens" or "fasting girls" moved self-starvation out of the religious realm. Although considered by the pious a sign of God's presence on Earth because they could eat virtually nothing yet stay alive, they were regarded by the general population more as curiosities than as divine manifestations. The popular media of the day publicized them. Thousands of people, including kings and other dignitaries, visited them, even offered them money, and in the process turned them into tourist attractions.

Physicians of the day took on the task of investigating these cases for their validity rather than for the purpose of treating them or discovering causes for their starvation. Many of these girls were unmasked as frauds and imprisoned or killed, but not all.

By the 17th and 18th centuries, according to Brumberg, religious reform and changes of attitude led to prolonged fasting's being taken as the work of Satan rather than God. "Women who exhibited anorexic symptoms were said to be possessed by the devil and persecuted as witches." During the 19th century, both the alleged extended fasts and the deceit of many of the maidens were labeled by physicians as signs of hysteria. From this point on, most self-starvation was looked upon as a medical-psychological problem.

It was not until 1873 that anorexia nervosa was established as a clinical diagnosis. In April of that year, Ernest Charles Lasègue, professor of clinical medicine at the University of Paris, claimed that *"anorexie hysterique"* was caused by emotional disturbances that the patient tended to disguise or conceal. He mentioned the patient's "state of quietude—I might almost say a condition or contentment truly pathological. Not only does she sigh for recovery, but she is not ill-pleased with her condition, notwithstanding all the unpleasantness it is attended with."

Then in October of that same year, Sir William W. Gull, one of London's most respected physicians, first used the term *anorexia nervosa* in a paper submitted to the London Clinical Society. He explained, "We might call the state hysterical. . . . I prefer, however, the more general term, 'nervosa,' since the disease occurs in males as well as females, and is probably rather central than peripheral." He did note that young girls were especially prone to the disease.

Lasègue and Gull were familiar with each other's work and recognized they were dealing with "the same maladie." They both insisted that anorexia was a mental rather than an organic disease and achieved a small degree of success by treating it with "rest, nourishment, separation from family and supportive therapy."

In 1879 a French physician, Naudeau (historians are unsure of his first name), published a lengthy description of a fatal case with significant similarities to modern anorexia nervosa. Then in 1883, another French doctor, Henri Huchard, differentiated between *"anorexie Gastrique"* and *"anorexie mentale."* Six years later, Jean M. Charcot, the famous French neurologist and teacher of Freud, recommended removal of his anorexic patients from their families. Although it was still relatively rare, the puzzling malady anorexia nervosa had become a recognized disorder affecting mainly the middle and upper class.

But recognizing anorexia nervosa as a disorder did not mean physicians agreed as to its causes; debates continued over whether it was a physical disease or a mental disease. During the early 1900s, medical experts for the most part considered all disease to stem from abnormal variation of the body's cells or organs. In the specific case of anorexia nervosa, Morris Simmonds, a pathologist at the University of Hamburg, during an autopsy observed lesions on the pituitary gland of a severely emaciated woman who had shown signs of pituitary failure and died. For the next 15 years, though anorexia was already in the medical literature, virtually all cases involving unexplained weight loss were diagnosed and treated as "Simmonds' disease."

Then in 1930, John Mayo Berkman of the Mayo Clinic in Rochester, Minnesota, published the first long-term report on large numbers of anorexia cases. His report outlined treatment of 117 patients at the clinic during a 10-year period. Even though the clinic treated anorexia as a metabolic disorder and rarely administered any kind of psychiatric treatment, researchers have credited Berkman with "rediscovery" of anorexia as a separate disorder.

During the 1940s, the theory that anorexia nervosa was a psychological disorder began to gain support, although disagreement as to its exact causes ran rampant for the next 20 years. These psychological theories ranged from fantasies to fears of oral impregnation to emotional disturbance to psychosexual dysfunction.

The start of the modern era in the treatment of anorexia nervosa has been credited to a paper delivered by Hilde Bruch in 1961 and published in *Psychosomatic Medicine* 24:2 (1962): "Perceptual and Conceptual Disturbances in Anorexia Nervosa." In her paper, Bruch differentiated between the classic form or "primary anorexia nervosa" described originally by Morton and Gull, and "atypical anorexia nervosa" or self-starvation due to other psychiatric illnesses.

Prior to the 1960s, reports of anorexia nervosa were rare, but since then they have been occurring at a rapidly increasing rate. In addition, anorexia has increased its geographic spread. Case have been reported in countries as far apart as the former Soviet Union and Australia, Sweden and Italy, England and the United States. Studies have indicated that the incidence of anorexia nervosa has more than doubled since 1960. Where hospitals typically admitted one anorexic a year during the early 1960s, they now handle 70 and more. Anorexia nervosa is so common today that it represents a substantial problem to high schools and colleges. With an increase in media attention, anorexia nervosa has become a fashionable disease among affluent adolescents and young adult women who are particularly susceptible to peer influence.

BULIMIA NERVOSA HAS A HISTORY, ALSO

Just as the incidence of anorexia nervosa has surged since the 1960s, bulimia also emerged during the last few decades as an increasingly common psychophysiological disorder—so much so that there is a widespread misconception that it is a "new" disease. In fact, bulimia has an extensive history.

Episodic overeating has been a common practice over the ages. Primitive peoples dependent on hunting went on one- or two-day binges after successful expeditions before spoilage could occur and to compensate for long periods of famine.

The Greek physician Galen (A.D. 130–200) was credited with defining the origins of boulimus, or the "great hunger." He considered it a digestive dysfunction, the primary symptom of which was a desire for food "at very short intervals." This, he said, was often coupled with fainting, loss of color, coldness in the extremities, oppressive feeling in the stomach and weak pulse. According to Galen, boulimus was probably caused by an acidic "humor" lodged in the stomach, causing intense but false hunger signals. In addition, he suspected that the disorder was associated with the too-rapid digestion of food, resulting in inadequate nourishment and chronic hunger.

Then during the early 1700s, other medical authors referred to "boulimous" in attempts to separate it from similar conditions associated with worms, ulcers and normal pregnancy. In *A Medical Dictionary* (1743), Robert James noted that shortness of breath and an intense preoccupation with food may be symptoms of true boulimus. Throughout the 1700s and first half of the 1800s, bulimia was classified as a subtype of anorexia nervosa.

Then in 1869, the Frenchman P. F. Blanchez identified "boulimie" as a distinct syndrome, although admitting that it might occur as an accessory to another disorder. He described boulimie symptoms as food being an obsession and major preoccupation, yet with hunger sometimes continuing even after enormous quantities of food are eaten. He described the patient as becoming lethargic after a binge until the intense hunger returns a few hours later.

Purging is also not a recent phenomenon. The ancient Egyptians thought all diseases originated in food and thus purged their bodies every month. Tilmann Habermas writes that "vomiting was one of the most popular nonspecific symptoms in the nineteenth century, so its absence was often noted in cases of anorexia. On the other hand, it was rather unexpected that patients might intentionally induce vomiting."

Many of the physicians reporting on anorexic patients from the 1800s on included purging of some kind to get rid of unwanted food as one of the illness phases. Some patients learned to vomit immediately after swallowing; at least one was reported to use "a kind of hose to empty her stomach" (Habermas). During the early 1900s, abuse of laxatives or thyroid medication for the purpose of weight control was first mentioned, although vinegar had been drunk as a laxative for centuries.

DIFFERENCES AMONG THE PRIMARY EATING DISORDERS

According to the *Diagnostic and Statistical Manual of Mental Disorders, Fourth Edition (DSM-IV™),* eating disorders are characterized by severe disturbances in eating behavior.

Anorexia Nervosa is characterized by a refusal to maintain a minimally normal body weight, an intense fear of gaining any weight, and a disturbed body perception (seeing one's body or a part of one's body as larger than it really is). In addition, postmenarcheal females (the majority of anorexia nervosa sufferers) are amenorrheic (their menstrual periods cease).

Bulimia Nervosa is characterized by repeated episodes of binge eating followed by inappropriate compensatory behaviors such as self-induced vomiting; misuse of laxatives, diuretics, or other medications; fasting; or excessive exercise.

Binge-Eating Disorder was first described as a syndrome in 1992 and is characterized by eating binges similar to those seen in bulimia nervosa, but not followed by some form of compensatory behavior. In *DSM-IV™,* Binge-Eating Syndrome was added to the appendix as a diagnosis needing further study.

Obesity, although technically not an eating disorder, is a much more common problem, affecting at least one-third of the U.S. population, up from about one-quarter a mere 20 years ago. According to a 1999 National Institutes of Health (NIH) report, *Clinical Guidelines on the Identification, Evaluation, and Treatment of Overweight and Obesity in Adults,* an estimated 97 million adults in the United States are overweight or obese. *Overweight* is defined as a body mass index (BMI) of 25 to 29.9, and *obesity* as a BMI of 30 or higher. However, overweight and obesity are not mutually exclusive because obese persons are also overweight. A BMI of 30 is about 30 pounds overweight and is equivalent to 221 pounds in a 6′0″ person and to 186 pounds in one 5′6″. The number of overweight and obese men and women has risen since 1960; in the 1990s the percentage of people in these categories increased to 54.9 percent of adults age 20 years or older. Overweight and obesity are especially evident in some minority groups, as well as in those with lower incomes and less education.

PROMINENT PEOPLE AND EATING DISORDERS/OBESITY

In recent years several well-known athletes, entertainers and other prominent people have come forward to discuss their eating-disorder problems or to raise the public's consciousness about ill-conceived obesity stereotypes.

The death in 1983 of Karen Carpenter, a popular singer, brought on by anorexia nervosa inspired many other women to make public their own bouts with anorexia and bulimia in the hope of influencing young people to seek treatment. Olympic athlete Cathy Rigby had been bulimic for four years when she retired at age 19, and her problems continued when she started her new career in sports broadcasting and commercials. She was 28 before she sought professional help.

Ballerina Gelsey Kirkland starved herself periodically while a teenager and later learned to vomit to keep her weight down. In her autobiography (*Dancing on My Grave,* Garden City, N.Y.: Doubleday, 1986), she talks about her pursuit of the body beautiful.

Cherry Boone O'Neill, daughter of singer Pat Boone, described her bout with anorexia in her book *Starving for Attention* (New York: Continuum, 1982). Actress and one-time political activist Jane Fonda was bulimic for many years. Actress Ally Sheedy was both bulimic and anorexic.

John Lennon, the late Beatle, has been described by biographer Albert Goldman (*The Lives of John Lennon,* New York: William Morrow, 1988) as being anorexic for most of his adult life. Goldman says that Lennon starved himself to what he perceived as perfection. The onset of his disorder can be traced to 1965, Goldman writes, "when some fool described him in print as the 'fat Beatle.' That phrase struck such a blow to his fragile ego that the wound never healed."

During 1988, Sarah Ferguson, the duchess of York, was lambasted in the media after her weight reached 203 pounds during pregnancy. Finally admitting to a long battle with her weight, Sarah Ferguson in 1997 became a spokesperson for Weight Watchers International and wrote a cookbook, *Dining With the Duchess* (New York: Simon & Schuster, 1998).

In 1999, actor Billy Bob Thornton said he developed anorexia after he lost 59 pounds for a movie role—then couldn't stop losing. He reported how he denied his eating problem to himself and others. At the time he acknowledged his problem, he said he had gotten it under control.

Obesity has been a problem for actress Camryn Manheim most of her life. More accurately, she has said, battling her own self-deprecation as well as the prejudices of studios has caused her career to be an uphill struggle.

But she reached the top in 1998 when she won both a Golden Globe and an Emmy for her acting abilities. Soon after her Emmy win, Manheim signed a book contract for *Wake Up, I'm Fat* (New York: Broadway Books, 1999), her story of growing up overweight in the United States.

HEALTH RISKS OF OBESITY AND EATING DISORDERS

Although being overweight is often considered a cosmetic problem, obesity is even more a health problem. An obese person is more likely to develop heart disease, stroke, diabetes, certain types of cancer, gout (joint pain caused by excess uric acid) and gallbladder disease. Being obese can also cause problems such as sleep apnea (interrupted breathing during sleep) and osteoarthritis (wearing away of the joints). A study of more than one million Americans published in the *New England Journal of Medicine* in 1999, the largest study ever done on obesity and mortality, found that overweight people run a higher rate of premature death. This was true even among people who did not smoke and were otherwise healthy. The more overweight a person is, the more likely that person will have health problems. Although losing weight can be difficult for some, and although continual dieting creates its own health risks, studies show that an obese person can improve his or her health by losing as little as 10 to 20 pounds.

Another study, published in the October 1999 *American Journal of Public Health,* looked at the lifetime health and economic benefits if obese people lost 10 percent of their weight and kept it off. Their life expectancy would increase by two to seven months, and the lifetime medical costs of five obesity-related diseases would fall as much as $5,300 according to researchers.

Many of the symptoms and problems of anorexia nervosa result from starvation. The anorexic person may suffer from constipation, abdominal pain, cold intolerance and lethargy. As weight decreases, the skin becomes pale and muscles cramp. As the body temperature decreases, some anorexics develop lanugo, a fine downy body hair that grows to keep the body warm. Those who induce vomiting may have dental enamel erosion. The starvation and purging can also lead to anemia, cardiovascular problems and osteoporosis. When the amount of fat drops below 20 percent of body weight, hormonal release is affected, which in turn can result in amenorrhea, or stoppage of menstruation for at least three menstrual cycles. Because they do not ovulate, many anorexics are infertile.

Persons with bulimia nervosa frequently suffer from low self-esteem or mood disorders, and some bulimics experience anxiety disorders. Substance abuse or dependence occurs in about one-third of individuals with bulimia nervosa. From one-third to one-half of bulimics also have personality disorders. Repeated vomiting eventually leads to a significant and permanent loss of dental enamel, especially from the front teeth. There may also be an increased frequency of dental cavities. In some bulimics who vomit frequently, the salivary glands and particularly the parotid glands become noticeably enlarged. Those who regularly use syrup of ipecac to induce vomiting may experience serious heart disease.

Persons with binge-eating disorder have varying degrees of obesity. In comparison with individuals of equal weight who do not do any binge eating, they report higher rates of self-loathing, disgust about body size, depression and anxiety. They are also more susceptible to major depression, substance abuse and personality disorders.

WHERE TO GO FOR MORE INFORMATION

Bell, R. M. *Holy Anorexia.* Chicago: University of Chicago Press, 1985.

Brumberg, Joan Jacob. *Fasting Girls: The Emergence of Anorexia Nervosa as a Modern Disease.* New York: Plume Books, 1989.

Bynum, Caroline Walker. *Holy Feast and Holy Fast.* Los Angeles: The University of California Press, 1987.

Oster, G., D. Thompson, J. Edelsberg, A. P. Bird, and G. A. Colditz. "Lifetime Health and Economic Benefits of Weight Loss Among Obese Persons," *American Journal of Public Health* 89 (October 1999): 1536–42.

Vandereycken, Walter, and Ron van Deth. *From Fasting Saints to Anorexic Girls.* Washington Square: New York University Press, 1994.

Walsh, B. T. and M. J. Devlin. "Eating Disorders: Progress and Problems," *Science Magazine* 280, no. 5368 (May 1998): 1387–90.

CHAPTER 2
BIOLOGY OF OBESITY

CAUSES

The age-old debate of heredity versus environment as the major influence on human development has also prevailed among the medical community in regards to obesity. Where one study will demonstrate how genes play a role, another will point to a sedentary lifestyle.

But according to the 1999 National Institutes of Health (NIH) report, *Clinical Guidelines on the Identification, Evaluation, and Treatment of Overweight and Obesity in Adults,* the environment is a major cause of both overweight and obesity conditions. Environmental influences are primarily related to food intake and physical activity behaviors. In countries such as the United States, there is an overall abundance of convenient, tasty, calorie-dense, relatively inexpensive food. In addition, aggressive and sophisticated food marketing in the mass media and supermarkets and the large "super-size" portions served today in restaurants, which are frequented by more Americans than ever before, promote high calorie consumption. Many of our cultural and social traditions, from holiday dinners to tailgate parties, also promote overeating, especially of foods laden with calories.

This increase in consumption of high-calorie foods comes at a time when physical activity is on the decrease. And as Hill and Peters wrote in *Science* magazine, "on the simplest level, obesity can arise only when energy intake exceeds energy expenditure." For many people, even when caloric intake is at or below the recommended level, the number of calories burned in physical activity is not sufficient to offset those taken in.

A primary reason for today's low calorie-expenditure rate is mechanization, which limits the necessity of physical activity in order to function in society. From electric can openers to gasoline-powered hedge trimmers to electric golf carts, machines today provide the energy our grandparents expended physically yesterday. Today's "couch potatoes" don't even have to walk across the room to change TV channels.

Adding to the increased use of mechanical and computerized devices and tools, many people today are entrenched in sedentary daily routines: They sit at work, they sit in traffic and they sit in front of a television or a computer monitor for most of their waking hours.

Then there are the gender, age and marital factors. Men generally avoid putting on weight until middle age when they slow down on their physical activity; they generally can get the weight back off more quickly and more easily than women. Because of their sex hormones, women run into more difficulty controlling appetite, energy expenditure and fat storage. When those hormones kick in, teenage girls go from 12 percent fat to 25 percent fat almost overnight. Later on, weight gained during pregnancy is often difficult to lose. The years after age 45 tend to put added weight on both men and women, but middle age hits men especially hard, with the frequently added weight settling around the middle, where it poses greater health risk. A Cornell University study found that married men were significantly fatter than men who had never been or were previously married. Causes given included married men eating more and spending less time playing organized sports. In old age, both men and women tend to lose weight gradually as appetite declines.

The NIH report cautions that although there are undoubtedly some variations in the genetic predisposition to become overweight or obese, several lines of evidence suggest that genetic factors alone cannot explain the demographic and ethnic variations in overweight and obesity prevalence. For example, different income levels have different rates of obesity, and studies have shown an increase in average body weight in those who move from a traditional to a Westernized environment.

Scientists on both sides of the Atlantic are studying the link between abdominal obesity and stress. According to researchers, persons exposed to stress day after day can put on pounds around the middle when the stress upsets the stress hormones—cortisol, thyroxine and adrenaline—even persons who eat a healthy diet and are lean elsewhere in the body. These researchers explain that when we are under a lot of stress, the body lets loose a surge of these hormones to help you fight the stress. The fact that the fat in our abdominal area has more receptors for stress hormones than anywhere else in the body is thought to be a possible cause of fat buildup there in people who suffer chronic stress.

Still another cause for some obesity, according to Johns Hopkins University School of Medicine researchers, is prescription medications. Although certain medications have long been known to cause weight gain, this is the first time specific data has been collected into a single report. Medications causing patients to gain the most weight were psychoactive medications (especially tricyclic antidepressants, lithium and some antipsychotics) and steroid hormones. Drugs for hypertension, diabetes and gastrointestinal disorders also caused weight gain. Researchers expressed special concern about the vicious cycle potential for medicine-caused weight gain. Even a small weight gain may require a patient to take more medication. Then that extra medication may cause the patient to gain even more weight. In one cited incidence, a man gained 240 pounds while taking a steroid that treats underactive adrenal glands. Among the reasons given for some drugs to cause weight gain are their tendency to cause stimulated appetite and retained fluid.

But what about the genetic influence on obesity? Although research has found that genetic factors can determine whether or not an individual is susceptible to obesity, the extent of genetic influences are not really clear; identification of the genes is not easily achieved in family or pedigree studies. Furthermore, whatever the influence of a gene on the cause of obesity, it is generally weakened or exacerbated by nongenetic factors.

A large number of twin, adoption and family studies have explored the level inheritance plays in obesity. The most recent studies of individuals with a wide range of Body Mass Index (BMIs) suggest that about 25 to 40 percent of the individual differences in body mass or body fat may depend on genetic influences. However, studies with identical twins reared apart suggest that the genetic contribution to BMI may be about 70 percent.

From the research currently available, variations of several genes seem to have the capacity to cause obesity or to increase the likelihood of becoming obese. Several studies have reported that a single major gene for high body mass was transmitted from the parents to their children; however, no gene has yet been identified. Evidence from several studies has shown that some persons are more susceptible to either weight gain or weight loss than others. For this reason, the NIH report advises doctors that weight gain cannot always be attributed to a patient's not following a diet or exercise regimen.

But scientists haven't given up in their search for obesity-causing genes. According to researchers attending the 1999 meeting of the North American Association for the Study of Obesity, probably only five to 10 genes exist that have a major impact on obesity—even though a few hundred genes possibly affect obesity in smaller degrees. Genes don't dictate weight, according to Anthony Comuzzie of the Southwest Foundation for Biomedical Research in San Antonio; instead, they help set the upper and lower weight limits. "They affect how your body is going to relate to the environment."

Despite scientific advances in the search for human obesity genes, authors such as Hill and Peters caution that heredity cannot explain the obesity epidemic. They remind us that our genes did not change substantially during the 1980s and 1990s, although overweight and obesity continued to increase at a higher rate than ever before.

But obesity is too complex to develop from a single cause. It is influenced by numerous factors—social, behavioral, physiological, metabolic, cellular and molecular. Our environment fosters behaviors that cause obesity, and those who have a family predisposition to gaining and retaining weight only face a greater challenge to overcome it.

FAT DEVELOPMENT AND METABOLISM

If fat is such a health problem, why do our bodies have any at all? Fat within our bodies is a connective fibrous tissue called adipose tissue. Fatty (or adipose) tissue is a layer of soft, solid, yellow, slightly greasy material lying just under the skin and around many internal organs, such as the heart and kidneys. Fatty tissue acts as a shock absorber, protecting organs from injury and cushioning areas such as the heels and buttocks against the frequent and sudden jolts they receive. Fatty tissue also functions as an insulating thermal blanket, keeping body heat inside, particularly in babies.

The evolutionary process early on favored survival of those who were able to convert food into fat efficiently for storage. Stored fat was available for use as an energy source during times of food deprivation—famine, pestilence and other disasters that have often beset humanity. But in societies like ours, where food is readily available, the body seldom has an opportunity to call on its fat reserves and gradually accumulates additional fat in its storage deposits. When these fat reserves are used during dieting, the body naturally becomes more "fuel efficient," lowering its metabolic rate and decreasing spontaneous activity to conserve the fat that, in ancient times, enhanced the ability to survive.

Metabolism is the means by which the body derives energy and synthesizes the other molecules it needs from the fats, carbohydrates and proteins we eat as food, by enzymatic reactions helped by minerals and vitamins. The rate of metabolism can be increased by exercise; by elevated body temperature (as in a high fever), which can more than double the metabolic rate; by hormonal activity, such as that of thyroxine, insulin and epinephrine; and by specific dynamic action that occurs following the ingestion of a meal. Reduction of caloric intake, on the other hand, will lower the rate of metabolism. Studies with animals have shown that the rate may drop during starvation to 60 percent of prestarvation levels. The lower the normal metabolic rate, the more, and the more quickly, it drops in response to caloric restriction.

Metabolism's role has gained increasing attention from researchers. In a year's time, for example, the average person of normal weight consumes more than one million calories, but there is little variation in body weight because a comparable number of calories is used in bodily maintenance and activity. Taking in 10 percent more calories or expending 10 percent less energy would lead to a 30-pound weight gain within a year. Researchers conclude that in normal weight individuals, body weight is regulated with extraordinary accuracy. Moreover, research suggests that the hypothalamus is directly linked to weight regulation, containing a feeding center that controls appetite and SATIETY and maintains body weight. Some studies have shown that, rather than causing obesity, metabolic and endocrinological abnormalities actually result from it.

About 95 percent of body fat is stored in the form of triglycerides, composed of fatty acids bound to glycerol. When our body needs energy metabolism, the triglycerides are broken down within the fatty cells. The fatty acid component then attaches to a specific protein in the blood (lipoprotein) for transportation to the muscles. Fat cells (adipocytes) are constantly active, dispensing fat into the bloodstream so it can be carried to the body tissues needing energy and extracting other circulating molecules for conversion into fat to replenish the storage deposits.

These fatty tissue deposits result when more food is eaten than is needed for other bodily functions; it sits there, in storage, waiting for our body to need energy. An average-size adult has between 30 and 35 billion fat cells. As a person takes in more food than needed, his or her fat cells increase in size so they can store more fat. But fat cells can expand only so far before they reach capacity and can store no more fat. If the person continues to take in more food than can be used by the body or stored within the current fat cells, additional fat cells develop.

The body cannot eliminate existing fat cells—once developed in your body, they become permanent residents. When you diet or exercise to "lose fat," these cells actually shrink in size; they do not disappear. This partially explains why once a person gains a significant amount of weight, it is difficult to lose it, yet easy to put it back on. Existing fat cells are primed to manufacture and store fat more efficiently once a normal diet is resumed. This is the reason for the "yo-yo" effect of rapid weight loss and gain experienced by so many dieters, especially those who do not combine dieting with exercise.

Until very recently, the only way considered to eliminate existing fat cells was through surgery, such as liposuction. But researchers are currently investigating medications that may destroy fat cells, as well as a theory that fat cells may decrease if a lower body weight is maintained for a prolonged period of time.

Scientists divide fat cells (or tissues) into two groups—brown and white. Brown fatty tissues act as a thermostat for the body, burning themselves up to produce heat to help regulate the body's temperature. Although fatty tissues are the body's fuel reserves, it's the buildup of these cells that eventually causes obesity. But an Italian researcher reported in November 1999 that under some circumstances, white fatty tissues can turn into the brown type and burn themselves up; for example, when people fast or are exposed to cold weather, the body dips into its white fat reserves and creates brown fat for immediate use. Correlating to this are recent studies discovering that rodents exposed to heat turn up to 20 percent of their white fatty cells into brown ones. Other animal experiments have determined that some drugs encourage the body to produce more heat and save less fat. The challenge for scientists will be to identify fatty tissue molecules in humans that respond to drugs the same as they do in the mice.

PREVENTING OBESITY

The best way to prevent obesity, whether it be in children or in maturing baby boomers whose metabolism is slowing down, is to expend more energy through physical activity than one takes in.

The Surgeon General's Report on Physical Activity and Health, released in 1996, emphasizes that the amount rather than the intensity of physical activity is important, which offers people more options for incorporating physical activity into their daily lives. A moderate amount of activity can be obtained in a 30-minute brisk walk, for example, or in separate periods of raking leaves and playing with the dog. This draws on research conducted by the Centers for Disease Control and Prevention (CDC) and the American College of Sports Medicine (ACSM) in 1995.

Exercise alone is not a magic bullet, however. Experts haven't changed their advice that balancing physical activity with food intake is the key to maintaining a healthy weight. This combined approach reaps other health benefits as well. "The health benefits of regular physical activity alone are real, and the Surgeon General's report confirms this," said John Foreyt, Ph.D., director of the Behavioral Medicine Research Center at Baylor College of Medicine and an obesity expert. "But the benefits of combining physical activity with calorie control are even greater, including helping America start to make significant progress in stemming the obesity epidemic."

The U.S. Department of Health and Human Services Dietary Guidelines for Americans recommend that people choose a diet low in fat, saturated fat and cholesterol.

Another diet staple that may help fight obesity is fiber, according to a 10-year study by Dr. David S. Ludwig of Children's Hospital in Boston, which he released in October 1999. The study found that young adults who ate at least 21 grams of fiber per day gained, on average, eight pounds less over the 10-year period than those who ate the least amount of fiber. Fiber promotes weight loss by helping to block the body's digestion of fat and protein and people absorb fewer calories when the fiber content of their meals is increased, according to USDA research physiologist David Baer, Ph.D., who was quoted in *Bottom Line.* He added that if you increase your daily fiber intake from 18 grams to 36 grams, you will absorb 130 fewer calories per day. Over the course of a year, that reduction will bring a loss of roughly 10 pounds.

A prime time to prevent future obesity is in early childhood. A German study published in 1999 in the *British Medical Journal* found that babies who are breast-fed exclusively for the first three to five months of life were 35 percent less likely to suffer from obesity by the time they reached school age. Those breast-fed exclusively for six months to a year fared even better—they were 43 percent less likely to be obese. The researchers studied nearly 10,000 children, ages five and six. Although a few of the children's weight could have been influenced by genetic traits, experts believe the large number studied would cause genetics to be ruled out as having any influence overall. What is unknown is the reason breast-feeding appears to be such a preventive measure. One suggestion is that bottle-fed babies tend to be "overfed" as mothers try to make children finish each bottle. The study's authors concluded that because obese children have a high risk of becoming obese adults, such preventive measures as breast-feeding may eventually result in a reduction in the prevalence of diseases related to obesity.

Beginning the prevention of obesity in early childhood is more imperative today than ever before. Children ages 10 and younger are getting fatter by the decade, with nearly 5 million of them fitting into the category of severely overweight according to the American Academy of Pediatrics. But growing children have huge nutritional requirements, particularly as they approach their teens, so waiting until they are heavy enough to diet before doing something about their weight only exacerbates potential health problems.

Because children need more fat and dairy in their diets than adults, a parent-supervised diet is not always best for the child. When trying to prevent obesity in children, a wiser course of action than restricting certain foods is to take a good hard look at the child's activity level. Find ways to incorporate more exercise into his or her life. Replace a few hours of television each week with activity that requires walking, running, jumping or bending.

Now that obesity has grown from a personal to a national problem, prevention becomes a community issue. In their 1999 Report on Obesity, the NIH notes that primary prevention of obesity should include environmentally based strategies that address major contributors to overconsumption of calories (such as food marketing practices) and inadequate physical activity like transportation patterns and lack of opportunities for physical activity during the workday. The report goes on to remind communities that people in lower socioeconomic levels living in urban areas lack access to physical activity sites. Such strategies will be essential for effective prevention of obesity for large numbers of individuals and for the community at large.

DIAGNOSING OBESITY

Height and weight tables have long been used to diagnose obesity. Insurance companies developed the first height and weight table in 1908 to establish insurance rates based on life expectancy studies (or mortality tables). The medical community subsequently adopted this table and similar tables for clinical use. In 1942–43, the Metropolitan Life Insurance Company introduced the term *Ideal Weights for Men and Women* for their table, and the medical community adopted a *percent above ideal weight* to determine obesity.

But controversy swirled over which height and weight table best measured actual obesity. According to the tables, muscular people, especially athletes, would often be rated as overweight—even though they would be in the best of health and have a low degree of body fat—and total body fat is the real measurement of obesity.

Also, critics have argued, the ideal height/weight tables were developed primarily from white, higher socioeconomic status populations and have not been documented to accurately reflect body fat content in the public at large. Critics have also pointed out that they were based on data from studies with inadequate follow-up and controls for factors such as age, smoking status, blood pressure, alcohol use, HDL cholesterol levels, triglycerides and the like. The NIH suggests now that these tables be used solely to follow weight changes, but not for diagnosis of obesity.

For actual obesity diagnosis (or assessment of total body fat), the NIH recommends Body Mass Index (BMI) as an acceptable approximation for the majority of persons. (BMI does overestimate body fat in persons who are very muscular and can underestimate body fat in persons who have lost muscle mass, such as the elderly.)

BMI is equal to a person's body weight in kilograms (1 pound equals 0.4536 kilograms) divided by height in meters squared (one inch equals 2.54 cm equals 0.0254 meters). Weight refers to a person with shoes off and clad only in a light robe or undergarments.

Underweight is defined as a BMI of under 18.5.

Normal weight is defined as a BMI of 18.5 through 24.9.

Overweight is defined as a BMI of 25 to 29.9.

Obesity is defined as an excess of total body fat that is documented by a BMI of 30 to 39.9.

Extreme Obesity is defined as a BMI of 40 or greater.

In addition to BMI, the presence of excess fat in the abdomen, out of proportion to total body fat, is used as an indicator of obesity. Relatively accurate measures of total abdominal fat can be made by magnetic resonance imaging (MRI) or computed tomography. These methods, however, are expensive and not readily available for most doctors. Research with these techniques, however, has shown that the waist circumference correlates with the amount of fat in the abdomen and therefore is an indicator of the severity of abdominal obesity. To diagnose obesity with abdomen (or waist) measurement, NIH guidelines suggest that men with waist measurements greater than 40 inches and women with waist measurements of greater than 35 inches have increased risk of obesity-related diseases.

But for completely accurate obesity diagnosis, actual percentage of body fat is ideal. Arriving at such accuracy has proven a challenge for more than 50 years. During World War II, the U.S. Navy sought submariners with low body fat for their greater ability to withstand nitrogen uptake and discharge, which protected them against the "bends." Thus began the search for a reliable means to measure body fat.

The direct method for measuring body fat is through biopsies. However, other measurements have been developed and are now used more frequently. Densitometric analysis (hydrostatic weighing) compares regular weight with underwater weight in calculating the amount of lean body mass and body fat. (Because fat weighs less than water, a fatter person weighs proportionately less underwater than a lean one.) This method has become the "control" against which other fat-measuring methods are compared and standardized. However, equipment to perform these tests can usually be found only at certain hospitals or university labs.

Anthropometric measurements such as body circumference and thickness of skin fold provide more practical assessments for measuring body fat. In particular, caliper measurements of skin folds have been advocated for use in behavioral research. In this procedure, calipers are used to measure the thickness of skin and underlying fat at several locations on the body, with results calculated in an equation. However, some researchers have found measurement of height and weight to have a smaller standard deviation than skin folds, so they are more frequently chosen to measure fatness. In addition, some clinicians have found height and weight measurements more convenient, practical and reliable in treatment than the caliper assessments.

Recently developed instruments offer the ability to determine an accurate measurement of body fat and lean body mass with no discomfort, with results in seconds. These fitness and body fat analyzers are based on a technology developed by the U.S. Department of Agriculture. By touching the biceps, a fiberoptic wand emitting infrared light senses a spectrum change (because fat absorbs more light than muscle or bone) and displays an accurate body fat percentage on a digital readout.

Still another recent development is the bioelectrical impedance analysis (BIA). This sends a mild electrical current through electrodes attached to the foot and hand; the greater the resistance to electricity, the more body fat. Although bioelectrical impedance devices are becoming more readily available, they lose accuracy in severely obese persons and are of limited usefulness for tracking changes in total body fat in persons losing weight. Researchers also do not agree about the reliability of the BIA and infrared tests.

More recent methods developed for measuring body fat include ultrasound, computed tomography, dual energy X-ray absorptiometry (DEXA), Bod Pod and magnetic resonance imaging (MRI).

Ultrasound machines frequently show up at health fairs, schools and health clubs. An ultrasound beam radiates through the body area (the biceps, for example), with the speed it takes to hit the bone and bounce back determining body fat percentage. Experts question its accuracy, which depends greatly on the expertise of the technician operating the machine.

Computed tomography shoots a beam of low intensity X rays through the (biceps) and then senses the strength of the remainder beam after it goes through the biceps. The machine rotates a degree and the process repeats. Once the scanner collects several of these readings, its computer processes the information and produces a graphical representation of the area.

Dual energy X-ray absorptiometry, a technique currently used to study osteoporosis has been demonstrated as a reliable tool for measuring body fat. It works by scanning the body from head to toe, using a filter to split the X-ray beam into two energy levels to measure bone or tissue density. Although the margin for error is only 2 to 3 percent, the cost for a test (around $400) restricts its use in most cases for research rather than for clinical purposes.

The Bod Pod, an orb-shaped, body enclosing chamber, differentiates fat and lean tissue through computerized pressure sensors that determine body density by measuring the quantity of air displaced by the person sitting inside the chamber. Developed with a grant from the National Institutes of Health, more than a hundred Bod Pods are in use nationwide. Its accuracy has been reported to correlate to that of hydrostatic weighing. Costs for a measurement run between $50 and $75.

Magnetic resonance imaging (MRI), the latest method of testing for body fat, is currently under study.

WHERE TO GO FOR MORE INFORMATION ON THIS CHAPTER

Comuzzie, Anthony G., and David B. Allison. "The Search for Human Obesity Genes." *Science Magazine* 280, no. 5386 (May 1998).

Eliakim, A., et al. "Fitness, Fatness and the Effect of Training Assessed by Magnetic Resonance Imaging and Skinfold-thickness Measurements in Healthy Adolescent Females." *American Journal of Clinical Nutrition* 66, no. 2 (August 1997).

Hellmich, Nanci. "Genetics May Streamline Obesity Fight." *USA Today,* November 17, 1999.

Hill, James O. and John C. Peters. "Environmental Contributions to the Obesity Epidemic." *Science Magazine* 280, no. 5386 (May 1998).

Lehmann, Annie. "Machine Measures Body Fat By Deducting Displaced Air." *Detroit Free Press,* March 24, 1998.

Lytle, Lisa. "How Tests Measure Body Fat, and Their Accuracy." *The Seattle Times,* October 2, 1996.

Mayo Clinic, "New Ways to Measure Body Fat." *Mayo Health Oasis,* June 5, 1996.

Piscatella, Joseph C., Bernie Piscatella, and William C. Roberts. *Fat-Proof Your Child.* New York: Workman Publishing Company, 1997.

Schultz, Stacey. "Why We're Fat." *U.S. News & World Report,* November 8, 1999.

Thomas, E. L., et al. "Magnetic Resonance Imaging of Total Body Fat." *Journal of Applied Physiology* 85, no. 5 (November 1998).

CHAPTER 3
PSYCHOLOGY OF OBESITY

PSYCHOLOGICAL EFFECTS OF OBESITY ON CHILDREN

Hilde Bruch painted a bleak picture of the obese child, writing that "the lot of fat children is a sad one." Researchers have long reported that because of the psychological trauma of feeling different, inferior, laughed at, unattractive and ashamed, obese children tend to withdraw from peer group situations and social activities. Tests have shown that personality characteristics of obese girls are similar to those of people who have been subjected to intense discrimination because of their race or ethnic origin: passivity, obsessive concern with self-image and expectation of rejection. These lead to awkwardness in social situations, social isolation and actual rejection, and thus less activity outside the home, increased eating and, consequently, greater obesity. Obese girls also consider obesity—and hence their own bodies—undesirable and in extreme cases repulsive. They consider obesity to be a handicap and the reason for all their disappointments.

When an adolescent feels inferior in group situations, he or she tends to withdraw to solitary and usually sedentary activities, such as TV viewing and eating. Food has been described as a "feel-good drug" for the apathetic and unsure adolescent, whose appetite is also increasing to accompany normal physical growth. Coupled with less-than-normal exercise, this usually leads to even more excess fat and often to severe obesity in adulthood. In extreme cases, the obese child may also suffer from depression, leading to total isolation and an incapacity to become attached emotionally to other persons.

A clothing-store owner was quoted in *The Wall Street Journal* as saying, "Routine and necessary activities like shopping for clothes can upset obese adolescents. Clothes made for 'typical' children don't begin to cover their frames. In order to locate pants that fit around his waist, the fat boy must shop in the men's department. But the rest of these pants are far out of proportion, creating a humiliating situation for already self-conscious children."

Summing up his findings in a study on childhood obesity, Jon K. Mills wrote, "Individuals who became obese during childhood have more psychiatric and psychological problems than those who become obese later in life."

Obesity in adolescence is frequently blamed for problems with sexual adjustment. Although being fat can prevent a person from being considered "attractive" in our weight-conscious society, Bruch cautioned that "it is not the weight excess itself but the attitude toward it, or more correctly toward oneself, that interferes with any personal relationships, most of all in the sexual area." Studies of adolescent obesity have described frequent cases of provocativeness and uncontrolled sexual behavior, even to the point of promiscuity.

Adolescents with severe personality problems who are desperately unhappy about being fat are especially easy prey for FAD DIETS and NOVELTIES. The promise and dream of changing a boring, uneventful life to one of exciting activity and romance make the advertised products appear magical.

Not all children who think they are obese—and thus are susceptible to these psychological problems—are in truth obese. More than half the girls who consider themselves overweight are not overweight, according to Dr. Richard Strauss, director of the Childhood Weight Program at the Robert Wood Johnson Medical School, New Brunswick, New Jersey. In his study of adolescents, he found that girls are twice as likely as boys to think they're fat when they're really not, and where 60 percent of white girls saw themselves as fat even when they were not, only about 30 percent of black girls did.

According to a 1999 report issued by the American Obesity Association, adolescent females who are overweight have reported experiences with stigmatization such as direct and intentional weight-related teasing, jokes and derogatory name calling, as well as less intentional, potentially hurtful comments by peers, family members, employers and strangers. Overweight children and adolescents report negative assumptions made about them by others, including being inactive or lazy, being strong and tougher than others, not having feelings and being unclean.

Although many researchers have written about the problem of magazines that feature ultrathin models encouraging teenagers to diet in unhealthy ways, University of Texas psychologist Eric Stice, for one, says that they do not spur teens to diet. Instead, he told the American Psychological Association in 1999, they increase the anxiety and depression of girls who already feel too fat.

The National Association to Advance Fat Acceptance (NAAFA), a nonprofit human rights organization (see Chapter 10), has taken strides to help overweight youth who face both societal discrimination and feelings of inferiority with their NAAFA Kids Project. This program provides speakers and curriculum materials on the issue of body image. It promotes healthy eating and exercise, combats weight-related teasing and boosts self-esteem for children of all sizes. It also works with teachers to address these topics in their classrooms.

Adolescent dieting can also be stressful socially because so much of teenage social life revolves around eating. Well-meaning but nagging parents may add to this stress, especially given adolescents growing independence. Experts suggest that, for this reason, parents may be most helpful in supportive roles.

Yet the psychological changes adolescents and teens go through can sometimes actually help in treating their obesity. Member of the American Society of Bariatric Physicians have reported little success in treating younger children for obesity, but they have had increased success with adolescents at about the age of puberty. Emerging interest in the opposite sex and a developing maturity level contribute to the motivation to follow eating restrictions.

PSYCHOLOGICAL FACTORS NOT A REAL CAUSE OF ADOLESCENT OR CHILDHOOD OBESITY

Theories of obesity as resulting from neuroticism or excessive emotional reaction to adolescent stress have been largely ruled out by recent studies. The evidence for psychological causes is considered less convincing than that for more sociological and culturally oriented explanations. However, numerous studies suggest that obese people, once they have become obese, may develop psychological symptoms and that these may become particularly apparent during weight reduction efforts. These symptoms are especially pronounced among those with an earlier age of onset and a greater degree of obesity. Such individuals are generally very sensitive about their condition. Because obese adolescents are discriminated against both in employment and in high-ranking college admissions, it has been suggested that these social selection factors, felt most strongly in late adolescence, tend to encourage obese adolescents into social environments more permissive of obesity; thus they become even fatter.

Theories based on family-centered learning emphasize the psychosocial interactions in the social environment of the family as important factors in the development of obesity. In some cases this may involve major disruptive events, such as long separation from the mother or an overly protective family environment, but these causes are considered much less common than a family disinclination to physical activity and exercise or a social, emotional and physical environment within the family that favors overindulgence. Family eating habits are often blamed for childhood obesity.

PSYCHOLOGICAL CAUSES AND EFFECTS OF OBESITY FOR ADULTS

Just what role psychological variables play in causing adult obesity is still not fully understood. Factors once thought to be important—lack of impulse control, inability to delay gratification or faulty eating habits—have not been supported by studies. Other factors, depression and anxiety, for example, appear to be consequences rather than causes of obesity, although they may serve to maintain and intensify weight-related problems. Dieting in response to weight concerns appears, perversely, to be implicated in increasing overweight. Response to food cues in the environment may also play a role in some cases of obesity.

Some people, when they are nervous, tense, angry, frustrated or upset, often indulge in overeating because food has become an emotional outlet for them. It acts as a sedative, giving them a feeling of well-being and security. Overindulgence in food helps to control the emotional stress they experience. Many of these people show signs of other exaggerated oral activity, such as excessive talking, laughing, giggling or nail biting.

Physicians have categorized four major types of so-called emotional overeating:

- Overeating as a response to tension, anger, upset, loneliness or boredom.
- Overeating as a substitute gratification for lack of sex or love or when faced with an intolerable life situation such as the hostility of a parent or spouse.
- Overeating due to addiction to food. (See BINGE EATING, COMPULSIVE EATING and CRAVING.)
- Overeating as a symptom of an underlying depression and hysteria.

Clinicians have reported a higher incidence of depression among obese patients, although it is not clear whether the depression stems from being overweight or is the cause of it. Depressed people have been found to have a more difficult time believing in a positive outcome from their weight-control efforts than those patients who are not depressed. They also often have very high standards for themselves, and when weight reduction does not go as they wish, their depression can increase, which further hinders success in weight reduction.

An increase in body weight resulting from overeating as a response to stressful life events is often referred to as "reactive obesity." It is widely accepted that all aspects of human growth, development and disease are conditioned by social and interpersonal environment, and case reports and surveys suggest that obesity is no exception. Obesity has been found to follow stressful experiences such as financial reverses, hospitalization, instances of social or intellectual failure, social isolation, marriage, failure of marriage, childbirth, illness or death of parents or close relatives.

Because of this, psychologists have suggested that abrupt weight gain, especially in puberty and early adulthood, be examined carefully from a psychosocial point of view. In many of these situations, patients benefit from both medical and psychological treatment, with the reasons for the weight increase being looked at as broadly as possible.

There have been numerous references in the medical literature to obesity as a possible symptom of nervous disturbance since the 19th century. These include women who, grieving over the loss of their loved ones during World War I, were observed to put on weight that could not be accounted for otherwise. Similarly, during World War II there were many instances of severe obesity in young women who had been exposed to bombing or other hardships. Clinicians have observed frequent cases of newly developed obesity following the deaths of family members, separations from home, breakups of love affairs or other situations involving fear and loneliness. Bruch observed that reactive obesity occurred more commonly in adults and infrequently in children.

Bruch also believed that obesity is an essential and desirable state for a considerable number of emotional overeaters. These people use their excessive fat like a security blanket—as a protective barrier against the world. For these people, loss of weight is fraught with psychological danger and may result in serious psychological consequences.

Thin fat people is a term used by Bruch to describe obese people who succeed in becoming and staying thin but whose problems are far from solved by having lost weight. On the contrary, their difficulties now have a chance to flourish because obesity no longer prevents them from putting their unrealistic dreams to the test. She was referring to those people who blame all their difficulties on being fat and who hope that their lives will change when they get thin. Such people, though no longer obese, are far from transformed. The term was originated by F. Heckel, who stated in 1911 that a fat person cannot be considered cured even though he has lost weight, unless all other symptoms of dysfunction have also disappeared.

WHERE TO GO FOR MORE INFORMATION

Abramson, Edward. *Emotional Eating: What You Need to Know Before Starting Another Diet.* San Francisco: Jossey-Bass Publishers, 1998.

Leblanc, Donna. *You Can't Quit Until You Know What's Eating You: Overcoming Compulsive Eating.* Deerfield Beach, Fla.: Health Communications, 1990.

Mills, Jon K., "A Note on Interpersonal Sensitivity and Psychotic Symptomatology in Obese Adult Outpatients With a History of Childhood Obesity," *The Journal of Psychology* 129, no. 4 (May 1995).

Shepherd, H., and L. A. Ricciardelli. "Test of Stine's Dual Pathway Model: Dietary Restraint and Negative Affect as Mediators of Bulimic Behavior." *Behaviour Research and Therapy* 36, no. 3 (March 1998): 34–52.

Strauss, Richard S. "Self-reported weight status and dieting in a cross-sectional sample of young adolescents." *Archives of Pediatric and Adolescent Medicine* 153, no. 7 (July 1999): 741–7.

Virtue, Doreen. *Losing Your Pounds of Pain: Breaking the Link Between Abuse, Stress, and Overeating.* Carlsbad, Calif.: Hay House, 1994.

CHAPTER 4

DIET, EXERCISE AND BEHAVIORAL TREATMENT OF OBESITY

IT'S YOUR DIET—NOT DIETING

The word *diet* probably brings to mind meals of lettuce and cottage cheese or days on end of nothing but fruit or protein. By definition, *diet* refers to what a person eats or drinks during the course of a day. A diet that limits portions to a very small size or that excludes certain foods entirely to promote weight loss likely will not be effective over the long haul; rather, you are likely to miss certain foods and will find it difficult to follow this type of diet for a long time. Instead, it is often helpful to change the type and amounts of food you eat gradually and to maintain these changes for the rest of your life. The ideal diet is one that takes into account your likes and dislikes and includes a wide variety of foods with enough calories and nutrients for good health.

Counting calories and restricting food intake has become an obsession with Americans. In fact, dieting has been called the fastest-growing industry in the United States. It is estimated that more than 20 million Americans are seriously dieting at any given moment, spending $33 billion a year in the process.

Also, dieting is no longer practiced only by adults. A study of fourth-grade girls in California found that 80 percent said that they were dieting. The practice of young girls' dieting to get from a size 8 to a size 7 can establish patterns of deprivation, binge eating and weight gain that will haunt them all their lives. The director of one hospital's eating-disorders unit estimates that more than 50 percent of the patients there—mostly women in their late teens and early twenties—began to diet before they were teenagers. A survey in London revealed that girls as young as 12 felt too fat, attempted to restrict food intake and expressed guilt about eating. Even nonobese girls of five and six express concern about their body image and fear of gaining weight. In extreme cases, children's attempts at dieting can actually stunt their growth: if they occur just before the main growth spurt of early adolescence, they can jeopardize the increase in height that would automatically rectify an obesity problem. Zinc deficiencies and anemia also can result from improper dieting.

A national survey of nearly 12,000 high school students conducted by the Centers for Disease Control and Prevention found that more than 43 percent of the girls reported they were on a diet—and that a quarter of these dieters didn't think they were overweight.

Remedies for obesity have always been a part of U.S. culture. But while there are fad diets, in the United States dieting itself is not a fad; rather, it is a culturally embedded practice, a permanent social feature.

The growing weight-consciousness of U.S. society became evident with the appearance of the first public penny scales during the 1890s. These had bells that rang and music that played when people stepped on them; the faces were large so that anyone could see the weight. Then charts began to appear with the scales. These initially showed the average weight for a given height and, later, the suggested weight. As scales and weight consciousness became more widespread, the faces shrunk. Soon, public scales were out of vogue and bathroom scales became popular—one could weigh in private, without clothes that added extra pounds.

THE VICIOUS CIRCLE

Dieting among the obese has a history of failure. When obese people are given dietary advice as the main source of help combined with programs of regular weighing and counseling, they generally lose weight—while attending. One study reported a mean loss of 25 pounds over an average 24 weeks of treatment. Long-term results are rarely reported. VERY LOW CALORIE DIETS, whether composed of ordinary or specially prepared food, achieve losses similar in size to those produced by starvation, but being safer, they can be employed with outpatients. However, studies of the long-term effects of very low calorie diets have found fairly rapid replacement of lost weight. Within two to five years, 40 percent of people who lose weight actually end up heavier than when they started. Jane R. Hirshmann, coauthor with Carol H. Munter of *Overcoming Overeating,* has been quoted as saying, "Every single diet results in a binge. It doesn't matter what you're on. Everyone who is involved with them knows they don't work."

The increasing evidence is that weight loss achieved exclusively through diet restriction can "prime" for future weight gain because a decrease in the resting metabolic rate occurs when energy intake is reduced, possibly as a result of the loss of lean body mass. A repeated cycle of weight loss and gain may lower the resting metabolic rate, and persons with a history of weight cycling may require significantly fewer calories than persons without such a history. (See SET-POINT THEORY; YO-YO DIETING.)

But a later study reported by the University of Pennsylvania Medical School disputes this "starvation response" theory. Researchers tracked 18 dieting obese women for 48 weeks, all of whom also increased their levels of physical activity. Half the women ate 1,200 calories daily; the other half took 420-calories-a-day OPTIFAST for 16 weeks, gradually returning to solid food.

The Optifast patients had a mean loss of 47 pounds, the others 22. The resting metabolism dropped dramatically for the very low calorie dieters early in the program, but it was only slightly lower by the end because of a reduction in lean body mass. The study determined that when dieters lose weight, they lose both fat and lean body mass; thus, for every 25 pounds lost, the dieter needs to decrease calorie intake by 100 calories a day.

There is some evidence that by dieting, the obese may actually shorten their lifespan. Japanese men in Hawaii who were heavy at age 25 but succeeded in losing weight by middle age had a higher mortality than those who maintained a high and steady weight. On the other hand, men who had been lean at age 25 and became even thinner fared no worse than those who maintained a low steady weight. Weight reduction was associated with a near doubling of mortality for fat men but was not nearly as hazardous for thin men. Nearly identical results have been obtained in studies of French government workers and Harvard alumni. In an American Cancer Society Study, persons who reported having lost weight by intent prior to entering the study were more likely to die of stroke and coronary artery disease over the ensuing five years of follow-up. In another study, victims of myocardial infarction who successfully lost 10 pounds or more were twice as likely to die as those who maintained stable weights. In a Dutch survey, obese women who were dieting to lose weight reported an average of 12 health complaints, whereas nondieters reported an average of only eight. These findings have raised questions about the widespread assumption that dieting for weight loss improves health.

Janet Polivy, professor of psychology at the University of Toronto, has been studying dieting for more than 20 years. She is convinced that dieting to lose weight can be as much of a problem as the one it is supposed to alleviate. Her research suggests that attempts to lose weight may result in both weight gain and poorer health, mental as well as physical. She and her research team have developed a picture of the chronic dieter as someone who is easily upset and easily distracted, who is obsessed with weight and eating, who is eager to please and generally has lower-than-normal self-esteem.

Polivy has also cautioned that fatigue, weakness, dizziness, irritability, changes in texture of hair and skin and occasionally more severe problems resulting from malnutrition occur as a result of inadequate caloric intake during dieting.

In addition to these physical effects, psychological aspects of dieting also are being studied by health professionals. A University of Vermont study attempted to correlate the daily and major life stress, psychological symptoms and dieting behavior in 143 adolescent girls aged 14 to 18 over a four-month period. The results of this study indicate that there is a correlation between stress and dieting behavior in adolescents, which was also found to be the case in previous studies of adults. The Vermont study also supported the idea that dieting behavior is related to certain psychological symptoms in adolescents.

Dieting has become an informal institution deeply embedded in Western culture and economy. The media, official bodies and product marketers ply the public with information, sometimes inaccurate, about ways to reduce weight. On the basis of such information as well as from personal experience, many people construct personal programs of eating practices and physical activity with the intention of losing weight. They also continue some of these practices, perhaps conceived as generally healthful eating and exercise, when they are no longer trying to lose weight.

Researchers have attempted to relate people's knowledge of diet and nutrition to issues of health and weight control. One study, for example, found that good knowledge of nutrition seldom correlated with good weight control in the overweight. Others have found differences between men and women in their use of dieting strategies. Women have been found to be more likely than men to use both physical activity and food-restriction strategies. However, another study, although noting that women more often used reduced-calorie diets than men, found that men engaged in physical activity for weight control more frequently than women.

A British research team led by Alan Blair reported in *Psychology and Health* on a study of the relationship between professed beliefs about dieting and reported body weight before and after dieting. Among respondents to their questionnaire, strategies of increasing exercise, avoiding alcohol and cutting down on fat were positively correlated with success in reducing weight. General avoidance of calories between meals was positively correlated with success in maintaining weight loss. Among practices whose use was not correlated with weight loss were conventional slimming strategies such as fasting, skipping meals, using liquid meal replacements and attending diet centers. In addition, effective weight control was directly related to high expectations of success, no matter the weight loss strategy. The researchers suggested that adjustments may be called for in the content of educational messages and clinical therapy for the overweight.

Other studies have reexamined the relationships between nutrient intake and overweight. In one, researchers found that high body-mass index was most strongly associated with low bread consumption and use of low-fat milk. Another found that average daily alcohol consumption was unrelated to fatness, and still another reported evidence that fat intake may contribute to overweight independently of total energy intake.

One researcher has hypothesized, on the basis of satiety physiology and surveys of sugar use, that calories in and with drinks consumed after and between meals make a major contribution to difficulties in weight control.

VERY LOW CALORIE DIETS

Very low calorie (VLC) diets are programs for achieving rapid weight loss through eating fewer than 800 calories per day. These diets can result in serious side effects, the most common of which are inability to tolerate cold, dizziness, diarrhea, constipation, dry skin, hair loss and gout. Mood changes ranging from elation to depression may occur, and acute psychosis has been reported.

Most VLC diets are not tailored for the moderately obese person's needs. Fatter people, for instance, can tolerate more drastic cuts in calorie consumption than less obese individuals. The best VLC diets are closely supervised and monitored by physicians, behavioral psychologists and dietitians. VLCs have been recommended as viable treatment for people whose obesity puts them at risk for such problems as diabetes, hypertension and heart disease (BMI greater than 30). It is best to consult a physician for more information on VLC diets.

WEIGHT LOSS: A SENSIBLE APPROACH

The U.S. Department of Health and Human Services suggests the following "sensible approach" to dieting:

Before embarking on any weight loss program, consult your physician to be sure there are no underlying medical problems and that the diet and exercise program you are contemplating is right for you. Talking to a registered dietitian or qualified nutritionist can also be helpful.

Women should be aware that they face more of a challenge in losing weight than men do. Because they generally need fewer calories than men simply to maintain their weight, women have to reduce calories to a lower level to lose. For example, most men can lose one to two pounds a week consuming 1,500 to 1,600 calories a day, whereas many women may have to cut down to 1,000 to 1,200 calories a day to achieve the same result.

Because she is consuming fewer calories, a female dieter needs to pay especially close attention to the nutrient value of the foods she eats. Anyone, male or female, considering a diet of 1,000 calories or less should discuss with a physician whether a vitamin/mineral supplement at the level of U.S. Recommended Daily Allowances is advisable.

Although women may have more of a battle than men when it comes to weight loss, the same basic principles apply to both:

- Aim for a moderate weight loss of one or two pounds a week. Research has shown that losses in excess of this tend to be losses not of body fat but of water and lean muscle.
- Reduce portion sizes, but maintain a balanced diet from the four basic food groups: grains and cereals; eggs and dairy products; fruits and vegetables; meat, poultry and fish.

- Limit intake of fats, sweets and high-calorie foods.
- Exercise regularly—increase exercise if possible.

Some dieters also find it helpful to count calories in order to keep track of how much they're taking in. It also can be helpful to eat several smaller meals, rather than three large meals a day. *Grazing* is a word used to describe the practice of eating six or more small meals throughout the day on the assumption that this will better lead to weight loss than the traditional three meals. Researchers remain divided in the debate; some studies have shown that "grazers" lose more weight than traditional eaters; in others the grazers have *gained* weight; in still others, there was no difference between the two groups. Counting calories will tell you whether you are taking in more calories or fewer with those six small meals a day.

DIET TRICKS AND TIPS

Eat and Drink "Airy" Food

According to a study by Pennsylvania State University nutritionists, you can trick yourself into feeling fuller if you increase the volume of the food you eat but not the calories, such as air-popped popcorn and puffed cereals. At the 1999 meeting of the North American Association for the Study of Obesity, the researchers explained how they had made several strawberry "smoothie" shakes with the same ingredients, but with different amounts of time in the blender. The resulting drinks varied in size, from half a glass to three-quarters to a full glass. Then 24 participants drank the shakes before eating lunch until they were full. Those who drank the largest shakes ate 100 fewer calories, yet did not make up the calories later in the day. *Caution:* Don't try to fill up completely with airy foods or you may end up with a stomachache and/or gas.

Eat Your Oatmeal

Results of a 1999 study by researchers at the New York Obesity Research Center at St. Luke's-Roosevelt Hospital Center suggest that eating oatmeal for breakfast can help with weight control by curbing appetite at lunch. For generations, mothers have insisted that oatmeal "sticks to your ribs," and apparently they have been right. Researchers theorize that what actually happens is that the fiber in oatmeal slows down the rate of emptying from the stomach, making a person feel fuller for a longer period of time. One surprising find during the study was that the people who ate sugared corn flakes for breakfast were just as hungry and ate as much lunch as the people who had no breakfast at all—only water.

Eat More Fiber

In *Sculpturing Your Body: Diet, Exercise and Lipo (Fat) Suction,* John A. McCurdy wrote, "The most effective method to assist in sculpturing your body by diet is to formulate a plan that is balanced but utilizes smaller portions of all basic food groups. If a diet is to be skewed in the direction of any one nutrient, it should be constructed to be high in complex carbohydrates because of the many benefits provided by these substances." He cited a study on a college campus that showed that overweight students effectively reduced on a diet *requiring* 12 slices of low-calorie, high-fiber bread per day in addition to virtually anything else they wished (except alcoholic beverages), including between-meals snacks. The high-fiber bulk of the bread appeared to reduce the intake of other high-calorie foods, presumably by increasing satiety or the feeling of fullness.

Drink Green Tea

According to a study published in the December 1999 *American Journal of Clinical Nutrition,* green tea appears to speed up calorie burning, including fat calorie burning. The study participants, 10 healthy young men who ranged from lean to mildly overweight, were on a "typical Western" weight-maintenance diet of about 13 percent protein, 40 percent fat and 47 percent carbohydrates. The group also taking green tea extract plus 50 milligrams of caffeine used more calories than the groups taking 50 milligrams of caffeine alone or a placebo. There was no difference between the caffeine users and the placebo users. The study's authors suggest that the caffeine interacted with natural substances in green tea called flavonoids to alter the body's use of norepinephrine, a chemical transmitter in the nervous system, and increase the rate of calories burning. Unlike some DIETER'S TEAS, green tea does not contain high doses of caffeine, and it did not affect the heart rate in the study participants.

Weigh and Measure

Dietitians see clients every day who are terribly confused about portion size, which is number 1 on the dietitians' hit-list for bad diet practices. They place much of the blame for this on the U.S. trend of all-you-can-eat specials and supersizing both restaurant servings and prepared food items. Too often, they say, people will dish out double and triple the amount of cereal the manufacturer intends as a "serving," to cite one example, so that they count the number of calories on the box for a serving, when in actuality they are eating two to three times that many. Dietitians suggest that instead of cutting out foods, simply cutting back to recommended portions will result in healthy weight reduction.

Drink Water—Lots of It

According to Donald S. Robertson, a bariatric physician and author of *The Snowbird Diet* (Warner Books), drinking at least 64 ounces of water a day can actually cause fat deposits to decrease. He explains that when the kidneys do not receive enough water, they do not function properly, resulting in some of their workload (carrying away waste products) transferring to the liver. When the liver then performs some of the kidney's work, the liver cannot effectively perform one of its primary functions: metabolizing stored fat into usable energy for the body. As a result, it metabolizes less fat and more fat remains stored in the body; weight loss stops. At the very least, drinking two or three glasses of water before every meal will fill you up; you will eat less.

BURNING UP THOSE CALORIES WITH INCREASED ACTIVITY AND EXERCISE

Exercise alone is not usually prescribed as a weight loss method, but physical activity is a key to any weight-control program. It burns calories, speeds metabolism and helps offset the dreaded "plateau" stage in which weight loss slows or stops temporarily. People who exercise and diet lose more fat and less muscle than people who only diet.

Achieving a negative energy balance—that is, using up more calories than one takes in—by exercise alone has been shown to cause some weight loss. One study showed an average weight loss of 16 pounds over 19 weeks, but no long-term follow-ups are available. Although changes of exercise (energy output) and/or altered metabolic efficiency can cause weight loss when one is over- or underweight, the amount is usually not significant unless accompanied by lowered food intake.

Most studies have shown that vigorous exercisers consume more calories than sedentary individuals, but they also weigh approximately 20 percent less on average to start with. There are no data supporting the contention that moderate activity of short duration used in weight-loss programs stimulates appetite. In fact, for many people, moderate exercise tends to have an appetite-suppressing effect. For this reason, many experts recommend that daily exercise be performed prior to the main meal of the day.

Researchers at Mt. Sinai Hospital in New York have reported that whereas fat people burn off more calories if they eat *after* exercising, thin people burn off more if they eat *before.* The researchers believe that fat people's cells are less sensitive to insulin, the hormone that admits fuel into body cells. Intense exercise, they say, may improve the insulin sensitivity of fat people.

Studies at Stanford University comparing food intake and weight of long-distance runners (those who run approximately 40 miles per week) with those of randomly selected sedentary adults of similar age show that despite ingesting an average of 600 more calories per day (2,959 vs. 2,361), the runners weighed 25 percent less than the sedentary group, evidence strongly suggesting that exercise lowers the set point. Numerous studies have documented the observation that a program of moderate exercise reduces body fat levels while preserving or increasing lean body mass. Animal studies show that exercise produces a specific fat-burning effect and that the animals maintain the new body fat levels, demonstrating that the set point has been lowered.

But the older we get, the more difficult it is for our muscles to burn fat, according to researchers at the Washington University of Texas Medical Branch in Galveston. Their study found that fat oxidation in older subjects (average age 73) was 25–30 percent lower than in younger subjects. The older people were more likely to burn carbohydrates during exercise.

The evidence establishing regular exercise as an important factor in weight control has convinced many health care professionals that one of the major causes of seemingly creeping obesity during middle age is the lack of physical activity, largely as the result of sedentary styles of life. The average American man between 35 and 45 years of age weighed six pounds more in 1980 than in 1960 (the average American woman of similar age showed an eight-pound weight increase) despite a 10 percent reduction in caloric intake over this period.

Three new studies presented at the November 1999 North American Association for the Study of Obesity confirmed the importance of exercise in weight reduction. In one study of more than 2,500 people who had lost an average of 60 pounds and kept it off for about six years, these people reported burning an average of 2,800 calories per week in walking, stair climbing and other activities. In another study, the people who lost the most weight burned 2,549 calories per week in physical activity. And in the third study, people who exercised more than 200 minutes per week (while burning 2,630 calories) lost more weight than people who exercised for 150 minutes or less per week (and burned 1,138 calories).

Yet a survey of more than 107,000 men and women, as reported in the *Journal of the American Medical Association* in October 1999, found that only 21.5 percent of men and 19.4 percent of women said they were using the recommended combination of fewer calories and added physical activity to lose weight.

Although several studies have demonstrated that fitness can be improved by short but regular exercise periods, researchers at the University of Pittsburgh and Brown University showed in a 1999 study that short bouts of exercise can also help overweight women shed weight and keep the pounds off just as well as longer workouts—critical for today's working moms who find it all but impossible to fit in the longer periods of time.

Then there is the simple physical activity of fidgeting. *Nonexercise activity thermogenesis* (NEAT) is the term used for physical activity associated with restless movement: fidgeting, jiggling your leg under the table, stretching, changing posture frequently, moving around, generally squirming and other activities of daily life. In a Mayo Clinic study in which people volunteered to stuff themselves with 1,000 extra calories a day for eight weeks, some gained as much as 16 pounds; others gained as little as two pounds. The difference, according to the researchers, was due to increased total daily energy expenditure through increased NEAT. Those people who had the greatest increase in NEAT gained the least fat, and those who had the least change gained the most.

TELEVISION—PSYCHOLOGICAL AND PHYSICAL EFFECTS ON OBESITY

With television watching the nation's most time-consuming activity after sleeping and working, the role it plays in the development of health-related attitudes and behaviors is of growing interest. Studies of this powerful medium suggest that many health messages are conveyed to viewers but that the information is sometimes unrealistic, distorted and misleading, particularly regarding food, nutrition and obesity.

William Feldman, medical professor at the University of Ottawa and author of a report in *Pediatrics* on children's attitudes toward weight, blamed television for most girls' belief that they are fatter than they really are. On television shows during the prime evening viewing hours, he said, women in prestigious positions are typically thin. Ubiquitous television imagery delivers the message that thinness equates with beauty and the good life.

Although many of these "lessons" to which Americans are regularly exposed promote misconceptions that may lead to unhealthy eating habits, television's primary offense may be simply its very existence, which has profoundly altered U.S. leisure. When the TV is on, activity ceases; time spent exercising is reduced significantly. The heart and other muscles are not strengthened, and CALORIES are not expended beyond the resting METABOLISM level during television viewing.

When Larry A. Tucker (then of Auburn University in Alabama) examined the relation between television viewing and physical fitness, he found that, among 379 high school males, as TV watching increased, multiple measures of physical fitness decreased markedly and systematically. Similarly, other researchers have shown that as TV viewing increases among children, obesity increases substantially.

Tucker and Glenn M. Friedman measured the extent of the association between TV viewing and obesity among adult males. Study subjects were 6,138 adult male employees of more than 50 different companies. Those who viewed TV more than three hours a day were twice as likely to be obese as those who viewed less than one hour per day.

Tucker and Friedman caution that with the growth of cable television, home video recording and video games, television viewing is likely to increase in the coming years. The findings of their study and other recent research show that the impact of television on fitness and health (especially obesity) cannot be ignored.

BEHAVIORAL TREATMENTS OF OBESITY

Behavioral techniques in treating obesity involve the manipulation of the physical and social environment to decrease the probability of overeating. This is achieved in the case of diet by keeping track of what is eaten, noting various internal and external cues that lead to eating, immediate positive reinforcements of desirable behaviors, dissociation of eating from other experiences and, in some cases, emphasis on eating styles. Behavior therapy in combination with diet restrictions has been shown in studies to be superior to diet alone, and maintenance of weight loss has been more successful. It is most helpful for those with one or more "obese eating style" problems: rapid eating, few but large bites, short-duration meals, exaggerated sensitivity to external stimuli.

When behavior modification is used in treatment for obesity, the therapist first analyzes the patient's current eating habits. Usually this involves the patient's maintaining a detailed food diary. Noted in the diary are the types and amounts of food eaten at various times of the day, where the food is eaten (at a desk, dining room table, living room, in a car, etc.), activities involved in at the same time eating takes place (e.g., reading, watching television, listening to the radio), the degree of hunger during each time food is eaten and the mood the patient is in when he or she decides to eat. The food diary helps identify particular eating patterns or situations in which the patient is likely to overeat.

After a thorough analysis of eating behavior has been made and recurring patterns identified, other behaviors are substituted for eating when a particular situation arises. For example, if the patient regularly snacks while watching television, he could substitute some other behavior such as chewing gum or sipping on a glass of water. If the patient routinely eats candy when she feels angry or depressed, she can instead do 10 repetitions of a simple exercise or go for a walk or express her thoughts on paper. In this way, a new habit is substituted for the established eating response to certain situations.

If the eating pattern analysis shows that the patient has poor eating habits, such as eating too rapidly, behavior modification is used to alter and control them. New eating patterns might include using smaller dishes, putting the fork down between bites and carefully chewing before swallowing to stretch out a meal and allow stimulation of the SATIETY mechanisms, substituting such low-calorie foods as fruits and vegetables for high-calorie snacks, eating meals at regular times or avoiding distractions such as television during meals.

A central element of most obesity behavior-modification programs is slowing down the act of eating. It was initially thought that doing so would interrupt the "chaining" of behaviors involved in eating: putting food on the fork, lifting it to the mouth and so on, which occurred largely outside a person's awareness. But it has since been found that slowing down the act of eating has an additional benefit because a larger proportion of the meal remains uneaten at the time when the stomach and intestine have begun to absorb nutrients, thus producing the physiological signals of fullness. These signals add to the effect of the techniques used to eat less.

There are specific techniques to help people slow their rate of eating, enabling them to become aware of all its components and gain control over them. The most frequently suggested one is setting down one's fork or spoon between bites. Another is to count each mouthful, chew or swallow. Those patients who have trouble slowing their eating rate are told to stop eating for one minute late in a meal when a delay is more readily tolerated. They are then instructed to increase the number and duration of delays and to begin them earlier.

Patients are also urged to make meals a time of comfort and relaxation and to avoid arguments and the rehashing of problems at the dinner table. They are encouraged to learn to savor food as they eat it, to make a conscious effort to become aware of it as they are chewing and to enjoy the act of swallowing and the feeling of warmth and fullness in their stomach. To the extent that they succeed with this, they may eat less and enjoy it more.

A system of rewards (positive reinforcement) is the key element in behavior modification. Although the ultimate reward is an improvement in health, personal appearance and self-esteem, interim rewards are important in encouraging patients to stay with the program. Examples include treating oneself to a movie after a three-pound weight loss or going on a trip after successfully shedding 10 pounds. Charts recording weight loss and changes in body measurements also provide positive reinforcement.

Although behavior modification appears to consist solely of tricks and games, a comprehensive treatment program involves much more, working on multiple areas, from exercise to personal relationships. The more thorough programs achieve weight losses of 30 pounds and more.

For many people, its easier to stick to a behavior-modification program if it's in a group setting. For this reason, groups devoted to weight loss have multiplied throughout the world. Two of the oldest and most successful are WEIGHT WATCHERS and TOPS (Take Off Pounds Sensibly).

Self-control therapy is a psychological treatment method in which clinicians help patients control their own behavior without the aid of drugs or other outside controls. Self-control treatment techniques for obesity attempt to help dieters achieve increased control over their eating to enable them to reduce their food intake. The self-control approach has been very widely adopted; nearly 80 percent of published studies of behavior therapy are of the self-regulation approach. Curing obesity "requires permanent changes in the overweight person's own habitual actions of eating, drinking, and physical exercise," according to British reseacher D. A. Booth. This self-management must be achieved if weight loss is to be permanent. The core components of the self-control approach to treating obesity are changing mealtime eating behavior, rearranging eating cues, self-monitoring and "deprogramming" inappropriate behaviors.

Weight loss with behavioral modification is slow and undramatic, and the amount of weight lost is usually moderate. Even though the goal of behavior modification is a lifelong change in eating habits, many people gradually return to their old eating behavior and regain the lost weight unless they continue participating in group or individual programs.

Behavioral approaches to obesity are considered by some to be even more important for children than for adults because it is usually easier to change the habits of children than those of adults, who are more set in their ways.

A child's level of involvement in a weight-loss program depends, in large part, on his or her level of mental development. Leonard H. Epstein outlined four age ranges as a guideline for placing increasing responsibility for weight control on a child. At ages one to five, any weight program must rely on parental control. A child is generally not able to read or write and thus is unable to keep track of calories consumed, calories burned through exercise and so on. Motivation to lose weight is absent. During this time, parents are the major influences on a child's eating and activity habits. At ages five to eight, a child's ability to monitor calorie consumption/expenditure and eating patterns is still limited, although simple diet control can begin. Children at this age can start learning nutritionally sound eating habits and can be trained to handle social situations in which food is offered. In addition, these children can also begin to learn to solicit praise and encouragement for healthy eating from adults close to them. Parents will still be involved significantly. At ages eight to 12, a child can set goals and self-monitor. Peer pressure may provide motivation to lose weight; however, children at this age still benefit substantially from parental involvement. From age 13 on, children can use programs similar to those of adults, though they may be helped through social groups. At this stage of development, children are becoming independent of their parents, and too much parental guidance or interference may be counterproductive.

In the attempt to monitor and control types and amounts of food intake, color coding of foods to show calorie amounts can be understood by children as young as age five. The nutritionally balanced TRAFFIC LIGHT DIET developed by Epstein in 1978 separates premeasured food portions into red, yellow and green categories corresponding to traffic signals (stop eating reds, be careful of the amounts of yellows, and go ahead and eat lots of greens). With young children, colored stars corresponding to foods eaten may then be exchanged for reinforcers. This method of encouraging healthy low-calorie eating by obese children has been shown to be useful in school as well as home settings. The New American Eating Guide, a color-coded poster similar in concept to the Traffic Light Diet, and the Nutrition Scoreboard (Center for Science in the Public Interest) have also been useful in programs of weight control and eating-habit change for children. The Food Exchange Diet prepared by the American Dietetic Association also can be used with children, with help from adults in learning the procedures. Pediatricians have used colored tokens to represent the food exchanges in this diet; tokens are transferred from one plastic box to another following consumption of food in their color groups. These color-coded systems provide effective visual representation of diet for children too young to read and write. Premeasured portions also eliminate the need for calorie counting.

INFANT FEEDING AND PREVENTION OF CHILDHOOD OBESITY

The incidence of obesity in infants has not been determined, but it appears to be increasing. Recent studies suggest that two trends in infant feeding may account for some of this increase—the trend toward bottle-feeding rather than breast-feeding, and the trend toward earlier introduction of solids. Whether bottle-feeding contributes to the development of obesity is controversial. Most available evidence indicates that breast-feeding does not prevent obesity, but it may help prevent overfeeding. Although infants are able to take solids at very early ages without apparent harm, they receive no desirable nutrients that cannot be provided by milk formula. Instead, such feedings usually result in the ingestion of more calories and protein than are required for optimum growth.

It is generally recommended that obese infants not be made to lose weight but that their weight be controlled. An obese infant's rate of weight gain should be slowed to parallel his or her linear growth. Recommended is a limitation of 50 to 55 calories per pound of body weight per day during the first six months of life, and 41 to 46 calories per pound of body weight per day from six to 12 months of age. Substituting skim milk for formula is not recommended, but water may be offered periodically in its place. Researchers believe that thirst is often mistaken for hunger.

A number of studies have claimed that rapidity of weight gain in infancy is a better guide to the risk of being overweight at the age of six or eight than is the weight of the parents. For example, in one study, adults whose obesity appeared to have begun in infancy had a higher number of fat cells than a group of equally fat adults whose obesity was of more recent origin. In addition, psychological problems encountered in attempting to lose weight have been more pronounced in patients with early onset obesity. An infant who becomes obese usually remains obese as an adolescent and as an adult.

Researchers at the University of Edinburgh investigated the learning experiences involved in HUNGER and satiety in early infancy, and their relation to eventual obesity and other eating disorders. Findings appeared to contradict an earlier theory that there might exist a critical period in early development when the number of FAT CELLS becomes fixed and predisposes a fat infant to become a fat child and ultimately a fat adult.

In 1999, a study by the National Institute of Child Health and Human Development said that babies who are undernourished in the womb often are fed too much when they're young to compensate, giving them excess fat to go with diminished muscle mass. Other babies born small react by storing more fat than the body needs. The result is small babies often grow into obese adults. The solution, according to lead author Mary L. Hedinger, is for parents to talk to their pediatrician about an exercise program for infants to increase blood flow and muscle.

One unconfirmed hypothesis is that dieting may begin accidentally during infancy, when dieting mothers unintentionally put their infants on and off diets by attempting to limit the children's food intake when they themselves are not dieting and by becoming more lenient when they're dieting. This theory derives from a single study in which mothers who reported the strongest inclination to diet were most likely to interpret tape-recorded episodes of a baby's crying as a reflection of hunger. The same study showed that fat mothers preferred thinner babies and planned to make more efforts to prevent obesity by limiting intake than thin mothers.

SCHOOL PROGRAMS TO TEACH NUTRITION

The U.S. Centers for Disease Control and Prevention (CDC) has issued *Guidelines for School Health Programs to Promote Lifelong Healthy Eating.* As the *Guidelines* explain: Young persons need nutrition education to help them develop lifelong eating patterns consistent with the Dietary Guidelines for Americans and the Food Guide Pyramid. Schools are ideal settings for nutrition education for several reasons:

- Schools can reach almost all children and adolescents.
- Schools provide opportunities to practice healthy eating. More than one-half of youths in the United States eat one of their three major meals in school, and one in 10 children and adolescents eats two of three main meals in school.

- Schools can teach students how to resist social pressures. Eating is a socially learned behavior that is influenced by social pressures. School-based programs can directly address peer pressure that discourages healthy eating and harness the power of peer pressure to reinforce healthy eating habits.
- Skilled personnel are available. After appropriate training, teachers can use their instructional skills, and food service personnel can contribute their expertise to nutrition education programs.

School-based nutrition education is particularly important because today's children and adolescents frequently decide what to eat with little adult supervision. The increase in one-parent families or families having two working parents and the availability of convenience foods and fast-food restaurants inhibit parents' monitoring of their children's eating habits.

Children's food choices are influenced by television advertisements for low-nutritive foods. Young people see about one food advertisement for every five minutes of Saturday morning children's shows. Most of the foods advertised during children's programming are high in fat, sugar or sodium; practically no advertisements are for healthy foods such as fruits and vegetables. Studies have indicated that, compared with those who watch little television, children and adolescents who watch more television are more likely to have unhealthy eating habits and unhealthy conceptions about food, ask their parents to buy foods advertised on television and eat more fat. Some studies of young persons have found that television watching is directly associated with obesity. Because youths in the United States spend, on average, more than 20 hours a week watching television—more time over the course of the year than they are in school—school-based programs should help counter the effect of television on their eating habits.

To request a copy of these *Guidelines,* contact CDC, MMWR MS(C-08) Atlanta, GA 30333; or go to http://aepo-xdv-www.epo.cdc.gov/wonder/PrevGuid/m0042446/m0042446.htm

WHERE TO GO FOR MORE INFORMATION

Dulloo, Abdul, et al. "Efficacy of a Green Tea Extract Rich in Catechin Polyphenols and Caffeine in Increasing 24-h Energy Expenditure and Fat Oxidation in Humans." *American Journal of Clinical Nutrition* 70, December 1999.

Epstein, Leonard H. "Treatment of Childhood Obesity." In *Handbook of Eating Disorders,* edited by Kelly D. Brownell and John P. Foreyt. New York: Basic Books, 1986.

Garrow, J. S. "The Safety of Dieting." *Proceedings of the Nutrition Society* 50, no. 2 (August 1991).

Hirschmann, Jane R., and Carol H. Munter. *Overcoming Overeating.* New York: Fawcett Books, 1989.

Larkin, Marilyn. "Ways to Win At Weight Loss." *FDA Consumer,* September 1997.

Levine, James A., et al. "Role of Nonexercise Activity Thermogenesis in Resistance to Fat Gain in Humans." *Science* 283 (January 1999).

Papazian, Ruth. "Should You Go On a Diet?" *FDA Consumer,* September 1998.

Safer, D. J. "Diet, Behavior Modification, and Exercise: A Review of Obesity Treatments from a Long-Term Perspective." *Southern Medical Journal* 84, no. 12 (December 1991).

Tucker, Larry A., and Glenn M. Friedman. "Television Viewing and Obesity in Adult Males." *American Journal of Public Health* 79 (April 1989).

Tulldah, J., et al. "Mode of Infant Feeding and Achieved Growth in Adolescence: Early Feeding Patterns in Relation to Growth and Body Composition in Adolescence." *Obesity Research* 7 no. 5 (September 1999).

CHAPTER 5

MEDICAL AND SURGICAL TREATMENT OF OBESITY

DRUG THERAPIES

Because of the poor long-term results often realized from behavior therapy, diet and exercise, there has been increased interest in drug treatment of obesity, and, as reported in the 1998 NHLBI *Clinical Guidelines,* drug therapy has undergone radical changes in the last few years. With the publication of the trials with phentermine and fenfluramine by Weintraub in 1992, drug therapy began to change from short-term to long-term use. Both dexfenfluramine and fenfluramine alone, as well as the combination of phentermine/fenfluramine, were used long term. The *Guidelines* reported that after 1995, the use of the prescription drugs fenfluramine or dexfenfluramine for weight loss increased to 14 million prescriptions during a one-and-one-half-year period. However, concerns about reported unacceptable side effects, such as valvular lesions of the heart causing significant insufficiency of the valves, led to the withdrawal of the drugs dexfenfluramine and fenfluramine from the market in September 1997.

In November 1997, the FDA approved a new drug, sibutramine, for use in obesity and is in the process of evaluating orlistat for long-term use. The drugs used to promote weight loss have been anorexiants or appetite suppressants. Appetite suppressant medications promote weight loss by decreasing appetite or increasing the feeling of being full. These drugs decrease appetite by increasing serotonin or catecholamine—two brain chemicals that affect mood and appetite. Appetite suppressants are effective but modest in their ability to produce weight loss. Net weight loss attributable to drugs generally has been reported to be in the range of 4.4 to 22 pounds, although some patients lose significantly more weight. Most of the weight loss usually occurs in the first six months of therapy, with a plateauing or actual increase in weight in the following six months. Weight-loss medications are recommended only for patients who are at increased medical risk because of their weight and should not be used for cosmetic weight loss. The potential for side effects from the use of weight-loss drugs is of great concern. There are no known pharmacologic agents whose specific effect is to reduce abdominal fat.

The *Guidelines* recommend that drugs should be discontinued if significant weight loss is not achieved (meaning a loss of at least four pounds in the first four weeks) or if serious adverse effects occur. Also, weight-loss drugs may only be used as part of a comprehensive weight-loss program including diet and physical activity for patients with a BMI of 30 or more or for patients with a BMI of 27 who also have obesity-related risk factors or diseases.

Some antidepressant medications have been studied for possible aid to treating obesity. Although these drugs are FDA approved for the treatment of depression, their use in weight loss is an "off-label" use. Studies of these medications generally have found that patients lost modest amounts of weight for up to six months. However, most studies have found that patients who lost weight while taking antidepressant medications tended to regain weight while they were still on the drug treatment.

Amphetamines and closely related compounds are not recommended for use in the treatment of obesity due to their potential for abuse and dependence.

Sibutramine

Sibutramine works to suppress appetite primarily by inhibiting the reuptake of the neurotransmitters norepinephrine and serotonin. Animal studies have shown that it also increases thermogenesis (expending of energy). Unlike dexfenfluramine, sibutramine does not cause an increase in release of serotonin from the nerve cell. In clinical trials, patients taking sibutramine while on a reduced-calorie diet, lost 10 to 15 pounds over six months. The average weight loss in persons on only the reduced-calorie diet was 3.5 pounds. The most common side effects associated with sibutramine include dry mouth, headache, constipation and insomnia. It can raise blood pressure, so the FDA recommends regular blood pressure evaluations for patients taking sibutramine. Sibutramine is manufactured and distributed by Knoll Pharmaceutical Company under the brand name Meridia.

Orlistat

This is the first in a new class of drugs known as lipase inhibitors, compounds that block the absorption (digestion) of roughly a third of the fat that the user consumes. In clinical trials, patients who took Xenical® (trade name of orlistat) lost about 10 percent of their body weight, more than three times the amount lost by those who took a placebo. Most of the patients taking orlistat reported such side effects as intestinal cramping, gas and oily or loose stools, but those usually were mild and lasted only a few weeks. The drug can also interfere with the body's ability to absorb vitamins A, D, E, K and beta carotene. FDA delayed approval for Xenical because one study showed an increase in cases of breast cancer, but researchers determined that many of those cancers were preexisting and that the breast cancer incidents were a statistical fluke. A large-scale follow-up study showed no increased risk of breast cancer. With this question settled, final FDA approval was granted on April 26, 1999. The drug is intended for treatment of severe obesity only. One concern, in addition to the side effects, is that people will quickly regain the weight they lost once they stop taking the drug. Almost everyone in the study did gain back their weight when they stopped taking the drug, so people may need to take it for life—at a cost of around $1,000 a year. But the study's high dropout rate (66 percent) suggests that patients will be unlikely to take the drug on a long-term basis. One of the reasons many patients drop out quickly is the need to cut fat in their diet—or suffer the embarrassment of loose stools and loss of fecal control. Clinical studies show that these side effects seem to be worse in the beginning and then improve later on—probably because the patients reduce their fat intake when they see what the consequences are.

SURGICAL TECHNIQUES FOR WEIGHT LOSS

Surgical treatment of obesity has aroused widespread interest and controversy. When used, it is most often as a last resort, after more conventional approaches have failed over a period of at least four years. It is not recommended for patients over the age of 50 and is suggested only for patients who are 125 pounds or more above their desirable body weight. With surgical treatments, the magnitude of weight loss varies widely, as does the number of patients who do not return for follow-up treatment or who require multiple operations. In a review of studies, the NHLBI *Clinical Guidelines* noted that weight loss due to surgical intervention ranged from 110.2 pounds to as much as 220.5 pounds in a period of six months to one year. The safety of this type of surgery and the recognition and successful treatment of side effects in cooperating patients have improved greatly in recent years.

According to the American Society for Bariatric Surgery, surgical treatment is medically necessary because it is the only proven method of achieving long-term weight control for the severely obese and therefore represent a legitimate, potentially lifesaving intervention.

Extremely obese persons often do not benefit from the more conservative treatments for weight loss and weight maintenance; obesity severely impairs quality of life, and these individuals are at higher risk for premature death. Because of this, the National Institutes of Health Consensus Development Conference consensus statement, "Gastrointestinal Surgery for Severe Obesity," concluded that the benefits outweigh the risks and that this more aggressive approach is reasonable in individuals who strongly desire substantial weight loss and also have other life-threatening conditions.

Following surgery, most patients lose weight rapidly and continue to do so for up to two years. Although most patients then begin to regain some of their lost weight, few regain it all.

In addition to the weight loss, surgery also improves most obesity-related conditions. For example, in one study blood-sugar levels of most patients with diabetes returned to normal after surgery. In another study, 60 percent of the patients who initially had obesity-related conditions were free of medication for these conditions three years after surgery.

Surgical treatment for the super obese (bariatric surgery) is not a cosmetic procedure, and it does not involve the removal of adipose tissue (fat) by suction or excision. Bariatric surgery involves reducing the size of the gastric reservoir, with or without a degree of associated malabsorption.

In 1991, a National Institutes of Health panel reversed an earlier negative view on surgical procedures for treating severe obesity as newer procedures with fewer complications have been developed. An estimated 35,000 Americans a year now have surgery to help them lose weight.

Obesity surgery basically is of two types: restriction and gastric bypass.

Restriction Procedures

These operations reduce the volume of food ingested. To be effective, they require patients to accept the premise of eating less. They are not recommended for patients who are food or cola addicts or alcoholics. All forms of gastric restriction operations fail in a certain category of patients who overeat the food provided in a liquid diet and in those who eat continuously; these patients find that they can consume as many milk shakes as they want as long as they drink them slowly, and consequently they do not lose weight. Even though such surgery has become reliable, it is not without drawbacks. People have to get accustomed to eating small meals and need to take vitamins for the rest of their lives to make up for the nutrients that the intestine no longer absorbs.

Edward Mason, professor of Surgery at the University of Iowa and a pioneer in the field of obesity surgery, divided the stomach so that a small pouch was formed, through which the food passed. The small size of the pouch and the small exit from it significantly decrease the amount of food that can be consumed at one sitting. His design was altered in the late 1970s by J. F. Alden, who partitioned the stomach rather than dividing it.

Restrictive operations lead to weight loss in almost all patients—on average from 50 percent to 80 percent of their excess weight; however, weight regain does sometimes occur. This usually happens with those patients who are unable to adjust their eating habits.

Gastric restriction procedures include gastric banding and vertical banded gastroplasty.

Gastric Banding. In this procedure, a band made of special material is placed around the stomach near its upper end, creating a small pouch and a narrow passage into the larger remainder of the stomach. A common risk is vomiting caused by the small stomach being overly stretched by food particles that have not been chewed well.

Vertical Banded Gastroplasty (VBG). This procedure is the most frequently used restrictive operation for weight control. Both a band and staples are used to create a small stomach pouch, which limits the amount of food the person can eat at one time. After a few bites of food, the person feels full. According to the NHLBI *Clinical Guidelines,* gastroplasty with diet had a favorable net outcome on weight loss after two years compared to diet alone. Vertical-banded gastroplasty was more effective than horizontal-banded gastroplasty. To avoid dehydration, the pouch must allow fluids to pass through it easily, which can be a problem if the person drinks high-calorie liquids, such as milk shakes, milk, soda pop or other sweets—any weight loss in that case would be negligible. Risks of VBG include erosion of the band, breakdown of the staple line and, in a small number of cases, leakage of stomach juices into the abdomen, which requires an emergency operation. Hospitalization usually is two to three days, with another 10 to 14 days before the patient can return to work.

Laparoscopic Adjustable Gastric Banding (AGB). Projected to be *the* obesity surgery of the future, this procedure is performed widely in Europe and Latin America but has not yet been approved by the Food and Drug Administration for use in the United States. AGB allows gastric banding with small incisions through a laparascope, a flexible fiberoptic tube and light source. The adjustable band is placed around the upper stomach where it squeezes the stomach, creating a small pouch. In addition to being minimally invasive (usually requiring only overnight hospitalization), its advantage is that the band can be adjusted later in the doctor's office, if the patient is not losing enough weight.

Gastric Bypass Surgery

This procedure has been in use since 1957 to reduce and control weight. First performed by Dr. Edward Mason, it offers a rapid weight loss without giving up food by reducing the amount of food that can be digested or absorbed. Gastric bypass divides the stomach, closing off a large segment by stapling it shut. Because the stomach is smaller, it cannot hold as much, and weight loss results because the patient becomes "full" rapidly. If he continues eating, vomiting occurs, frequently reason enough for the patient to eat less.

Bypass surgery is intended to reduce calorie intake without necessarily reducing food consumption. It is reserved for extremely obese persons and produces substantial and lasting losses of as much as 100 pounds. Side effects such as frequent diarrhea are common, and there is a mortality rate of about 3 percent. In addition, acid-related gastroduodenal disease may occur in the bypassed gastrointestinal tract. Some bypass patients develop bulimia, and others become obese again. Gastric bypass operations may also cause "dumping syndrome," whereby stomach contents move too rapidly through the small intestine. Symptoms include nausea, weakness, sweating, fainting and diarrhea after eating. When eating sweets, the patient may become so weak and sweaty as to be forced to lie down until the symptoms pass.

Despite these side effects, gastric bypass is the most effective method for controlling morbid obesity. The Swedish Obesity Study (SOS) found that gastric bypass produced greater weight loss than gastroplasty (93.3 pounds versus 67 pounds) at one year. Studies have indicated the need for standardized long-term data and methods to correct hernias and diarrhea caused by the procedure.

These operations can cause a 38 percent weight loss within 12 months, and long-term experience suggests that weight loss is maintained for as long as five years in these patients. Complications include gastric outlet obstruction, vomiting, dumping syndrome (sweating and weakness after eating, associated with rapid emptying of stomach contents into small intestine), gastric leaks and wound infections.

COSMETIC SURGERY TO LOSE FAT AREAS

After a person loses a large amount of weight, either because of low-calorie dieting or following stomach surgery, he or she may choose to have cosmetic surgery to remove folds of skin or excessive fat "pockets."

Abdominoplasty

This is a shaping of the abdominal area by surgery, popular since the 1960s. Frequently referred to as a "tummy tuck," this surgery gets rid of stomach fat and tightens flabby muscles and loose abdominal skin. Frequently following a significant weight loss, the skin that had stretched as the abdomen grew during weight gain will hang down over the beltline and even over the pubic area. Not only can this be unsightly, but it may lead to skin irritation or even skin breakdown. When this happens, abdominoplasty may be recommended. During an abdominoplasty, the surgeon makes an incision of from seven to 15 inches across the body at the bikini line, lifts the skin, uses sutures to tighten the abdominal muscles and tissue, pulls the skin back down over the tightened area, cuts off excess skin and then closes the incision, making a new "belly button" in the process. The length of the incision depends on the looseness of the skin. There is some pain and a scar, which usually fades to a thin line within a year. Costs generally range between $1,200 and $8,500. Once an indulgence of the wealthy, such surgery is now advertised to the public. It is now even possible to finance such surgery through an easy monthly payment plan—as a New Mexico plastic surgeon's Web site proclaims, "Many doctors accept several methods of payment, including credit cards. Some participate in local and national programs to help you finance the cost of surgery." According to the American Society of Plastic and Reconstructive Surgeons (ASPRS), performance of abdominoplasty procedures increased 215 percent between 1981 and 1988. The ASPRS reported 20,213 such procedures in 1990.

Abdominoplasties are not always without problems. When fat above the incision is not completely removed, bulges can occur above the scar line. These bulges can also appear if circulation is impaired during surgery, resulting in an accumulation of fluid. Because removing fat from the upper part of the abdomen can lead to bleeding and can interfere with the skin's blood supply, fat is frequently left in this upper area, giving unsatisfactory results, with the upper abdomen sticking out over the more-flattened lower abdomen.

These complications have led to a more frequent use of liposuction for abdominal fat removal. However, because successful liposuction depends on normal elasticity to shrink the skin after surgery, this procedure isn't always satisfactory either where there is excess skin or loose muscle. In many such cases, surgeons first use liposuction to remove the fat and then follow with abdominoplasty to tighten the abdominal muscles and remove excess skin.

Liposuction

This surgical procedure was pioneered in Europe in the 1970s to remove localized deposits of excess fat. It is also called liposculpture, lipoplasty or lipectomy. The surgeon inserts a long, thin, hollow blunt-edged tube called a cannula through a quarter-inch incision. This tube is attached via another hollow tube to a machine with a powerful vacuum apparatus that sucks out subcutaneous (beneath the skin) fat. The collecting tube is transparent, allowing the surgeon to see the tissue being removed. Liposuction has been referred to as "maid service for your fat: The surgeon vacuums the areas you didn't have the time or energy to clean up yourself." Though once controversial, it has become an increasingly common type of cosmetic surgery today.

Giorgio Fischer, a surgeon in Rome, was the first to devise an instrument to remove fat by suction and the first to perform liposuction surgery. The original procedure removed fat almost totally from the suctioned area, creating a large cavity that filled with body fluids. Because the skin overlying it did not shrink correspondingly, the procedure left an unsatisfactory result.

To combat this problem, Yves-Gérard Ilouz, a French surgeon, devised a method for dissecting fat with a blunt tube (cannula) that removed fat in a regular series of tunnels created sequentially by probing the fat deposit to be treated. In this new procedure, both the adjacent fat and the small blood vessels running through the area remained intact, allowing continuous contact between the skin and the underlying tissue. This helped the skin to shrink slowly and regularly over the newly contoured area, with less likelihood of developing ripples and depressions. Keeping original blood vessels in the area helped fluids that leak into it during the postoperative period to be more easily absorbed into the body. This shortened the prolonged wound drainage that characterized earlier suction procedures.

Liposuction was developed to remove from a healthy, normal-weight person localized, genetically derived fat deposits that do not respond to diet or exercise. It is not intended to be a treatment for obesity. The most frequently treated areas include the hips and thighs and the abdomen. Liposuction can also be done on the neck, face, arms and legs.

According to American Academy of Cosmetic Surgery statistics, 372,857 liposuction surgeries were performed nationally in 1998, compared to 292,942 in 1996 and 226,744 in 1994; a 64 percent increase from 1994 to 1998. The average physician fee in 1998 was $2,686, with the average total cost $3,304.

Results: While fluid shifts restricted fat removal to about two pounds during a single liposuction in the early days, recent advances in liposuction techniques, such as tumescent liposuction, allow doctors to safely take out three to four times that amount and to remove up to 15 inches off a person's girth. Tumescent liposuction injects the area to be suctioned with a special fluid/anesthesia combination prior to suctioning. The fluid constricts the surrounding blood vessels, making the procedure nearly bloodless, while minimizing the pain. According to the American Academy of Cosmetic Surgery, 91 percent of liposuction surgeries today are tumescent.

Not all fat is removed from a location. The surgeon leaves some fat cells behind because fat cells grow and shrink, depending on nutrition and the age of the patient. Removing all the fat cells would result in a disproportionately flat area.

Not everyone achieves satisfactory results, mainly because there is no control over how the skin will contract over suctioned areas. Some patients end up with "dents" and more uneven skin and sagging than they had before surgery. Others have dropped two full clothing sizes.

Liposuction surgery differs from fat loss through dieting and exercise. When fat is lost in those ways, fat cells become smaller, though their number throughout the body remains constant. These "starved" fat cells send messages to the brain indicating their depleted state, stimulating hunger. When they receive extra calories, these cells once again store fat for future needs. Liposuction, in contrast, actually removes fat cells from the treated area. These are not replaced unless there is a subsequent weight gain large enough to fill the remaining cells to their capacity. For this reason, patients who have undergone liposuction surgery must monitor their caloric intake to maintain positive results. Reaccumulated fat is not necessarily deposited in the same locations that have been suctioned. This new fat generally tends to spread itself evenly throughout the body.

Liposuction also removes fat from specific, targeted areas, but diet and exercise may reduce nonpreferred areas while leaving other areas virtually intact. Women with large thighs, for instance, are often frustrated by the persistence of this phenomenon even when their diet and exercise regimes lead to virtual emaciation of their faces and upper bodies, and men with "spare tires" around their middles are often unable to eliminate them entirely by dieting despite considerable weight loss.

Limitations: Liposuction surgery is not the ultimate answer to dieters' prayers, though. The procedure does have distinct limitations.

Good skin tone is important for continued success because once fat is removed, the skin must shrink to fit a new contour. Assuming that prolonged accumulation and drainage of body fluids does not occur, skin that is sufficiently elastic will heal without dimples, dents or ripples. But skin that has lost its elasticity may not contract as rapidly or satisfactorily.

Liposuction can be performed under local or general anesthesia. At the present time, the surgery is commonly performed on an outpatient basis in an office surgical suite or ambulatory surgical facility. However, medical opinions differ about whether the procedure should be done in an office or in a hospital. Dr. Pierre F. Fournier, a past president of the International Academy of Cosmetic Surgery, has stated that "anyone who is going to have a large amount of fat removed should be operated on in a hospital and observed overnight. Such patients will probably need intravenous fluids and may need blood transfusions."

Liposuction surgery is a body-contouring operation, not a weight-loss procedure. Only small amounts of fat in terms of weight, one-half to two pounds, are actually removed during an operation, and this fat is considerably lighter than the solutions administered intravenously during the surgery. It is not uncommon for a patient actually to observe a weight gain of several pounds in the first few days following surgery because of this fluid replacement. But the kidneys rapidly eliminate excess fluid, and body weight soon returns to its preoperative level. Most patients with small to moderate fat bulges lose only a few pounds but may drop two to three clothing sizes. Many patients, however, report continuing weight loss for several months following liposuction, stabilizing at a loss of five to 10 pounds.

Complications: Early reports of problems, including loss of limbs and a dozen deaths, led to investigations of liposuction procedures by the American Society of Plastic and Reconstructive Surgeons. In 1987 the society issued a report stating that "suction-assisted lipectomy is normally safe and effective" when performed by a properly trained, experienced surgeon with board certification in plastic surgery and a proven track record of success in liposuction. Legally, any surgeon can perform liposuction.

This fact was brought out during a 1989 hearing held by the U.S. House of Representatives Small Business Committee's Subcommittee on Regulation and Business Opportunities. Chairman Ron Wydan (D-Oregon) concluded that a liposuction surgeon "can buy $4,000 worth of equipment on Monday morning, do two procedures in the afternoon and make money all day Tuesday," even if he or she lacks accreditation.

But proponents of liposuction cited its safety record. John McCurdy, Jr., in his 1987 book, *Sculpturing Your Body: Diet, Exercise and Lipo (Fat) Suction* (now out of print) wrote that a compilation of more than 5,000 cases performed through 1983 showed only six complications, most minor (loss of skin and limbs was blamed on untreated infection; deaths occurred when liposuction was performed along with other surgery or by unqualified surgeons).

Liposuction is major surgery and, as such, carries all the inherent risks, including potential problems with anesthesia, infection, discomfort, recovery time, side effects, complications and, of course, high cost. Minor complications associated with liposuction can include bruising, swelling and local sensory changes. Some complications can be permanent, such as bodily lumps, craters, asymmetry and permanent creases and furrows where the fat is removed. If the suction occurs too close to the skin's surface, it may tug at the skin tissue, causing it to ripple. The worst complications are excessive bleeding and loss of body fluids. Patients who have large amounts of fat removed (two liters or more) run the risk of shock if fluids are not adequately replenished during the surgery.

Bleeding was the most common complication following liposuction surgery in its early days. Removal of large amounts of fat can still result in moderate blood loss, but for the routine liposuction, these problems today are unusual.

Most serious complications today are associated with large-volume (more than 10 pounds) liposuction.

As with any procedure involving incisions in the skin, liposuction does leave scars. Usually these are small, about one-quarter inch, and are camouflaged by placement within natural skin lines. However, surgeons caution that persons predisposed to "overactive" scars need to discuss this problem with their doctor prior to surgery.

Early complaints of dents, depressions and skin waviness were blamed on the uneven removal of fat during liposuction. Today's specialists claim to have solved most of the problem by leaving a pad of fat on the undersurface of the skin and confining fat removal to deeper areas. Most surgeons now use smaller cannulas to make smaller, more numerous tunnels through the fat. This results in a smoother, more even shrinkage of skin over the suctioned area. The most troublesome area is the inner thigh, where skin does not contract as well as skin in other areas.

When uneven contours do exist after swelling has gone down, a second liposuction procedure is usually performed under local anesthesia.

Surgeons say it is far easier to remove small amounts of excess fat than to fill in depressions caused by excessive fat removal.

The newest liposuction technique is ultrasonic liposuction (or ultrasound assisted lipoplasty—UAL), which was introduced in the United States in 1994 and was FDA approved in 1996. UAL uses sound waves to liquefy the fat so that it can be vacuumed out of the body faster than it might with other methods. There is less trauma to the body with UAL. Plus the ultrasound leaves blood vessels and nerves intact, so there is significantly less bleeding and postoperative pain. UAL may make fat easier to remove in certain dense areas of the body, such as the upper back. UAL is used in combination with the tumescent technique. American Academy of Cosmetic Surgery statistics show 3 percent of liposuction surgeries being ultrasound.

WHERE TO GO FOR MORE INFORMATION

Ackerman, Norman B. *Fat No More: The Answer for the Dangerously Overweight.* Amherst, N.Y.: Prometheus Books, 1999.

Davidson, Michael H., et al. "Weight Control and Risk Factor Reduction in Obese Subjects Treated for 2 Years With Orlistat." *Journal of the American Medical Association* 281 (January 1999).

Engler, Alan M. *Body Sculpture: Plastic Surgery of the Body for Men & Women.* Hudson Pub., 1998.

Freeman, J. B., et al. "Weight Loss After Extended Gastric Bypass." *Obesity Surgery* 7 no. 4 (August 1997).

Hansen, D. L., et al. "Thermogenic Effects of Sibutramine in Humans." *American Journal of Clinical Nutrition* 68 (December 1998).

Hellmich, Nanci. "Fat Blocker Weighs In A Drug For Obese." *USA Today,* January 20, 1999.

———. "New Fat-blocking Obesity Drug Approved." *USA Today,* April 27, 1999.

———. "Drastic Measures for the Desperate." *USA Today,* November 16, 1999.

Mason, E. E., et al. "A Decade of Change in Obesity Surgery." *Obesity Surgery* 7, no. 3 (June 1997).

Pollnar, Fran. "Obesity Surgery Regaining Favor." *Medical World News,* May 1991.

Powers, P. S., et al. "Outcome of Gastric Restriction Procedures: Weight, Psychiatric Diagnoses, and Satisfaction." *Obesity* 7 (December 1997).

Weintraub, M., P. R. Sundaresan, M. Madan, et al. "Long-term Weight Control Study. I (weeks 0 to 34). The Enhancement of Behavior Modification, Caloric Restriction, and Exercise by Fenfluramine Plus Phentermine Versus Placebo." *Clinical Pharmacology and Therapeutics* 51 (1992).

CHAPTER 6
ANOREXIA NERVOSA

WHO ARE ANOREXICS?

Anorexia nervosa has always been overwhelmingly a disorder of upper-class adolescents (the usual age range is from 12 to 25), but studies show it to be increasing in older women and in other social classes. Ninety to 95 percent of anorexics are female; in 85 percent of patients, onset occurs between the ages of 13 and 20.

It is estimated that in the United States, between one and two females in late adolescence and early childhood of every 200 is starving herself (source: *Diagnostic and Statistical Manual of Mental Disorders,* 4th ed., Washington, D.C.: American Psychiatric Association, 1994). The Anorexia Nervosa and Related Eating Disorders Organization (ANRED) estimates that approximately one in every 100 females between the ages of 10 and 20 suffers from anorexia. The number of children between 8 and 11 years old with anorexia is said by ANRED to be increasing. For girls over 16 in private schools or in universities, the figure may be as high as 1 in 10. Until recently, anorexia was rare among African Americans, low incidence explained by experts as due to less concern among African Americans with dieting and being thin. They reason that the recent increase in anorexia in black women is due to their assimilation of the ideals of the middle and upper classes.

Anorexia nervosa has been said to develop only in the face of plenty, that it exists only where food is abundant. However, today's researchers are beginning to discover that the stereotype is inaccurate and that it may have come about because such a large proportion of the studies done were of college students and patients who could afford treatment. In a 1989 survey of more than 2,000 adolescent girls and their mothers, University of Michigan psychologist Adam Drewnowski discovered that the frequency of eating disorders was the same in lower-income communities near Detroit as it was in the city's wealthy suburbs—about 2 percent.

Family Dynamics

Researchers have noted that there is a greater risk of a person developing anorexia nervosa when another member of the family has had the disorder or when a parent is either very thin or obese. What has not been established is whether this risk is genetic. Studies reported in 1998 from Toronto Hospital, Ontario, and University of Pittsburgh School of Medicine concluded that genetic factors may influence predisposition to eating disorders but do not prove that it is actually inherited. Because a few sets of identical twins have been found in which both twins succumbed to anorexia, and because several cases are known of adopted family members matching the patterns of their biological families' histories, this family tendency is believed to be more environmental than inherited. However, research in this area has been sparse; much more needs to be learned.

Anorexics do tend to come from families placing strong emphasis on food. In their book *Anorexia Nervosa and Bulimia: A Handbook for Counselors and Therapists* (now out of print), Patricia A. Neuman and Dr. Patricia A. Halvorson explained that "this concern may be the result of the special dietary needs of a family member, an emphasis on nutrition, and/or previous power struggles over eating. The family may also have used food for purposes other than nourishment. Eating may be used when members face problems or unpleasantness, as a sign of love and caring for the providers, to fill time, or to keep the family together and 'happy.'"

Clinicians have found that certain personality types seem to appear frequently among parents of anorexics. Mothers are often found to be domineering, intruding in the anorexic's hour-to-hour life. Mothers of anorexics also frequently suffer from depression, and fathers are described as "aloof or passive." Alcoholism and other addictions, of one or both parents, are not uncommon. However, none of these patterns is always present; some cases even show the exact opposite family dynamics.

But there are medical experts who still insist that family dynamics play an important role in generating the disorder. They cite those family features most likely to encourage anorexia as enmeshment (entanglement in one another's affairs), rigidity, overprotectiveness and inability to resolve conflict within the family. One suggestion is that a father's emotional or physical absence from the family may be a major influence on both anorexia nervosa and bulimia in adolescent girls. Thirty-six of 39 young female patients questioned in one study described their fathers as emotionally distant.

Child Anorexics

Anorexia nervosa has been reported in children as early as age four; it is estimated that 3 percent of reported anorexia cases occur before the age of puberty. Because children, especially girls, have less body fat than adolescents, they become emaciated more quickly than older anorexics. GERALD F. M. RUSSELL examined a series of 20 girls whose anorexia nervosa began before their first menstrual period (menarche), concluding that anorexia nervosa can be devastating to physical development. There is prolonged delay of puberty (late menarche) and interference with growth in stature and breast development. Young children with anorexia have exhibited clinging behavior upon entering school, difficulty in maintaining peer relations, physical and psychological immaturity, depression and an inability to translate feelings into words. Also, according to DSM-IV, any associated mental disturbances may be more severe among children who develop anorexia nervosa.

SYMPTOMS & FEATURES—WHAT TO LOOK FOR

The person with anorexia nervosa typically begins to diet with a simple goal of losing weight, but over time the achievement of that goal becomes an expression of mastery, control and virtue. The anorexic may find dieting easy and rewarding from the start or at least discover that in a sense she is good at it. Typically she ends up by continuing to diet despite having gone past her target weight. The desire for slenderness becomes secondary to the need for control and mastery over the body and develops into a real fear of fatness and a drive to remain small and childlike.

Because anorexia nervosa patients do not see themselves as abnormal, they do not want any help in reversing their weight loss. When told they cannot live on such a small amount of food, they will insist that they feel better as they become thinner. Because they do not suffer, they must be well. This denial of illness is an important feature early in the disorder. The clinical picture of anorexia nervosa centers on a three-fold denial—denial of hunger, of thinness and of fatigue.

Even if they admit to some weight loss, anorexics will feel that although they may have lost weight generally, some particular part of their body is still too large. When family pressures or social obligations force anorexics to eat, most will use deception to hide their extreme dieting. They'll slip food to the dog, flush it down the toilet or throw it into the garbage. Teenagers will tell parents, "I'm not hungry; I ate at a friend's house." Many will induce vomiting after meals. When undergoing treatment, anorexics will resort to all kinds of deceptions to lead doctors to believe that they are gaining weight. Among the documented deceptions are drinking enormous amounts of water before being weighed, recalibrating scales and inserting weights in the rectum and the vagina.

The central feature of anorexia nervosa is the overriding pursuit of thinness. This may seem to begin innocently with ordinary adolescent self-consciousness—dieting to lose extra pounds put on during puberty's growth spurts. But after several months, the restrictor anorexic will stubbornly refuse to eat normal amounts of food. Typically she limits her intake to about 600–800 calories per day, resulting in a loss of 25 percent or more of body weight. In extreme cases, the loss may be as high as 50 percent.

When questioned about her loss of weight, an anorexic will deny that she is too thin or that there is anything wrong with her. This denial can be an obstacle for doctors. Because they don't perceive themselves as ill or abnormal, anorexics refuse help. Denial is a typical characteristic of anorexia nervosa and is seen as an early sign of the disorder.

One of the fundamental characteristics of anorexia nervosa is a disturbance in body image, "feeling fat" even when emaciated. During treatment, the anorexic claims that her body is larger than it really is. She seems genuinely unaware of her changed body proportions. Even though her body may appear starved, she may stubbornly insist that she is not as thin as another anorexic who is as thin or thinner than she; yet she will recognize the other anorexic as too thin. A few will admit to their emaciated state and even recognize the health dangers, but they will still refuse to eat. Many anorexics argue that their thin bodies are still too fat. Others consider their stick-figure legs and arms to be attractive and "just right."

Overestimation of body size may indicate greater severity of disorder with less hope of recovery. In studies, patients who most grossly overestimated were also those who were the most malnourished, were previous treatment failures, indicated a greater loss of appetite, had a greater tendency to deny their illness, vomited, were more depressed and in general exhibited more symptoms of anorexia nervosa.

In addition to the misperception of body size, the anorexic's body image disturbance can involve her attitude toward her body. Frequently the maturing anorexic expresses self-loathing, particularly of her developing female body parts, such as the normal slight curve of stomach or rounding of hips or buttocks.

Hunger is usually denied, even in the presence of stomach pains. When she does eat a small bit of food, an anorexic will complain that it causes her acute stomach pain.

In contrast to starving nonanorexics, who generally attempt to conserve energy by reducing activity and who usually show symptoms of listlessness and indifference, anorexics are often hyperactive, tending to indulge in heavy or prolonged exercise. Instead of being exhausted while starving, these young women enjoy boundless energy until late in their illness. The anorexic begins to exercise to burn up calories and lose additional weight. As with dieting, however, exercising over time becomes an issue of self-discipline and control; anorexics cannot allow themselves to miss even one day of the highly structured regimen that they have assigned themselves.

If an anorexic was already involved in a sport, she will likely become driven, almost obsessed to excel at it. Anorexics may appear to be in perpetual motion—constantly busy, moving about restlessly until late into the night, almost never sitting down. Studies have shown that anorexics walk an average of 6.8 miles a day compared with the average of 4.0 miles walked by women of normal weight. This hyperactivity is not generally present before the onset of anorexic illness. Just as the anorexic denies hunger, she will deny any difficulty in sitting still and attending to her work.

Often compulsive behavior is exhibited in excessive orderliness, cleaning and studying. As Neuman and Halvorson explained, "Anything less than perfection is upsetting to the anorexic, and everything undertaken seems to be done in excess."

Several years ago anorexia was generally interpreted as reflecting a wish not to grow up, to return to a prepubertal stage; therapists now say that many anorexics appear anxious to exercise authority and to control their lives through regulation of body weight.

Anorexics have been described as suffering from a "weight phobia." Regardless of the original reason for dieting, subsequent weight gain by the anorexic causes severe anxiety and weight loss reduces it. This "phobia" about "normal" body weight appears to intensify as the patient becomes thinner. She weighs herself frequently, becoming anxious if the scales show an increase over the previous reading. In her mind, each drop in weight becomes a new barometer; next time she must weigh less to be normal. Anorexics seem to have a greater fear of becoming obese than of dying from starvation. As the anorexic's weight drops, her fear becomes more entrenched: the thinner she gets, the fatter she thinks she is.

In addition to a phobic attitude toward weight, the anorexic develops another phobia toward food. At first, she fears only high-carbohydrate foods and so deletes them from her diet. Soon she systematically eliminates fats and other foods until only a few vegetables and fruits remain. She also controls food portions rigidly; she must restrict intake to a specific number of pieces or bites a day. If she does exceed her allotted daily portion, the anorexic suffers severe anxiety and sets about to control her eating even more severely.

She may exhibit oral expulsion syndrome—attempting to lose weight by chewing food and spitting it out instead of swallowing it. Some anorexics become compulsive about it, spending hours doing it in secret and, in time, developing intense anxieties about swallowing. As a consequence, they become isolated, fearful and seriously malnourished.

Some researchers maintain that the core psychopathology of anorexia nervosa is cognitive; that is, such individuals have extremely distorted ways of thinking and distorted and irrational beliefs about food, themselves and the world. They may have completely irrational ideas regarding the caloric content of foods, even to the extent of worrying about gaining weight from licking a stamp. Such individuals may also have all-or-nothing beliefs about eating; for example, believing that eating one piece of candy is as bad as eating the whole box. The anorexic individual may equate self-worth with physical appearance. To put on weight means to be worthless. Similarly, the anorexic individual may have attitudes about the world and others such as believing that others evaluated them only in terms of body size and shape. Although this belief is distorted, it's merely an exaggeration of some of the attitudes that are shaped by the popular media.

Anorexic patients often become experts in devious behavior. They will conceal their eating habits by lying about what, when and where they eat. Usually they do not like to eat in front of others and come up with excuses to avoid eating with the family, partly to avoid the food itself and partly to avoid confrontations about their eating habits and their appearance. Because of family pressure to eat, they may take food onto their plate, surreptitiously slipping it to the dog under the table or hiding it in their napkins to flush down the toilet or throw away later. Many pathological behaviors occur in secret: hiding food, self-induced vomiting, laxative and/or diuretic abuse and excessive exercising.

Also accompanying anorexia nervosa is delayed psychosexual development. Although anorexics may express a desire to have boyfriends, it is only in a fairy-tale sense—to live "happily ever after." Anorexics exhibit virtually no sexual interest, with low estrogen in female anorexics and low output of testosterone in males. During therapy, anorexics cannot even talk about sex, not out of embarrassment but because it is so foreign: anorexics are totally out of touch with the sexual part of their being.

Anorexics also gradually narrow their interests. Many entirely restrict their activities to exercise, schoolwork and dieting, and all other activities fall by the wayside. Most girls lose interest in their friends early in their dieting; this loss is considered a most important early signal of the problem. By the time the weight loss has progressed to the point of requiring medical attention, an anorexic may be totally isolated from others. This isolation results in loneliness and a sense of social inadequacy.

Other warning signals include dizziness and fainting spells, nervousness around mealtime, excuses during mealtime for not eating, cutting food into small pieces or playing with it, an increased interest in collecting recipes and cooking for others, weighing frequently and wearing multiple layers of clothing (anorexics are frequently cold as a result of the loss of fat and muscle tissue). In some cases obsessive interest in food will result in an anorexic's insisting on cooking for and overfeeding her immediate family. Anorexics have been reported to hoard and conceal food, including food that is rotten or moldy, while refusing fresh food.

Another established feature of anorexia is amenorrhea (absence or suppression of menstruation). In a high percentage of cases, this is the first sign of the disorder, appearing before any noticeable loss of weight. Ultimately, it occurs in nearly all cases as weight plummets.

Anorexics have frequent mood swings; when they are most hungry and their blood sugar levels the lowest, they may become quite irritable. They also will sometimes demonstrate an inability to concentrate, and this may be coupled with confused thinking. Initially they will deny all problems, including mood changes; anorexics display a stubborn defiance about most matters, along with a noticeable lack of concern for personal problems. They tend to be highly perfectionistic, particularly about physical appearance, as well as highly self-critical. They tend to be overachievers. They will frequently seem angry, irritable, indecisive, stubborn, tense or overly sensitive. Depression or obsession is common when the disorder becomes chronic.

When asked to describe their anorexic daughters as children, parents refer to most of them as "model children," using such terms as *introverted, conscientious* and *well behaved.* They are usually nonassertive, reacting passively to others. But although an anorexic may appear outwardly smiling and happy and is usually a people pleaser, she may actually be miserable. Neuman and Halvorson stressed that although a passive personality has been found to be consistently among the most common of anorexics' traits, it is not always present. Anorexics can display irritability, indecisiveness, stubbornness and defiance.

Restricting anorexics demonstrate significant immaturity and inhibition in sexual and social experience; however, in their attempt to meet all social expectations, they sometimes present a facade of good social adjustment.

Some women marry while anorexic, even though they are likely to be infertile. The anorexic will often choose a partner who suits her as the kind of person she has become rather than as she was before becoming anorexic. For instance, the husband may be quiet and sexually undemanding, or alternatively superficially glamorous but privately wary of personal or sexual involvement. The marriage may be stable while the wife remains anorexic, but it will often be strained and tested if and when a process of recovery begins.

COMPLICATIONS: WHAT CAN HAPPEN WITHOUT EARLY DIAGNOSIS AND TREATMENT

Most of the medical complications of anorexia are those caused by starvation. The body defends its vital organs, the heart and the brain, against a lack of nutrients by slowing down: menstrual periods stop, breathing, pulse and blood pressure rates drop and thyroid function slows.

Particularly critical are the fluid and electrolyte (sodium, potassium, hydrogen, etc.) imbalances that commonly occur, especially among anorexics who induce vomiting or use laxatives extensively. Potassium deficiency can lead to muscle weakness, abdominal bloating, nervous irritability, apathy, fatigue, drowsiness, dizziness, mental confusion and irregular heartbeat. Death from kidney or heart failure may occur. Such electrolyte imbalances are not always outwardly apparent; the person suffering from them may appear to be in relatively good health.

In addition to an emaciated appearance, an anorexic usually has dry, cracking skin and may lose some hair from her scalp. Her nails become brittle. A fine downy growth of fetallike hair (lanugo) over the cheeks, neck, forearms and thighs is common. Yet she will keep her pubic and underarm hair as well as the shape of her breasts, thus ruling out glandular insufficiency as the root cause of her symptoms. The anorexic's hands and feet usually have a bluish tinge, which may also appear on her nose and ears. Other likely results of anorexia include a slow heartbeat, low blood pressure (hypotension) and a low basal metabolic rate. An anorexic may also have trouble sleeping when the loss of fat tissue padding makes sitting or lying down uncomfortable.

Those anorexics who frequently and over a long period resort to vomiting as a way to control food intake can develop a variety of dental problems, including loss of enamel, decay and enlarged salivary glands. They typically have decreased salivary flow as well. Fear and depression decrease salivary flow and affect its composition, thus potentially contributing to the formation of caries (cavities). Often this decreased flow of saliva is multiplied by the misuse of laxatives and diuretics or by antidepressant drugs. These drugs decrease total fluid volumes and affect electrolyte balance, causing an even further diminished salivary flow.

Mild anemia, swelling joints (from edema), reduced muscle mass, dizziness and lightheadedness are also results of anorexia. If the disorder becomes severe, osteoporosis, kidney failure, irregular heart rhythm and heart failure can occur. The anorexic who turns to purging to limit weight is in particular danger; the abuse of drugs to stimulate vomiting (see IPECAC), bowel movements and urination increases the risk of heart failure. In addition, there is a possibility of temporary or even permanent edema (accumulation of fluid in the body's cells, tissues or cavities) once the use of diuretics as an aid to weight reduction is stopped.

Osteoporosis (a loss of bone mass accompanied by mineralization of the remaining bone) is another consequence of anorexia nervosa. A study of anorexics by Massachusetts General Hospital researchers found that adults with anorexia nervosa had bone density that was 30 percent lower than normal. Those whose menstruation stopped before age 18 had even weaker bones—20 percent weaker than the bones of the older anorexia victims. In another study, in 24 anorexic patients who were severely malnourished, the ovaries were small and shapeless, and some hormone levels were very low.

Depression, weakness and obsession with food also accompany starvation. Personality changes can occur. Outbursts of hostility and anger or social withdrawal may surprise those who have become used to the typical "good girl" anorexic. Other complications can include amnesia, generalized fatigue, lowered body temperature (hypothermia), low blood sugar, low white blood cell count and lack of energy.

To determine the range and severity of medical complications encountered in younger patients, a study was made of the medical records of 65 adolescents and preadolescents in the Eating Disorders Clinic of the Children's Hospital at Stanford University. A total of 55 percent of anorexic patients required hospitalization for medical reasons during the study period.

George Patton reported in the *British Medical Journal* (July 15, 1989) that in an assessment of 481 anorexia nervosa patients, half of those who died killed themselves, either accidentally or intentionally through drug overdoses. This challenges the earlier view that death in anorexia nervosa is always a direct consequence of malnutrition.

There have been no clear, consistent predictors of worsening conditions without eventual improvement in anorexia nervosa cases, but factors most often found in these cases include extremely low weight, long periods with the illness, older age at onset and disturbed family relationship.

TREATING ANOREXIA NERVOSA

Because anorexics and their families tend to deny the presence of the disorder or its severity, the results of treatment of anorexia have been among the most unsatisfactory in clinical medicine. Even patients in treatment tend to resist prescribed medical and psychiatric care; because they don't consider themselves to be ill, or because they don't want their efforts to lose weight thwarted, they make those trying to help them "the enemy."

Virtually every type of therapy known to psychiatry has been proposed and tried at some time in the treatment of anorexics, but no one has been found distinctly effective or definitive. Part of the reason for this is the lack of agreement about the relationship between food and its "host." We know very little of the chemical processing of food by the body and how dieting and purging may affect the appetite center of the brain. To make matters worse, there is body image distortion and an interoceptive (internal sensory receptor) problem. (See INTEROCEPTIVE DISTURBANCE.) In addition, the treatment needs of different patients can vary widely; considerable flexibility is necessary.

Because anorexia nervosa patients differ widely in psychological, social, behavioral and biological functioning, treatment centers most frequently offer integrated and multifaceted programs. Both the physical and psychological aspects of the disorder have to be addressed: the physical aspects take precedence when the weight is low and the starvation strategy is most dominant, and the psychological aspects take precedence later, after weight concerns have been addressed and eating habits have been stabilized. Ideally, internists, nutritionists, individual or group therapists, psychopharrnacologists, psychiatrists and family therapists may all be involved in treatment.

Weight gain must occur if psychological treatment is to be meaningful. In their 1982 book, *Anorexia Nervosa: A Multidimensional Perspective*, Paul Garfinkel and David Garner explained the two reasons for this. First, the effects of starvation must be reduced for the patient truly to benefit from psychotherapy, a learning process that cannot proceed well when a patient's mental functioning is impaired. Second, patients have developed a phobic attitude toward weight and must learn to face it as a precondition for dealing with underlying psychological issues. "As long as a low weight is maintained through rigid dieting, the phobia is being reinforced, as is the avoidance of dealing realistically with significant life problems."

The concept of weight phobia has been questioned by experts such as Arthur H. Crisp, who argues that what a patient dreads is facing herself at a normal weight. He believes that what is being reinforced when weight is kept very low is the "advantage" of being "prepuberty" thin so this dread doesn't become an actuality. Other researchers have concluded that modern Western anorexia nervosa with weight phobia is clearly distinct from other groups of cases of extreme fasting without weight phobia.

The most difficult and critical factor in treatment is engaging the patient in therapy. The problem here is that many anorexics deny their illness; they insist that there is nothing wrong with them if only others would leave them alone. They mistrust themselves and especially mistrust medical people who they think are interested only in getting them to gain weight or who represent parental authority. Anorexics feel that treatment represents a betrayal of their trust, fearing a return to being what they consider overweight.

Although controversy has surrounded almost every means of weight restoration, the issue of hospitalization has been far less controversial. Historically, hospital admission has been advocated both to allow the physician to control the situation and to separate the patient from her parents.

Hospitalization should be considered if there are numerous physical complications, if the patient is suicidal or extremely unmotivated and/or if there is no outpatient treatment available.

Frequently, even when emergency care is not necessary, several days of unstructured hospital rest are ordered to give physicians and psychiatrists a chance to observe the patient. The treatment team can thus learn whether she is a starver or a vomiter, whether she hoards food or secretly throws it away, whether she drinks water or not before weigh-in. They also observe how much walking and exercising she does and whether hospitalization has resulted in her becoming agitated and manipulative or passive and withdrawn.

Length of hospitalization usually varies between two and four months. Brief hospitalization of 10 days to two weeks can be helpful for anorexics who are not severely malnourished but who suffer from laxative withdrawal (e.g., dependence on the laxative drug in place of normal bowel action) or uncontrollable binge eating and vomiting.

Application of EXPOSURE AND RESPONSE PREVENTION treatment principles to anorexia nervosa requires a patient to face the twin fears of eating and gaining weight. Reports have shown that psychological improvement does occur with weight gain; to realize it, several approaches to treatment may be effective, including forced feedings and structured diets.

Forced feeding is the most dramatic treatment for anorexia. In severe cases, in which body weight falls to dangerous levels, parents and physicians may decide to admit an anorexic to a hospital for forced feeding on the grounds that it will prevent her death and restore her to a mental state that will make meaningful therapeutic interaction possible. In these critical cases physicians recommend "renourishment" or "refeeding" because they believe that the biological effects of starvation create a psychological prison from which patients cannot escape. In this view, the anorexic must gain a certain amount of weight before she can progress in psychotherapy or make rational decisions about treatment.

Forced feeding through a tube inserted into the stomach via the nose is a method sometimes used to supplement nutrition and replace body fluids in anorexic patients. Many clinicians find several disadvantages to this method: it represents a direct intrusion into the gastrointestinal tract of someone who is already preoccupied with (and misguided about) bodily functions; it may be perceived as an assault or act of hostility that will only serve to confirm the patient's sense of her own worthlessness; it is done with minimal patient cooperation and may lead to increased mistrust; and the physiological side effects are not insignificant. Usually tube feeding is only recommended in life-threatening situations.

Response prevention can be used to treat anorexic "rituals" such as vomiting after meals, food fads, use of laxatives, compulsive exercising and frequent weighing. Response prevention entails forced avoidance of these rituals; for example, the patient might agree to delay vomiting for an increasing amount of time after meals eventually to stop vomiting altogether.

In general, it is felt that patients must retain as much control as possible as long as the desired result is achieved. Patients discharged from the hospital although the medical staff is still in control via structured enforced diets or tube feeding usually relapse.

Those patients better motivated to change will sometimes benefit from outpatient treatment. Education about the effects of starvation and application of the principles of exposure and response prevention, coupled with simple support, sometimes will produce weight gain. Individual psychotherapy is the approach most commonly prescribed for outpatient treatment, especially when the patient has stable relationships and adequate self-esteem.

Also beneficial can be the use of behavioral techniques that the patient can apply herself: keeping records of food intake, using structured meal plans and practicing "nonanorexic" eating. In cases in which certain foods are feared, the person in charge of treatment may recommend that these be left out of the diet initially but introduced later. Eventual exposure to feared foods is important; to avoid it would be to reinforce anorexic behavior. Cognitive behavioral therapy is designed to help the patient gain control of unhealthy eating behaviors and to alter the distorted and rigid thinking that perpetuates the syndrome.

The goals of individual therapy are to help the patient regain physical health, reduce symptoms, increase self-esteem and proceed with personal and social development. Long-term individual therapy may be indicated when the patient has a mild personality disorder, such as irritability, anxiety, depression, mood swings or sleep disturbance.

Group therapy can be helpful to motivated anorexics, allowing them to feel less alone with their symptoms, to get feedback from their peers and to build their social skills. It has been found useful to have patients at varying stages of improvement in a group. The role modeling done by recovering anorexics, as well as the support and appropriate confrontation by an entire group, has proven to be quite powerful.

Family therapy attempts to establish more appropriate eating patterns, facilitate communication and permit family members to feel more connected with one another. It may be helpful even if a patient is able to achieve only a limited degree of autonomy because of disturbed family relationships.

Anorexics often retreat into denial when experiencing anxiety in therapy and may flee treatment early on.

Many drug therapies have been tried, either as the major focus of treatment or as adjuncts to general support and psychological therapies. The primary aim of such treatment has been to promote food intake and weight restoration. Although drug treatments do have a place in the *management* of eating disorders, they have not yet attained a high enough degree of effectiveness to be considered as useful as they are in the treatment of such disorders as mania or depression.

In a 10-year follow-up of 76 anorexic women in Iowa and Minnesota who had been treated in hospitals and released at normal weight, Cornell University Medical College researchers found that only three women kept their weight within normal range during the 10-year study period. Thirty-one of the 76 women were still below minimum weight for their age and height at the 10-year mark. Five women in the study had died; their average weight at death was 58 pounds.

RECOVERY

Recovery from anorexia nervosa does occur, but it isn't always the same for every patient—or for every treatment center. Generally, recovery involves many factors and may vary from partial to full recovery. The criteria most usually associated with recovery are weight gain, resumption of menstruation and social/emotional maturity. Because different criteria are used by different researchers to indicate recovery, and because different treatment centers select different types of patients, studies reporting recovery rates can be confusing and contradictory.

It is tempting, because it is so noticeable, to consider only weight gain as a measure of recovery, but weight restoration alone is not always a good barometer. Returning a patient to normal weight is certainly important, but it is relatively easy to accomplish simply by hospitalizing the patient and controlling her food intake. The critical and more difficult task is to get the patient to maintain the higher weight in her normal environment. For this reason, the length of time reported in studies between "recovery" and follow-up is important. The longer the time from treatment to follow-up, the higher the reported mortality rates, the more frequent the rehospitalizations, the greater the continuing psychological problems, the more inadequate the marital and social adjustments and the lower the recovery rates. However, researchers hope that newer treatment methods, along with earlier detection (due to educational efforts and publicity), will result in more permanent recoveries.

In terms of nutrition, researchers have correlated various studies to determine that 50 percent of diagnosed and treated anorexics can be expected to recover completely within two to five years. When those anorexics who demonstrate *some* nutritional improvement are included, the rate of recovery increases to 66 percent. Approximately 90 percent of treated anorexics go on to become employed. Between 50 and 87 percent of these anorexics resume menstruation, usually a year or more after body weight has stabilized. Even for those anorexics who do not experience the return of menstrual periods, the possibility of bearing children remains if the ovaries are still active.

On the other hand, recovered anorexics may continue to experience problems relating to their disorder. Anorexia can become chronic. In their research, Neuman and Halvorson found that as many as half those affected have a relapse, and up to 38 percent may have to be rehospitalized within two years. But rehospitalization can actually be a step toward recovery; sometimes several setbacks occur before real progress is apparent. Nevertheless, approximately 18 percent of diagnosed anorexics do remain ill and unchanged. Death from complications of the disorder or from suicide has been estimated to occur in anywhere from 3 to 25 percent of cases. Psychologically, approximately 50 percent of anorexia victims, on follow-up, show problems with phobias, depression and social adjustment.

A comparison of several studies indicates that recovery rates may be predicted when body weight is low at the time treatment begins; the older the age at the onset of the disorder, the longer the duration of the illness. Other predictors are disturbed family relationships, binge eating and/or purging or a history of previous psychiatric treatment or childhood adjustment problems.

WHERE TO GO FOR MORE INFORMATION

Hall, Lindsey, and Leigh Cohen. *Anorexia Nervosa: A Guide to Recovery.* Carlsbad, Calif.: Gurze Books, 1998.

Harmon, Dan, and Carol C. Nadelson. *Anorexia Nervosa: Starving for Attention.* Broomall, Pa.: Chelsea House Publishers, 1998.

Sargent, Judy Tam. *The Long Road Back, A Survivor's Guide to Anorexia.* East Sandwich, Mass.: North Star Publications, 1999.

CHAPTER 7

BULIMIA NERVOSA

WHO ARE BULIMICS?

Bulimia has been called the disease of success because the typical bulimic is a professional woman in her mid- to late-twenties, college educated, single and working and living in a big city—an overachiever. In moments of stress, bulimics turn toward food, not away from it as anorexics do. Bulimic patients are usually more distressed and humiliated by their behavior than anorexics, swinging between intense feelings of self-control while dieting and total self-loathing when bulimic.

Sometimes eating behavior becomes bizarre. A young woman from a financially secure background may search through garbage for food. Another may shoplift food or steal money from friends and family to buy it. The behavior that supports the "habit" of recurring bulimia can resemble that of alcoholism, and its cost may also be similar.

Bulimics usually control their eating while busy with other things, but during solitary leisure time they may eat to the point of exhaustion. Enormous amounts of food may be eaten at one time, as many as 20,000 calories a day. Some studies have shown the average binge to last slightly less than one-and-a-quarter hours and to include slightly more than 3,400 calories. However, research also demonstrates that there is great variability in the amount of food persons with bulimia nervosa call a binge. What seems to be the most prominent feature is the feeling of lack of control during the eating episode. Nevertheless, the DSM-IV does now specify that to meet the diagnostic criteria for the disorder, the person does have to engage in objectively large binges at least twice per week. This bingeing will be followed by purging via vomiting (induced by gagging, emetics or simply willing it), diuretics or laxatives (from 50 to 100 or more tablets at one time).

The disorder can go undetected for years, even by close family members. Both the bingeing and purging are carried out in secret, with all evidence destroyed. Because the bulimic appears outwardly to be quite successful in school or career, no one suspects that she doesn't feel as good as she may appear to be. It is not unusual for a diagnosis not to be made until a patient is well into her thirties or forties.

Bulimia typically begins during the late teens or early twenties, after the patient has unsuccessfully tried to lose weight via several reducing diets, especially when restrictive dieting results in hunger. The hunger is satisfied by bingeing. Either through reading about it or hearing a fellow student or coworker talk about it, the patient learns that self-induced VOMITING or laxative use will get rid of the extra calories, thereby relieving feelings of guilt brought on by the binge eating. However, self-induced vomiting leads to further hunger. Ultimately, a vicious cycle is established, perpetuated by emotional disturbances and the continuing desire to lose weight. Some bulimics begin with vomiting after regular meals to lose weight and only binge eat later when their hunger and cravings increase because of the lowered energy intake. During a binge, bulimics typically eat foods high in CARBOHYDRATES, foods they would normally not be allowed to eat on healthy or weight-reduction diets, setting aside time each day for solitary, secret binge eating. However, therapists have reported patients eating salads, vegetables, cheese, meat and yogurt during a binge.

SYMPTOMS AND FEATURES—WHAT TO LOOK FOR

Typical physical signs of bulimia include dark circles under the eyes, tooth decay, puffiness around the face (eyes and below cheeks), facial pallor, red knuckles, dull and lifeless hair and loss of hair. In many bulimics, the menstrual cycle becomes irregular. Bulimics may be—but rarely are—emaciated; they are most usually of normal weight but sometimes are overweight.

Researchers comparing normal-weight bulimic and obese individuals have found many similarities between them. Common characteristics include a greater tendency to guilt, alienation, impulsivity, obsessive thinking and preoccupation; there are similarities in eating habits as well. Bulimics, however, display greater distortions in both cognitive and mood disturbances, as evidenced by more pervasive impulsivity as well as body image disturbance, anxiety and depression. The disorders of both groups represent needs from more than one level—physical (the need for weight control) and psychological (the need for increased psychosocial development).

Bulimics (and anorexics) who vomit repeatedly to purge themselves of consumed food risk erosion of the enamel of their teeth, particularly on the inner surfaces, from hydrochloric acid in the vomit. This erosion may result in severe gum disease, cavities and tooth loss. The dentist may be the first to encounter actual indications of bulimia. Although not life threatening and not evident until the later stages of illness, dental cavities are side effects of eating disorders that cannot be reversed.

Bulimic behavior can be suspected where there is evidence of consumption of unusually large amounts of high-calorie foods, especially if consumed alone or secretly. Other signs include excessive exercise or fasting, a preoccupation with food, weight and bodily concerns, frequent weight fluctuations due to alternative binges and fasts or purges, increased time spent alone and less with family and friends, theft of money for binges and frequent trips to the bathroom, especially after meals. Sexual interest may also diminish, but not always.

Emotionally, bulimic patients have feelings of depression and self-loathing after eating binges, feel unable to control eating behavior and may appear embarrassed, angry, tense and oversensitive. The following COGNITIVE DISTORTIONS may also exist:

- *Denial.* Bulimics seek acceptable reasons for unacceptable behavior. Whereas others say that obesity results from a simple lack of willpower, the bulimic will have excuses or even lie about her overeating ("I eat because . . .") ("I don't know why I'm fat. . . . I never eat."). Bulimics hide their purging by using breath sprays, mints and chewing gum. They will often seek "magic" cures for their problems (depression or obesity) through such gimmicks as mail-order BODY WRAPPING.
- *Distorted Body Image.* Although more anorexics than bulimics appear to have body image disturbances, the bulimic also may not have an accurate grasp of her weight. Bulimics sometimes believe themselves fatter than they actually are. (See BODY IMAGE DISTURBANCE.)
- *Fictional Finalism.* Bulimics often believe that there is a "magic" weight and that once they attain it, they will have happiness and success ("If I were 120 pounds, everything would be perfect").
- *Demandingness.* Bulimics often make infantile demands ("I want what I want when I want it"). The demands are often not met, and they develop an oversensitivity to rejection and a childlike insecurity. Bulimics' demandingness usually provokes the most anger in others involved in their lives.
- *Rigidity and Inflexibility.* Bulimics develop an attitude of intransigence, characterized by an air of "I'm right and you're not." This is most obvious in their refusal to try suggested cures or in their rigid persistence with diets that do not work.

In a March 1989 *Journal of Counseling and Development* article, psychologists Barbara Bauer and Wayne Anderson identified nine irrational beliefs commonly held by bulimics that are related to these emotional distortions: (1) Becoming overweight is the worst thing that can happen to me. (2) There are good foods, such as vegetables and fish, and bad foods, such as sweets and carbohydrates. (3) I must have control over all of my actions to feel safe. (4) I must do everything perfectly, or what I do is worthless. (5) Everyone is aware of, and interested in, what I am doing. (6) Everyone must love me and approve of what I do. (7) External validation is crucial to me. (8) As soon as a particular event such as graduation or marriage occurs, my bulimic behavior will disappear. (9) I must be dependent and subservient yet competitive and aggressive.

The most universal belief and the one most difficult to modify appears to be the fear of becoming fat and the failure it represents. Bulimics obsess about and belittle themselves over the slightest weight gain. Although not everyone with bulimia holds all these beliefs, therapists say all are likely to believe in some of them.

A bulimic's weight may fluctuate but not necessarily to the dangerously low levels seen in anorexics. Also unlike anorexics, bulimics are commonly upset by their actions and willing to accept help; they frequently join self-help groups or even seek medical help. Furthermore, they are usually outgoing and have developed attachments, whereas anorexics are isolated and asexual.

According to researchers, bulimics often have a history of other compulsive behaviors, such as alcohol or drug abuse, and some have features in common with drug or alcohol addicts. They may spend $50 or more a day on food to support their habitual bingeing and often resort to stealing money or shoplifting food.

The way in which bulimics often tackle exercise and schoolwork also resembles addiction. Alcohol, over-the-counter diet pills, caffeine, barbiturate and amphetamine addictions have been noted by many researchers to be commonly associated with bulimia. In a 1981 study done at the University of Minnesota Adult Outpatient Psychiatric Clinic, bulimic women reported using alcohol to avoid depression associated with binge purging, to relax and to delay or prevent overeating.

In a 1984–85 survey of 1,100 patients at Hazelden, a Minnesota chemical dependency treatment center, approximately 7 percent of female patients and 3 percent of males reported enough symptoms to be classified as bulimic under clinical guidelines criteria.

A later Hazelden report, posted on their Web site (http://www.hazelden.org) states that 30–40 percent of the women in residential treatment for alcohol and other drug dependence have an active eating disorder or one in recession. Among men, the incidence is about 5 percent.

Hazelden reported that its bulimic female patients experienced more adolescent behavior problems and self-destructive behavior than nonbulimic patients. The typical chemically dependent female bulimic at Hazelden is more likely to "be a polydrug user; have had adolescent behavior problems such as school suspension or expulsion, stealing, and fighting; exhibit self-destructive tendencies through self-inflicted injury, suicide attempts, or suicidal thoughts during treatment; have had outpatient or inpatient mental health treatment or medication."

According to DSM-IV, chemical abuse or dependence occurs in about one-third of individuals with bulimia nervosa. Such stimulant use often begins in an attempt to control appetite and weight.

Although less sexually and socially mature than borderline women, bulimic women are more so than anorexic women. But bulimia usually results in a sharp decrease in sexual desire, attributed to both psychological and physiological causes. Even when bulimia sufferers are sexually active, they will have times of withdrawing from their partners and ceasing sexual behavior. Bulimic patients often have irregular menstrual cycles, pointing to disruption of the pattern of sex-hormone secretion. Their obsession with food leaves them little time to think about other aspects of life, and they characteristically feel worthless and flawed. They also often fear that if anyone becomes closely involved with them, they will learn their secret. Likewise, psychiatrists contend that many people overeat to cover up feelings of sexual inadequacy. If they do not seem attractive to the opposite sex, they will avoid occasions of stress and humiliation. However, it is not unusual for those bulimics who lack control over their impulses to participate in sexual promiscuity and extramarital affairs.

Many bulimics vow to give up binge eating and purging once they are married, hoping that marriage itself will magically transform their lives. This does happen for some, but others resume their habit in secret, feeling more guilty and ashamed than ever. Bulimics have been known to keep their behavior a total secret from their husbands for as long as 15 years. But the deception often destroys a marriage. Some husbands conclude that their wives must be carrying on affairs because of their exaggerated sense of privacy. When they finally do find out that it's "only" an eating problem, they are relieved and often don't realize that it is even more significant than the affair they had suspected.

COMPLICATIONS: WHAT CAN HAPPEN WITHOUT EARLY DIAGNOSIS AND TREATMENT

Menstrual irregularities occur in more than 40 percent of bulimics; for those whose weight falls below 92 percent of ideal body weight, there is an increased likelihood of amenorrhea. Repeated vomiting dissolves tooth enamel and makes the gums recede, can tear the esophagus and stomach and may cause the salivary glands to swell. Binge eating can overload the stomach, causing it to expand and even rupture. Low potassium in the blood can lead to heart problems and death and can upset the body's balance of electrolytes (sodium, magnesium, potassium and calcium), causing fatigue, seizures, muscle cramps, irregular heartbeat and decreased bone density (see OSTEOPENIA). Other complications include digestive problems, bursting blood vessels in the eyes and cheeks, headaches, rashes, swelling around the eyes, ankles and feet, weakness, kidney failure and heart failure. Bulimia can also cause scarring on the backs of hands when fingers are pushed down the throat to induce vomiting. Also, bulimic patients sometimes show evidence of abrasions of the lining of the throat due to use of the fingers or foreign objects to induce vomiting. The caustic gastric acid brought up during the purging process inflames esophageal, pharyngeal and salivary gland tissues. For diabetics, bingeing on high-carbohydrate foods and sweets is particularly hazardous because their pancreas may not be able to metabolize properly the starches and sugars.

Many bulimics suffer from serious depression, which, combined with their impulsive tendencies, places them at increased risk for suicide. Depression is a problem especially among bulimic students, whose self-esteem plummets when they engage in these extreme behaviors. When they become depressed, their grades fail and they lose their self-confidence.

To determine the range and severity of medical complications encountered in younger patients, researchers reviewed the medical records of 65 adolescents and preadolescents in the Eating Disorders Clinic of the Children's Hospital at Stanford University. Twenty-two percent of bulimic patients required hospitalization for medical reasons during the study period.

TREATING BULIMIA NERVOSA

Although bulimic patients are for the most part more likely than anorexics to accept, even seek, treatment, they usually expect quick solutions and become frustrated if treatment does not produce immediate relief of their symptoms. They may deal with their frustration and anxiety in therapy through increased binge eating and may also leave treatment prematurely. GROUP THERAPY is particularly useful for bulimics who feel isolated by their symptoms.

The psychological treatments that have been studied the most are behavior and cognitive behavioral approaches. These treatments use behavioral interventions such as self-monitoring and stimulus control to normalize eating behavior and use cognitive interventions to challenge the distorted thinking and belief systems of the individual. Research suggests that these treatments can be very effective, as effective as antidepressants and more effective when one considers follow-up. Another psychological treatment that has recently been found to be effective for bulimia nervosa is INTERPERSONAL PSYCHOTHERAPY.

In a British study, a cognitive-behavioral approach was applied to the individual treatment of 11 bulimic women. First the binge-purge cycle was interrupted, and then cognitive strategies were taught for self-control. Next the patients were helped to modify abnormal attitudes toward food, eating and body weight and shape. Normally restricted foods, such as carbohydrates, were gradually introduced into the diet to lessen the desire to binge on these foods. Patients were also helped to identify situations in which loss of control occurred. Finally, patients were prepared for future relapse events. Duration of treatment was seven months. Nine of the 11 patients reduced their binge eating and vomiting from three times daily to less than once a month. Anxiety and depression decreased, as did dysfunctional attitudes concerning shape and weight. At a one-year follow-up of six of the patients, one had stopped bingeing and vomiting completely, four reported that these behaviors occurred two to three times a month, and one showed no improvement. Follow-up data were not available for the other five patients. The research team later reported that subsequent experience with more than 50 patients has confirmed that the majority do indeed benefit from the cognitive therapy approach, with most remaining well and requiring no further treatment. Currently there is more empirical support (practical experience) for the use of cognitive and/or cognitive behavior therapy with bulimia nervosa than any other treatment.

Antidepressant medication has been used in treatment for bulimia. The three classes of antidepressant drugs most commonly used in the treatment of bulimia have been the monoamine oxidase inhibitors, the serotonin-reuptake inhibitors (fluoxetine, clomipramine) and the tricyclics. Some controlled studies of antidepressants in bulimia have been promising; imipramine and phenelzine have been shown to be significantly successful in reducing bulimic and depressive symptoms.

During controlled testing, the tricyclic antidepressant imipramine produced, on average, a 70 percent reduction in binge frequency. A similar drug, desipramine, resulted in a mean reduction of 91 percent in binge frequency. A third tricyclic antidepressant, amitriptyline, was associated with a 72 percent reduction in binge frequency. A controlled trial of phenelzine, a monoamine oxidase inhibitor, found a 66 percent reduction in binge frequency. However, the long-term outcome of drug treatment for bulimia remains unknown.

Medication has proven useful when a bulimic patient also has an associated mood disorder and has failed to respond to psychotherapy. Treatment for bulimia nervosa is most successful when medical therapy and psychotherapy are combined.

Canadian scientists reported that preliminary studies showed bulimic patients also suffering from seasonal mood swings and treated with light therapy (exposure to bright light) improved both in their depression and in their bulimia. However, these studies have thus far been too limited to yield any serious data.

Although normal-weight bulimics are the most common, there are substantial numbers of overweight bulimics who run into difficulties when seeking appropriate treatment; for example, because they binge eat and purge, they are often grouped by providers of therapy with emaciated bulimics or anorexics, or they are classified simply as obese individuals. Overweight bulimics vehemently reject these classifications and the treatment approaches that go with them. In treating overweight bulimia, clinicians promote the use of self-help groups in developing self-regulatory abilities. They suggest that it is the development of these abilities that encourages the maintenance of any weight loss that is achieved.

Professor P. J. V. Beumont, presenting a paper on "Dietary Advice" at the BASH VII International Conference in April 1989, stated that nutritional counseling is an important component of the treatment of all bulimic patients and is usually essential if therapy is to be effective. He gave the following reasons why nutritional guidance is so important:

- Eating behavior is often so erratic in bulimics that patients need to regain control of their habits before they become involved in other forms of treatment such as psychotherapy.
- Bulimics view their problem as one of overeating and do not understand that gorging is a response to prior restrained eating practices.
- Bulimics have many fears and misconceptions about food and weight control that need to be identified and corrected. (They firmly believe that if they eat regular meals or high-energy foods, they will inevitably get fat.)
- Bulimic patients have had disordered eating habits for so long that they need to learn to recognize when they are hungry and when they are satisfied.

WHERE TO GO FOR MORE INFORMATION

Burby, Liza N. *Bulimia Nervosa: The Secret Cycle of Bingeing and Purging.* New York: Rosen Publishing Group, 1998.

Cooper, Peter J. *Bulimia Nervosa & Binge-Eating: A Guide to Recovery.* New York: New York University Press, 1995.

Sobel, Stephen V. "What's New in the Treatment of Anorexia Nervosa and Bulimia?" *Medscape Women's Health* 1, no. 9 (1996).

Stanley, Debbie. *Understanding Bulimia Nervosa.* Minneapolis: Hazelden Information Education, 1999.

Tobin, David L. *Coping Strategies Therapy for Bulimia Nervosa.* Washington: American Psychological Association, 2000.

CHAPTER 8

SPECIAL EATING DISORDER–RELATED PROBLEMS

BINGE-EATING DISORDER

Binge-eating disorder (BED) resembles bulimia nervosa. Like bulimics, individuals with BED have recurring episodes of uncontrolled eating or bingeing. (A binge occurs when one eats more food than most people would eat during a similar time period and under similar circumstances, plus exhibits a lack of control during the bingeing episode—cannot stop eating or cannot control what or how much one is eating.) However, binge-eating disorder differs from bulimia because its sufferers do not purge their bodies of excess food.

Even though they may not be hungry, people with BED do not stop eating until they are uncomfortably full, and they tend to eat much more rapidly than normal. Invariably, this eating will occur in secret due to shame and embarrassment over the amount being eaten. Yet after a binge, they will feel distressed, depressed, disgusted and/or guilty after overeating. To meet clinical diagnosis as BED, their binges must occur at least twice a week for a minimum of approximately six months.

Usually, BED persons have more difficulty losing weight and keeping it off than do people with other serious weight problems. Many people with the disorder are obese and have a history of weight fluctuations. Binge-eating disorder is found in about 2 percent of the general population—more often in women than men. Recent research shows that binge-eating disorder occurs in about 30 percent of people participating in medically supervised weight control programs. BED usually begins in late adolescence or the early 20s, but onset can be as early age seven or in the 30s and 40s.

Medical complications with BED include heart disease, respiratory problems and psychological problems. The binge eater is likely to be addicted to alcohol or drugs.

NIGHT-EATING DISORDERS

Night-Eating Syndrome (NES)

Albert J. Stunkard identified this syndrome in 1959 as an eating pattern in which an obese person succeeds in keeping his eating-disordered behavior under control during the day in the interest of normal functioning but is unable to resist it at night when alone. NES sufferers exhibit a lack of appetite in the morning, overeat during the evening and suffer agitation and insomnia overnight.

In a study reported in 1996, Stunkard and his team concluded that the frequency of night-eating syndrome is comparable to that of binge-eating disorder. This was followed in 1997 by a University of Florida study that found prevalence of night-eating syndrome to be higher among post-operative obesity patients than among a randomly selected sample of adults but within the range reported for binge-eating disorder. They concluded that night-eating syndrome may warrant consideration as a distinct eating disorder.

In August 1999, Dr. Grethe Stoa Birketvedt from the University of Pennsylvania School of Medicine and colleagues there and in Norway published two clinical studies on NES. In their research, night eaters had 9.3 eating episodes per 24 hours, compared with 4.2 episodes for the BMI and age-matched control group. Between 8 P.M. and 6 A.M., night eaters consumed 56 percent of their daily calories, compared with 15 percent consumed during those hours by controls. On average, night eaters woke 3.6 times during the night compared with only 0.3 times for controls. About half the time, night eaters consumed a carbohydrate-rich snack during these awakenings. In comparison, none of the controls ate during the few times any of them awoke. Contrary to the usual pattern found in depression, the mood of the night eaters fell during the evening. Dr. Joel Yager from the University of New Mexico School of Medicine called the findings "potentially interesting," but emphasized that NES is in its early stages of study.

Night-eating syndrome is believed to occur in 1.5 percent of the general population but in 10 percent of obese people seeking treatment for their obesity, which means that about 10 million people may be affected.

Sleep-Related Syndrome

In this recently recognized syndrome, people wake in the night and binge but don't always remember doing it. In one of the few studies published on this disorder, 83 percent of the patients were female, and for most of them the condition had begun in adolescence and had been chronic—they suffered from it for an average of 15.8 years before it was diagnosed. Thirty-five percent of those studied also had a lifetime eating disorder (anorexia, bulimia or binge eating). Nearly all the patients reported eating one to six times on a nightly basis, and all episodes followed a period of sleep. All patients described their eating as out of control. Many reported being totally asleep during these episodes and could not recall them; only a messy kitchen, food in the bedroom or testimony from another family member convinced them it was happening. Those who could recall the sleep-eating episodes said they were half-awake, half-asleep during them.

Foods eaten during these sleep-related eating episodes has been reported to run toward high-fat, high-sugar foods that people have restrained themselves from eating while awake. Bizarre combinations and ingestion of nonfood items have also been reported.

MALES WITH EATING DISORDERS

Boys and men do develop anorexia nervosa but much less commonly than girls and young women. Generally, men have been found to be more comfortable with their weight and perceive less pressure to be thin than women. However, for male bodybuilders, long-distance runners and wrestlers, emphasis on body and physical appearance approaches the levels seen generally in women in our culture and puts these men at higher risk for developing eating disorders. It is believed by many experts in the field that anorexia may be more common in males than it seems to be but is not readily recognized by doctors because of its reputation as a female disorder. Recent estimates are that 5 to 10 percent of all cases occur in males. Based on the number of those who seek treatment, experts estimate that at a minimum, several hundred thousand men are affected by eating disorders.

Studies of male anorexics tend to agree that in general the behavior of males resembles closely that of their female counterparts with a few exceptions. One is that males who become anorexic tend to do so on average at an earlier age than females. In addition, relatively more males come from working-class homes. Some studies have found that a family history of anorexia nervosa is particularly common in male cases. The anorexic male tends to be massively obese before becoming emaciated. Finally, there is an impression that male anorexics respond to treatment less well and may be more likely to become chronic or drop out of treatment programs.

HILDE BRUCH wrote that male anorexia "occurs in youngsters who seemingly were doing well but whose accomplishments were a facade, an expression of compliance, and not of self-initiated and self-directed goals. In their desperate struggle to become 'somebody' and to establish a sense of differentiated identity, they become overambitious, hyperactive, and perfectionistic."

Arnold E. Andersen, associate professor of psychiatry at the Johns Hopkins School of Medicine, reported that 76 males had presented themselves for consultation or treatment to the Johns Hopkins Eating and Weight Disorders Clinic over approximately 10 years. This was almost exactly 10 percent of the patients seen there.

According to Dr. Andersen, males and females were similar in many ways, all meeting the essential diagnostic criteria of self-induced starvation and morbid fear of fatness. Males did differ from females, however, in a number of ways: in contrast to women who in general felt fat prior to dieting, men on the average actually were obese. More than 50 percent of them were medically obese, usually mildly to moderately.

Men were seldom as concerned about clothing size or weight as females. Instead, they were intensely concerned with body shape. This has been confirmed in independent studies comparing the relative frequency of occurrence of articles, advertisements and the like on dieting and change of shape in magazines read primarily by men and those read primarily by women. Men more than women attempted to change body size and shape by way of athletic activities. Finally, men more often dieted to avoid medical consequences of overweight, such as heart disease.

Families of boys aged nine to 12 who develop anorexia are often described as psychologically disturbed or distressed, the child having an unsatisfactory relationship with both parents.

Most males with anorexia begin weight loss during adolescence. These boys are more often mildly to moderately obese before onset than girls who become ill at the same age. Many but not all adolescent boys with anorexia show confusion about sexual identity. In personality tests they present a spectrum of disorders from perfectionistic and obsessive to borderline personalities not capable of maintaining stable relationships, and they display rapid and inappropriate mood changes.

Because few suspect eating disorders among teenage boys and men, the problems often go undiagnosed and untreated for many years. When finally recognized, the disorders are often far advanced and that much more difficult to treat.

Andersen has noted that understanding the lower frequency of eating disorders in males may lead to more effective means of protecting girls from these disorders and from the culturally induced distress about normal body size and shape that burdens adolescent development and adult life.

Occasional binge eating on high-calorie, easily ingested foods may be done by as many as 30 percent of male college students, according to studies. The percentage of males meeting the DSM-IV criteria for bulimia nervosa, however, is approximately 1 to 3 percent. In one report, male students reporting to a university psychiatric clinic represented 10 percent of patients diagnosed as bulimic.

The figures could be artificially low. In tests, men have freely acknowledged "frequent consumption of large quantities of food at times other than during meals"; unlike women, however, they tended not to label this behavior as binge eating.

A past history of obesity is a risk factor for males. Obese young males, being a minority in our society, are often targets of cruel verbal and physical taunting. They might easily become preoccupied with their body and their physical appearance.

In some bulimia studies, the rare men with the diagnosis of bulimia nervosa all had a history of dieting from their mid- or late teens; indeed, this was all they had in common—only some had been anorexic, only some obese.

According to researchers, it appears more difficult for the male bulimic to seek help, perhaps because the socialization of men discourages help-seeking and because bulimia has been described as a "woman's problem."

Many of these men form a bona fide subgroup of overeaters and compulsive exercisers. Rather than following the typical binge-purge cycle, they are preoccupied with physical activity. After exercising for hours, they will become ravenously hungry and eat uncontrollably. Sometimes the food will be a reward for the frantic workout, but afterward the thought of the calories ingested will cause them to begin the cycle again with even more exercising.

In a 1997 Massachusetts General Hospital study of 135 males with eating disorders, 62 were bulimic. Of these, 42 percent were identified as either homosexual or bisexual. The study concluded that while most characteristics of males and females with eating disorders are similar, homosexuality/bisexuality appears to be a specific risk factor for males, especially for those who develop bulimia nervosa. The authors said that future research on the link between sexual orientation and eating disorders would help guide prevention and treatment strategies.

HOMOSEXUALITY AND EATING DISORDERS

When psychiatrist Joel Yager of the University of California, Los Angeles found that nearly 50 percent of the men who enter treatment for anorexia nervosa describe themselves as homosexual, he questioned whether there might be a link between homosexuality and anorexia or bulimia. In a comparison study he conducted of homosexual with primarily heterosexual males, the gay men were more fearful of being fat and were more likely to feel fat despite others' perceptions. They also reported a higher incidence of binge eating and purging. The homosexual men also scored higher on the EATING DISORDERS INVENTORY scales for drive for thinness, INTEROCEPTIVE DISTURBANCE, bulimia, body dissatisfaction, maturity fears and ineffectiveness.

Yager also found that gay men had a different body image preference. Heterosexual men preferred a more muscular or "macho" physique; gay men preferred being slender. Yager speculated that homosexual men may be more likely to develop eating disorders because of this concern with slim bodies, a traditionally feminine attitude.

A 1996 study of 203 lesbians by the Rutgers University Eating Disorders Clinic to assess bulimia nervosa risk factors found that the rate of bulimia nervosa among lesbians was similar to that of heterosexual women, but binge-eating disorder was more frequent. Lesbians were not significantly different from heterosexual women in attitudes concerning weight, appearance or dieting.

ATHLETES AND DANCERS WITH DISORDERED EATING

Some of the best-known bulimics are those who started purging because thinness is important to them vocationally. In this category are models, actresses, athletes and dancers who use vomiting or laxatives as a means of weight control and become dependent on it. Vocational bulimics present a special obstacle to treatment because it would be unreasonable to try to convince a dancer, for instance, that she doesn't have to weigh 90 pounds when that is the current standard for dancers.

Athletes who compete in certain sports in which body thinness is stressed along with high performance expectations, such as gymnastics, wrestling, swimming and figure skating, have shown frequent symptoms of eating disorders, as have dancers. Likewise, bulimia and other drastic weight-control measures have been described as common among jockeys, who must meet low weight requirements.

Female cheerleaders often experience pressure to attain and maintain weight that is lower than other adolescents of the same height. A study reported in 1986 by Lundholm and Littrell examined cheerleaders' desire for thinness in relationship to disordered eating and weight-control behaviors. A total of 751 high school cheerleaders from the Midwest were tested. Cheerleaders who expressed a strong desire for thinness had significantly higher scores on seven of eight eating-disorder scales. The greater the desire for thinness, the more likely the tendency to report disordered eating and weight-control behaviors associated with bulimia.

A 1989 Associated Press story stated that an "alarming number" of women athletes at the University of Texas had eating disorders, with the problem especially prevalent among members of the swimming team. According to the report, during a period of 18 months, one of every 10 female athletes at the university, a total of 12, had been diagnosed as having a serious eating disorder. Another 20 to 30 percent had shown symptoms of an eating disorder, and 50 to 60 percent expressed above-average concern about their weight. Current and former swimmers blamed the pressure to meet weight guidelines for their routine fasting, induced vomiting, laxative and diuretic abuse and excessive exercising: Tiffany Cohen, a swimmer who won two Olympic gold medals in 1984, was quoted as saying that her fear of being overweight when reporting to workouts led her into bulimic cycles of binges and purges that resulted in a nine-week hospitalization. Many women on the professional tennis circuit also are known to suffer from eating disorders, including Zina Garrison and Carling Bassett-Seguso.

According to an American College of Sports Medicine study, eating disorders affected 62 percent of females in such sports as figure skating and gymnastics. Olympics gymnasts who have admitted to eating disorders include Nadia Comaneci, Kathy Johnson and Cathy Rigby. In 1976 the average gymnast weighed 105 pounds, and in 1992 the average dropped to 88 pounds.

A 1997 study of NCAA student athletes in 11 sports disclosed that binge eating occurred at least weekly in 13 percent of male student athletes and in 10 percent of female student athletes.

Some coaches may be contributing to the development of eating disorders in their athletes by putting too much pressure on them to achieve a preset weight or body form without taking the individual's condition into consideration. Many coaches and athletes estimate optimal body weight to be much lower than what physicians believe to be healthy and consider a well-formed and graceful body to be much leaner than the medically defined healthy body.

A study published by the American College of Sports Medicine in 1999 that compared 85 junior high and high school wrestlers with 75 nonwrestlers found that although the wrestlers tended to use risky weight-loss measures to meet certain weights during wrestling season, they had no greater degree of clinical eating-disordered behavior than the nonwrestlers. Once the wrestling season was over, most of them returned to normal eating patterns.

Effects of eating disorders on athletes include stress fractures, fatigue, iron deficiency anemia, electrolyte imbalances and cardiac arrhythmia. Because athletes are already putting above-average pressure on their bodies, they are at a greater risk than nonathlete patients for these complications.

According to various reports in medical journals, between 7 and 38 percent of female dancers in competitive settings have been found to have serious eating problems: classical ballet demands the same high standards of technical proficiency of its dancers as competitive sports do of first-class athletes. As in wrestling, gymnastics and swimming, the right body shape and weight are primary concerns. Because ballet is basically nonaerobic and has a low caloric expenditure, weight reduction cannot be achieved and low weight maintained through dancing alone.

In a study of 49 female dancers who performed in national ballet companies in the United States and in the Republic of China (Taiwan), 11 percent of the U.S. dancers and 24 percent of the Chinese reported they had an eating problem. Those dancers were chosen from general auditions but showed significantly more anorexic, bulimic or purging behavior than those taken from a company school such as the School of American Ballet, where a strict selection process over a number of years weeds out those who do not meet the rigid body shape and weight requirements. The study's authors contend that dancers selected from company schools may be less susceptible to the development of eating problems because they are more naturally suited to the thin ideal required by the profession. This has been suggested as the reason for the wide disparity of eating disorders reported in different studies of ballet dancers.

In a 1996 study comparing ballet dancers with students, the dancers were more preoccupied with thoughts of eating and body weight, abused laxatives for weight control, and reported disordered eating more than the students—even though the dancers were at lower body weight and had less body fat. Another study in 1998 indicated a high distortion of body image among 10 professional female ballet dancers.

EATING DISORDERS IN THE ELDERLY

Although eating disorders are most commonly thought of as occurring during adolescence, the process of aging brings many changes that can influence such illnesses as anorexia nervosa and bulimia. After the age of 50, physical changes such as a decrease in the basal metabolic rate, a decrease in lean body mass and an increase in percentage of body fat combine with common changes in psychosocial conditions to affect nutrition; for instance, decreasing financial resources and increasing social isolation may promote the development of poor eating patterns. Favorite foods may be financially out of reach; boredom may lead to decreased interest in meals; aging people may simply lack understanding of what their bodies require. Life stresses and trauma may also have an effect on the development of eating disorders in the elderly; for example, research indicates that women who are newly grieving over the deaths of their husbands are likely to skip meals and resort to junk food.

As with adolescents, there is an increase in body fat in those over 50. Changes in the body's energy requirements may coincide with changes in daily routine due to such events as illness, relocation or retirement. If physical activity is decreased but the amount of food consumed is not, there will be a gain in weight, another common variable in already changing bodies.

Along with a decline in metabolism, the aging process brings changes in nearly all other body systems. The aging may experience changes in sight and hearing, as well as declining sensitivity to temperature, touch and taste (gustatory villae [taste buds] begin to atrophy in women in their early forties and men in their early fifties). The neurological system, especially the brain, the digestive system and the musculoskeletal system are all noticeably affected. Such physiological changes affect the body images of aging individuals, and body image is often an important variable in the initiation of dieting behaviors that may lead to eating disorders.

Clinicians at Northeastern Ohio University reported on three case histories of onset of anorexia nervosa in geriatric patients. Geriatric research has demonstrated neurotransmitter changes that may predispose the aging population to anorexia. These include a decline in norepinephrine as well as B-endorphin levels; these changes are also seen in anorexia.

Some researchers have theorized that eating disorders are becoming more common among the elderly for two reasons: first, there has been a dramatic increase in the incidence of eating disorders in the last three decades, and because at least 20 percent of patients become chronic and not all of them shed their illness as they age, some are likely to remain anorexic or bulimic into old age; second, it is possible that even elderly women are beginning to succumb to the social pressures to be slim, and some may use vomiting to control their weight.

According to John E. Morley, a professor of geriatric medicine at St. Louis University Medical School, depression is the most common cause of weight loss and anorexia in older persons.

WHERE TO GO FOR MORE INFORMATION

Abraham, S. "Eating and Weight Controlling Behaviors of Young Ballet Dancers." *Psychopathology* 29, 1996/4.

Andersen, Arnold E. *Males With Eating Disorders* New York: Brunner/Mazel, 1990.

Andersen, Arnold E., and J. E. Holman. "Males With Eating Disorders: Challenges for Treatment and Research." *Psychopharmacology Bulletin* 33 (1997).

Birketvedt, G. S., et al. "Characteristics of the Night-Eating Syndrome." *JAMA* 282 (1999): 657–663.

Carlat, D. J., et al. "Eating Disorders In Males: A Report on 135 Patients." *American Journal of Psychiatry* 154, August 1997.

Deutsch, Nancy. "National Eating Disorders Screening Program." *Sports Sciences Newsletter,* 1997.

Giannini, A. James, James I. Collins, and Denise Lewis. "Anorexia Nervosa in the Elderly—Case Studies." *American Journal of Psychiatry* 146, no. 2 (February 1989).

Hahn, Cindy. "Why Eating Disorders Pervade Women's Tennis." *Tennis,* December 1990.

Hamilton, Linda H., J. Brooks-Gunn, Michelle P. Warren, and William G. Hamilton. "The Role of Selectivity in the Pathogenesis of Eating Problems in Ballet Dancers." *Medicine and Science in Sports and Exercise* 20, no. 6 (December 1988).

Heffernan, K. "Eating Disorders and Weight Concern Among Lesbians." *International Journal of Eating Disorders* 19 (March 1996).

Lundholm, J. K., and J. M. Littrell. "Desire for Thinness among High School Cheerleaders: Relationship to Disordered Eating and Weight Control Behaviors." *Adolescence* 21, no. 83 (fall 1986): 573–79.

Manni, R., et al. "Nocturnal Eating: Prevalence and Features in 120 Insomniac Referrals." *Sleep* 20 (September 1997).

Miller, Peter M. *Binge Breaker!: Stop Out-Of-Control Eating and Lose Weight.* New York: Warner Books, 1999.

Morley, J. E. "Anorexia in Older Persons: Epidemiology and Optimal Treatment." *Drugs and Aging* 8 (February 1996).

Nash, Joyce D. *Binge No More: Your Guide to Overcoming Disordered Eating.* Oakland, Calif.: New Harbinger Publications, 1999.

Perrone, Vinnie. "Pound for Pound, a Most Dangerous Sport." *Washington Post,* April 28, 1991.

Pierce, E. F., and M. L. Daleng. "Distortion of Body Image Among Elite Female Dancers." *Perceptual and Motor Skills* 87 (December 1998).

Rand, C. S., et al. "The Night Eating Syndrome in the General Population and Among Postoperative Obesity Surgery Patients." *International Journal of Eating Disorders* 22 (July 1997).

Rucinski, Ann. "Relationship of Body Image and Dietary Intake of Competitive Ice Skaters." *Journal of the American Dietetic Association* 89, no. 1 (January 1989).

Schnitt, Diana. "Psychological Issues in Dancers—An Overview." *Journal of Physical Education, Recreation and Dance* 61, no. 9 (November 1990).

Stunkard, Albert J., et al. "Binge Eating Disorder and the Night Eating Syndrome." *International Journal of Obesity Related Metabolic Disorders* 20 (January 1996).

Thompson, Colleen. "Athletes and Eating Disorders." *Eating Disorders Shared Awareness* (November 1998).

Thompson, Ron A., and Roberta Trattner Sherman. *Helping Athletes With Eating Disorders.* Champaign, Ill.: Human Kinetics Publishing, 1993.

Winkelman, John W. "Clinical and Polysomnographic Features of Sleep-related Eating Disorder." *Journal of Clinical Psychiatry* 59 (January 1998).

PART II

ENTRIES A TO Z

A

Academy of Eating Disorders (AED) This multidisciplinary professional organization was founded in 1993 and focuses on Anorexia Nervosa, Bulimia Nervosa, Binge-Eating Disorder and related disorders. A guiding principle of the organization is that effective treatment for eating-disorder patients requires that professionals from various disciplines work together. The AED brings these professionals together to: (1) promote the effective treatment and care of patients with eating disorders and associated problems; (2) develop and advance initiatives for the primary and secondary prevention of eating disorders; (3) disseminate knowledge regarding eating disorders to members of the Academy, other professionals and the general public; (4) stimulate and support research in the field; (5) promote multidisciplinary expertise within the academy membership; (6) advocate on behalf of patients, the public and eating-disorder professionals; (7) assist in the development of guidelines for training, practice and professional conduct within the field; and (8) identify and reward outstanding achievement and service in the field.

acupressure A technique similar to and derived from ACUPUNCTURE, this treatment involves the application of manual pressure to the body rather than the insertion of needles. Acupressure has been recommended by some practitioners to control APPETITE. It is administered by applying pressure with the ball of the thumb and sometimes the fingers to specific points on the body. The main pressure point is on the upper lip; a point midway between the breastbone and navel is said to control HUNGER. Other points on the elbow and the knee are said by practitioners to control the emotions that lead to overeating. Not an instantaneously effective treatment, according to specialists, it is said to take three days for the reflex passages to the brain to become programmed by acupressure. Acupressure is even less well documented and scientifically tested than acupuncture. A review of four studies advocating acupuncture and acupressure for weight reduction, published in the January 1997 Austrian journal *Wiener Klinische Wochenschrift,* found that all four studies had significant flaws and contradictory results.

acupuncture An ancient practice, used especially by the Chinese, of piercing the skin with extremely fine needles at strategic places on the body, its aim is to treat disease or relieve pain. Acupuncturists believe that vital energy (*chi*) flows through the body along 12 main pathways (channels or meridians) connected to internal organs and systems like the kidney and respiratory system. They believe that disease occurs when there is an imbalance of energy in one of these systems and that acupuncture needles inserted at specific points (numbering more than 1,000) on the body correct the flow of energy through the channel and help the body to heal itself. Some medical doctors speculate that acupuncture may produce a state of painlessness partly by stimulating the release of endorphins (natural painkillers). Acupuncture as a treatment has some respectability based on observations and experience but almost no scientific basis for acceptance. A very few medical doctors use acupuncture to supplement standard treatment.

The origin of acupuncture is unknown, but it is believed to have been practiced in China for more than 3,000 years. When acupuncture is used to help lose weight, the needle is placed in the area of the external ear known as the concha. The vagus nerve, which extends from the brain down the neck and chest to the stomach, branches to the concha. When the sharp point of the needle finds this branch of the vagus nerve, it acts to inhibit the contractions of the stomach.

The acupuncture treatment to the ear does not itself cause a person to lose weight; rather, it causes the person to feel less HUNGER. Doctors in the United States have used staples and small needles, which are left in the ear to be jiggled when the patient feels the urge to overeat.

Published studies evaluating acupuncture as a treatment for obesity have thus far been inconclusive. In one, the author claimed a good response from 75 percent of 1,030 patients, but few details were given. In another study of 120 volunteers, it was reported that 70 percent treated at the "hunger" point experienced decreased appetite, compared with only 20 percent who had a stud (needle) in another part of the ear, and in a study of 350 obese subjects treated with acupuncture, 66 percent of them lost weight after seven treatment sessions. However, subjects had a differing numbers courses of treatments of varying duration. There were also no control subjects for comparison, so no final conclusions could be drawn. However, researchers Richards and Marley did use a control group in a study involving 60 overweight subjects. Of those who responded, 95 percent of the active group experienced less APPETITE, whereas none of the control group noticed such a change. After reviewing several studies, Vincent and Richardson concluded that even though there are no clear indications for or against the use of acupuncture, an individual patient might derive psychological benefit from belief in the treatment.

In practice, acupuncturists have reported compulsive eaters to be most open to acupuncture.

Richards, D., and J. Marley. "Stimulation of Auricular Acupuncture Points in Weight Loss." *Australian Family Physician* 109, suppl. 2 (July 1998).

Vincent, C. A., and P. H. Richardson. "Acupuncture for Some Common Disorders: A Review of Evaluative Research." *Journal of the Royal College of General Practitioners* 37 (February 1987).

addiction This term may refer to a wide range of different behaviors depending on whether it is used in scientific or popular media. In strictest scientific terms, an addiction requires the development of tolerance (a need for more of a substance to achieve the same effect) and/or withdrawal (characteristic physiological effects associated with termination of the use of a substance). A similar term in the scientific literature is *substance dependence,* and highly "addictive" substances include nicotine, alcohol, cocaine and opium derivatives. In the popular literature, the term *addiction* is often applied to unwanted habits that are hard to break (for example, shopping) or to substances (e.g., chocolate) that do not elicit the core characteristics of addiction (i.e., tolerance and withdrawal). Addiction has also been described as physiological or psychological dependence on some substance (for example, alcohol or a drug) or practice, with a tendency to increase its use. Addictions such as smoking and alcoholism share characteristics with binge eating and purging, but the eating-disordered person is addicted to the illness itself rather than to a substance. Food is the agent the addicted eating-disordered person uses to cover up or forget a weight problem (either real or imagined), fear of losing control over eating or other behavior, distorted body image, negative self-image, dissatisfaction in sexual or interpersonal relationships or lack of independence. There is great controversy over whether or not eating disorders are a form of addiction. According to Vandereycken, addictionlike behaviors exhibited by bulimics include "craving, preoccupation with obtaining the substance, loss of control, adverse social and medical consequences, ambivalence towards treatment, and risk of relapse." In addition, persons with eating disorders often have substance use disorders (i.e., alcohol or drug abuse) along with the eating disorder. If eating disorders are considered addictions, the substance or behavior to what the person is addicted is unclear. Some experts argue that it is food or specific types of food (for example, sugars or white flour), while others contend that persons with eating disorders are addicted to dieting, exercising and/or purging.

Because of the strong association between addictions and eating disorders, Hazelden, a Minnesota treatment center, conducts a comprehensive assessment for eating disorders for all its patients.

Although the medical community agrees that both chemical and food disorders must be treated for either illness to be treated successfully, disagreements exist over whether to treat them together or separately. Hazelden quotes Dr. Elke Eckert, professor of psychiatry and director of the Eating Disorders Clinic at the University of Minnesota, as believing the chemical dependency must be treated first and then the eating disorder.

In addition to chemical addiction, eating-disordered patients can also exhibit a general tendency toward addiction to running and level of running intensity. Estok and Rudy found that 25 percent of the women studied who ran more than 30 miles a week indicated a high risk for anorexia.

See also MULTICOMPULSIVE.

Davis, C., and G. Claridge. "The Eating Disorders as Addiction: A Psychobiological Perspective." *Addictive Behaviors* 23 (July/August 1998).

Ertock, P. J., and E. B. Rudy. "The Relationship Between Eating Disorders and Running in Women." *Research in Nursing and Health* 19 (October 1996).

"Study Suggests Some Bulimia Manageable During Chemical Dependency Treatment." *Hazelden Professional Update,* September 1988.

Vandereycken, Walter. "The Addiction Model in Eating Disorders: Some Critical Remarks and a Selected Bibliography." *International Journal of Eating Disorders* 9, no. 1 (1990).

addiction model of eating disorders and obesity See ADDICTION.

adoption and eating disorders There is some interest in discovering how adoption and the incidence of eating disorders may correlate because both anorexia and the internal conflicts faced by adoptees manifest themselves in early adolescence and around puberty. However, reports on anorexia nervosa in adopted children are sparse.

A case was reported in 1985 in which three biologically unrelated individuals in one family had severe anorexia: a father, his adopted daughter and an unrelated person living with them. This case suggests the possible importance of environmental factors in the generation of anorexia nervosa and also reveals the special problems underlying the development of the condition in adoptees.

Researchers have been calling for twin, family and adoption studies to help determine which causes of eating disorders can be inherited and which are due to family circumstances or individual environments.

Fry, Richard, and Arthur H. Crisp. "Adoption and Identity: A Case of Anorexia." *British Journal of Medical Psychology* 62 (1989).

Hewitt, J. K. "Behavior Genetics and Eating Disorders." *Psychopharmacology Bulletin* 33 (1997).

adult-onset obesity Obesity that starts at about the age of 25, usually from overeating (especially of high-calorie snack foods) and frequently because of emotional frustration, stress or boredom, adult-onset obesity is generally seen in people who did not have weight problems as children. Some of the more common emotion-charged events that can lead to first-time obesity in adults include leaving home for college or career, marriage, pregnancy, divorce, death of a close family member, extended illness or serious injury. In one study, 68 percent of obese adults related the onset of their weight problems to inactivity because of injury or illness; frequently these traumatic events result in unusually excessive eating of high-calorie foods combined with long periods of inactivity. Because these rather common and relatively sudden increases in weight frequently remain even after the stress and and the excessive eating stop, one theory suggests that there may be a resetting of the set-point mechanism during these eating/exercise pattern changes (see SET-POINT THEORY).

aerobic exercise Aerobic exercise conditions the heart and lungs by increasing the efficiency of oxygen intake by the body, usually through an activity in which oxygen reaches the muscles at the same rate at which it is used up. This type of physical activity is also recommended for weight control and body conditioning. Such exercise involves the large muscles of the upper body, arms and legs; to be effective it should be continued for periods of at least 20 minutes at least three times a week. Typical aerobic exercise is not too strenuous and can be performed slowly for a long period of time. Such exercise includes walking, jogging, swimming, bicycling, ice skating, roller skating, rowing, aerobic dancing, ballroom dancing, rope skipping and cross-country skiing.

Aerobic exercise is effective for weight reduction because it increases the muscles' ability to use oxygen to burn energy from stored fat. Although the exercise itself may seemingly expend few calories, the expenditure is cumulative and continues after exercise ends.

The effectiveness of aerobic exercise in reducing fat deposits depends upon several elements, including body weight and the frequency, intensity and duration of exercise. According to the Exercise Physiology Laboratory at the University of Massachusetts Medical School, the average 150-pound person burns approximately 100 calories walking a mile. Its tests have shown that the average person who takes a brisk 45-minute walk four times a week for a year and does not increase food intake will burn enough calories to lose 18 pounds. Virtually all of this weight loss will be fat because regular aerobic exercise preserves muscle mass.

Usually, aerobic exercise tends to decrease appetite. Some fitness experts claim that exercising aerobically during the lunch hour reduces appetite sufficiently that a bowl of soup or a cold drink will satisfy hunger; they also claim that some people have lost as much as 20 pounds within five weeks. (See ANAEROBIC EXERCISE.)

Cooper, Kenneth H. *The Aerobics Program for Total Well-being: Exercise, Diet, Emotional Balance.* New York: Bantam Doubleday Dell, 1985.

Cotton, Richard T. (editor), and Robert L. Goldstein. *Aerobics Instructor Manual: The Resource for Fitness Professionals.* San Diego: American Council on Exercise, 1993.

Kan, Esther, and Minda Goodman Kraines. *Keep Moving!: It's Aerobic Dance, 2nd Edition.* Mountain View Calif.: Mayfield Publishing Company, 1991.

Malkin, Mort. *Aerobic Walking, the Weight-Loss Exercise: A Complete Program to Reduce Weight, Stress, and Hypertension.* New York: John Wiley & Sons, 1995.

amenorrhea A suppression or absence of at least three menstrual cycles, amenorrhea is considered normal after menopause, during pregnancy and during lactation (secretion of milk after childbirth). Primary amenorrhea is failure of menstruation to occur at puberty; secondary amenorrhea is cessation of menstruation after its establishment. Among the causes of abnormal amenorrhea are metabolic disorders (diabetes or those stemming from OBESITY or malnutrition) and emotional disorders (ANOREXIA NERVOSA or those stemming from excitement, shock, fright or hysteria).

When the amount of fat drops below a critical percentage of body weight (20 percent) for any reason, hormonal release is affected, which in turn results in amenorrhea. Because of this, it is usually present in and generally considered to be a symptom of anorexia nervosa. At one time the presence of amenorrhea was considered necessary for anorexia nervosa to be diagnosed. However, many persons who are at an extremely low body weight do not develop amenorrhea, and sometimes persons who are actually overweight develop amenorrhea while losing weight. Although drastic weight reduction generally leads to amenorrhea, there have been cases in which amenorrhea has occurred prior to weight loss. In many of these cases, the amenorrhea continues even after the weight has been regained, sometimes for years. For this reason, some suggest that amenorrhea is a response to psychic stress or indicative of an underlying hypothalamic (body temperature) disorder. Others suggest that perhaps poor nutrition or abnormal psychological development can affect hormonal functions and cause these different results. Currently amenorrhea is one of the required diagnostic criteria for anorexia nervosa, but many researchers have recommended that it be eliminated as a criterion.

Irregular menstrual cycles and amenorrhea in bulimic women have been reported by nearly a dozen authors in medical journals, with irregular menstrual cycles reported in as many as 50 percent of cases studied and amenorrhea in 7 to 20 percent of cases studied. (See BULIMIA NERVOSA.)

Garfinkel, Paul E., et al. "Should Amenorrhea Be Necessary for the Diagnosis of Anorexia Nervosa?" *British Journal of Psychiatry* 168 (April 1996).

American Anorexia/Bulimia Association (AABA) This association of support groups and other programs is designed to assist anorexics, bulimics and their families. There are several chapter affiliates and task forces; total membership is about 3,000. AABA was founded in 1978 by Estelle Miller, a clinical worker. Its board is comprised of pediatricians, psychiatrists, parents, recovered anorexics and bulimics, teachers, school nurses, social workers and members of the lay community. The organization is tax exempt and nonprofit. Its newsletter (*AABA Newsletter*) is published three times a year and is mailed to all interested persons in the United States and elsewhere. The organization sponsors free support groups. Meetings are not regularly scheduled, so it is suggested that one call first

(212–575–6200). At the meetings, professionals present current theories about eating disorders and hold communication workshops; the latter are led by mental health professionals and recovered anorexics or bulimics or parents of recovered anorexics or bulimics.

The most active advocacy group for eating disorders, AABA has lobbied the U.S. Food and Drug Administration against over-the-counter sales of IPECAC. The organization works energetically to keep anorexia and bulimia in the public eye.

AABA offers anorexics and bulimics, family members and professionals the opportunity to participate together in the effort to cope with and overcome these life-threatening conditions. Membership is open to all interested persons.

amitriptyline This tricyclic ANTIDEPRESSANT has been used to treat bulimic patients for depression and BINGE-EATING behavior. In one study, amitriptyline (trade name Elavil) was tested against a PLACEBO in a sample of 32 bulimic subjects. Even though it was discovered that as many as half the subjects receiving amitriptyline may have been inadequately treated, amitriptyline still proved to be significantly superior to the placebo on one rating scale for anxiety and depression but not significantly superior on another rating scale.

Other studies have reported less-favorable results in treating ANOREXIA NERVOSA. Because amitriptyline has been shown to produce cathohydrate cravings in nonanorexics, Garfinkel and Garner cautioned that there may be a significant risk of triggering BULIMIA in anorexics (see CARBOHYDRATES and CRAVINGS). In a 1985 study comparing the effects of amitriptyline and placebo on weight gain, depression, eating attitudes and obsessive-compulsive tendency over a five-week period, no significant differences favoring amitriptyline were found in any of the outcome variables.

Side effects include increased appetite and thirst and constipation.

Currently, its use is being superseded by the newer SEROTONIN reuptake inhibitors such as fluoxetine (PROZAC).

amphetamines Amphetamines are central nervous system stimulants whose effects resemble those of the naturally occurring substance adrenalin. They have the temporary effect of increasing energy and apparent mental alertness. Until recent years amphetamines were widely prescribed by physicians for obesity because they lessen the appetite.

Amphetamines were originally formulated in a German laboratory in 1887 but were largely ignored until they were rediscovered in 1932 by Gordon Alles of the University of California, who transferred his patents to the pharmaceutical firm of Smith, Kline & French (SKF) Laboratories. By 1937, amphetamines were being recommended for certain patients whose obesity was accompanied by low-level depression on the grounds that a patient whose mood improved would no longer need to overeat and thus would lose weight. It wasn't long before amphetamines were being hailed as a painless way to lose weight through appetite suppression. By the time the federal government stepped in to control the manufacture and sale of amphetamines, SKF was selling $30 million worth each year. (See APPETITE SUPPRESSANTS and OBESITY.)

Their use does initially reduce appetite and increase energy levels. Because they induce conditions in the body that mimic a state of alarm or arousal, they may inhibit the digestive functions, causing the body to use fat rather than food for energy. Some practitioners believe that this theory shows that weight loss from amphetamines is the result of a lowering of the set point rather than appetite suppression (see SET-POINT THEORY). It has also been suggested that the anorexic effect of these drugs is a consequence of their inhibition of the salivary glands, which causes dry mouth, makes food less palatable and results in a loss of appetite. Amphetamines are frequently misused by anorexics, who experience intense hunger on the one hand, yet terror on the other at giving in to the impulse to eat. Amphetamine abusers have experienced difficulty in swallowing, an extreme way to suppress the appetite.

All of these appetite-control mechanisms have only temporary effects. The body soon draws on its immense recuperative powers, learns to adapt to the chemical and restores digestion, salivation and appetite to normal, thus preventing any more loss of tissue. Those who adhere to the lowered-set-point theory also say that the resultant weight loss is temporary: after use of the drug is stopped, the set point returns to its previous level, so weight also rises to its previous level, or higher.

The American Medical Association (AMA) has evaluated amphetamines as hazardous because of their undesirable effects, including a tendency to produce psychic and, occasionally, physical dependence when used indiscriminately and in large doses. The AMA suggests that physicians prescribe them only for temporary use of four to six weeks. The Food and Drug Administration affirms that these common drugs are of limited usefulness and that their use for prolonged periods in the treatment of obesity can lead to drug dependence and abuse and must be avoided.

Amphetamines are marketed under a variety of trade names; Dexamyl, Fastin, Pondmin, Preludin, Sanorex and Tenuate are among the more popular. All of them are closely related chemically. Phentermine (one of the ingredients of fen/phen) is an amphetamine. (See FEN-PHEN/REDUX)

Bayer, Linda N., and Steven L. Jaffe (editor). *Amphetamines & Other Uppers (Junior Drug Awareness).* New York: Chelsea House, 1999.

Czerwinski, W. P. "Amphetamine-related Disorders." *Journal of Louisiana State University Medical Society* 10 (October 1998).
Snyder, Solomon H., (editor) and Scott E. Lukas. *Amphetamines: Danger in the Fast Lane.* New York: Chelsea House, 1992.

amylin A recently isolated hormone discovered in high levels in the pancreas of Type II (non-insulin-dependent) diabetics, amylin appears to be responsible for the obesity, the reduced insulin secretion and the reduced effectiveness of insulin observed in Type II diabetes. Until this discovery, obesity had been considered by many to be a major contributor to the disease rather than a result of it.

anaerobic exercise Anaerobic exercise demands brief spurts of intense effort, such as calisthenics, weight lifting and sprinting. (Tennis and basketball are largely anaerobic because of their stop-and-go nature.) Anaerobic exercise is so intense that the oxygen supplied to the muscles by the blood is insufficient, forcing the muscle cells to work without it. For this reason, it does not burn as many calories as AEROBIC EXERCISE does. Anaerobic exercise is important to include in an overall fitness program because it helps to improve flexibility, toning and firming of the muscles, but it will not contribute a great deal to a weight reduction program. According to Dr. Michael O'Shea, founder of Sports Training Institute, when you begin to exercise, your body is always in an anaerobic mode—you use the "fuel" stored in your muscles and other parts of your body. After two or three minutes of exercise, your body switches to an aerobic system, using oxygen to keep you going.

anorexia mirabilis The term used by physicians during the High Middle Ages to describe "miraculously inspired" loss of appetite, anorexia mirabilis was a fairly common occurrence in medieval Europe, especially between 1200 and 1500. It was considered miraculous when women survived prolonged periods of fasting; many insisted they were actually unable to eat normal "earthly fare." Fasting was critical to female sainthood during this time, given medieval culture's association of the female body and food. Catherine of Siena (1347–80) restricted her diet to a daily handful of herbs; whenever she did partake of other food, she would cause herself to vomit by forcing a stick down her throat. Other female saints became ill or felt their throats close up around food, fasted for days at a time, ate only orange seeds and even died of starvation. Anorexia mirabilis, unlike anorexia nervosa, was not restricted to adolescent or young adult women, and today's anorexic strives for the modern ideal of physical perfection or beauty rather than the medieval ideal of spiritual perfection or beauty.

As the Protestant Reformation revolutionized medieval culture, prolonged fasting became a negative practice; it was considered a work of the devil rather than of God. Where fasting females were once venerated as saints, they were now denounced as evil, possessed by the devil or insane.

Brumberg, Joan Jacobs. *Fasting Girls.* New York: Plume Books, 1989.

anorexia nervosa A serious psychological disorder characterized by intense fear of gaining weight, anorexia nervosa sufferers refuse to maintain even a minimal body weight and are pathologically preoccupied with food and dieting. *Anorexia* literally means "lack of appetite," which is actually a misnomer, but it is the generally accepted name for the condition. Anorexics do experience hunger, but they simply refuse to give in to it for fear of becoming fat. Anorexia nervosa affects chiefly young women in their teens and twenties.

Of those patients being treated for anorexia, about 15 of every 100 will actually die. Of the remainder, only half will recover to lead normal lives; the rest are likely to relapse. Arthur H. Crisp has reported patients relapsing after being in remission for 50 years. Morbidity and mortality rates in anorexia nervosa are among the highest recorded for psychiatric disorders. The mortality rate of 6 to 18 percent reported frequently in medical journals would make anorexia the most lethal psychiatric illness. Across multiple studies, mortality rates vary, but on average there seems to be approximately a 1 percent-per-year mortality rate.

Causes There is no known specific cause of anorexia. Several theories do exist, but they are based on individual clinical observations and histories, so none has been accepted as definitive. Researchers do agree that anorexia nervosa is probably a negative response to a number of psychological, environmental and physiological factors rather than a disease that can be traced to a single cause. Although these influencing factors affect virtually all individuals, the anorexic appears to lack the skills necessary to cope with them.

Anorexia nervosa was once believed to be a disorder of Western culture, a belief recently reconsidered by researchers. A 1996 Chinese University of Hong Kong study determined that Western patterns of body dissatisfaction and disordered-eating attitudes are now common among Chinese adolescent girls. One theory is that these attitudes are grounded in the "transitional culture of modernity" due to increased affluence in parts of the world rapidly becoming more urban. In most Western societies, a strong cultural emphasis is placed on individual success. Neuman and Halvorson explain that, until recently, Western women's social success was judged by their affiliations—by whose daughter or wife they were. Today's woman has new demands. "Thus many maturing females find themselves caught up in the 'Superwoman' syndrome, trying to be all things to all people."

And, they add, girls who are already perfectionists and not good at making decisions can become overwhelmed by feelings of powerlessness. College-age anorexics especially have reported to Neuman and Halvorson these feelings of confusion and being out of control of their own future.

Other cultural factors influencing the rise of anorexia nervosa include the growing concern about nutrition and physical fitness and a national obsession with calorie counting and being thin. Television, magazine and newspaper messages bombard women and girls with advice on how to lose weight more quickly, exercise more and eat less to be thinner. The messages blatantly state that being thin will make a woman more attractive, improve her popularity, lead to success on the job and snag her an ideal mate because she will then be sexier and more desirable. Fashion models display small waists and busts, narrow hips and thin thighs. This has resulted in a cultural focus more on the physical being than on the inner person. Small wonder, experts say, that some girls in the highly vulnerable adolescent and young adult years take these "thin-or-sorry" messages to heart and carry their responses to them to extremes. (See CULTURAL INFLUENCES ON APPEARANCE and CULTURAL INFLUENCES ON EATING DISORDERS.)

In a 1999 study, Swedish researchers showed that premature birth and birth trauma may increase the risk of development of anorexia nervosa. The authors concluded that anorexia nervosa is probably caused by multiple factors and that preterm birth and birth trauma may cause subtle brain damage, which, in conjunction with other individual or environmental factors, may result in the inability to identify hunger and satiety sensations correctly. Because this study was restricted to inpatients, researchers warned that these results may not apply to less severe cases of anorexia.

Cnattingius, Sven. "Very Preterm Birth, Birth Trauma, and the Risk of Anorexia Nervosa Among Girls." *Archives of General Psychiatry* 56 (July 1999).

anorexia research In response to congressional requests, the National Institute of Mental Health (NIMH) has embarked upon a program of professional education to improve the diagnosis and treatment of eating disorders. To ensure that educational efforts are based on established research findings, NIMH established an Eating Disorders Scientific Advisory Group to review research findings in the areas of epidemiology, etiology and risk factors, course of illness, comorbidity and psychosocial and pharmacological treatments. NIMH continues to focus attention on the need for research-based knowledge in the diagnosis and treatment of eating disorders, both through encouraging research and incorporating research knowledge into curricula and course presentations.

To understand the course and outcomes of eating disorders better, NIMH began to support a longitudinal study of anorexia and bulimia nervosa in the early 1990s. In this ongoing research, a large group of women with these disorders are being interviewed at six-month intervals. Most of the women had other mental disorders along with the eating disorders; the majority had current major depression and at least one anxiety disorder. The women participated in a variety of treatments—primarily individual therapy—but also group therapy, family therapy, pharmacotherapy and nutritional counseling. At this point in the study, indications are providing valuable knowledge of the comorbidity and outcomes in anorexia and bulimia nervosa that not only helps us to unravel the largely unknown origins and nature of these disorders but also has practical clinical applications for treatment.

NIMH investigators are also currently conducting studies to determine if patients with anorexia nervosa have abnormalities in the genes involved in regulating function of the neurotransmitter serotonin, including serotonin receptors and the rate-limiting biosynthetic enzyme tryptophan hydroxylase. It is thought that dysregulation of brain serotonin could contribute to restricted eating, behavioral overcontrol, obsessive behaviors and negative affective states that are evident in the clinical phenotype of individuals with anorexia nervosa. Ongoing studies of the neurobiological and genetic mechanisms that contribute to the etiology of anorexia nervosa will lead to improvements in the treatment of the disorder.

anorexic behavior Researchers Garfinkel and Garner use this term to describe the behavior of young women who have weight concerns that interfere with their psychological well-being but do not have full-blown anorexia nervosa. Garfinkel and Garner speculate that these women may be using weight control to deal with issues similar to those of anorexics—the regulation and expression of self, autonomy and self-control; they correspond to Bruch's THIN FAT PEOPLE. Among the features of so-called anorexic behavior are intense preoccupation with food, food fads, mixing unusual food combinations and dawdling over meals.

anorexic bingers Anorexic bingers are technically referred to as anorexia nervosa, binge-eating/purging type. According to DSM-IV, most anorexics who binge engage in these behaviors at least weekly, but sufficient information is not available to justify the specification of a minimum frequency. Anorexia accompanied by binge eating and purging has been found to affect older age groups more frequently than it does adolescents. Bingeing anorexics display less self-discipline and act more impulsively than RESTRICTOR ANOREXICS. They also have greater incidence of MULTICOMPULSIVE behavior such as alcohol and drug abuse and shoplifting, as well as more SUICIDE and SELF-MUTILATION attempts. There is also more VOMITING and LAXATIVE ABUSE among bingers.

In comparing anorexic bingers and nonbingers, researchers have found that anorexic patients who binge tend to be more depressed, anxious, guilt ridden and preoccupied with food than nonbingers. Anorexic bingers also complain more about aches and pains and have more trouble sleeping, resulting in more complaints of fatigue. Bingers also tend to be more outgoing and sensitive to others. In one study, 86 percent of the anorexic bingers were described as outgoing as children in contrast to only 57 percent of the anorexic nonbingers. Besides being more outgoing, anorexic bingers are often sexually active and concerned with physical attractiveness and attention from the opposite sex, in marked contrast to the restrictor, who denies or avoids sexual feelings. Perhaps not coincidentally, poor father-child relationships have been reported more often in the lives of anorexic bingers than nonbingers.

Restrictor anorexics are able to ignore and even deny hunger, but bingers report stronger appetites that are more difficult to control. Possibly because of this feeling of lack of control, the binger is more likely to seek treatment. Yet, anorexia accompanied by bingeing is more difficult to treat because it occurs intermittently and persistently over a longer period of time.

In a study of 120 adolescents under treatment for eating disorders, those patients with binge/purge symptoms exhibited significantly more behavioral disorders and had a higher frequency of depression than those who were restrictors.

ANRED (Anorexia Nervosa and Related Eating Disorders, Inc.) This national nonprofit organization collects information about eating disorders and distributes it to anorexics, bulimics, families, school personnel, students and medical and mental health professionals. The ANRED staff leads workshops and seminars across the United States, helping people identify and understand anorexia nervosa and bulimia. ANRED also participates in professional conferences, helping physicians, psychotherapists and other human services personnel learn effective ways of working with eating-disordered people.

ANRED also works closely with Sacred Heart Hospital in Eugene, Oregon, where its offices are located, to provide an integrated, comprehensive eating-disorders program. The program incorporates inpatient, day-hospital and aftercare modes. The *ANRED Alert,* a monthly newsletter containing research updates, self-help tips, stories by recovered anorexics and bulimics, encouragement for families and descriptions of therapy techniques, is available for $10 per year.

ANRED provides speakers and educational presentations for schools, clubs, civic organizations, churches, counseling agencies and other groups. It also provides training for counselors and psychotherapists who work with anorexic and bulimic clients.

anticonvulsant treatment Anticonvulsants are drugs that suppress convulsions. These include diphenylhydantoin (Dilantin), mephenytoin (Mesantoin) and trimethadione (Tridione). They are used in the treatment of epilepsy and in psychomotor (muscular action resulting from mental activity) and myoclonic (involuntary twitching or spasms of muscles) seizures. A relationship between binge eating and seizure disorders has been suggested because binge eaters typically describe their binges as episodic and uncontrollable. Binge episodes are also frequently preceded by a change in mental state that could be interpreted as an aura (flashes of light, unusual smells, increased tension or fear), a phenomenon that sometimes occurs in nervous disorders. A number of compulsive eaters have had abnormalities of their electroencephalogram (EEG) pattern (an EEG measures electric current generated in the brain). Because of these findings, some doctors have treated bulimic patients with anticonvulsant drugs and have reported success. However, others have found these drugs to be of no use, and there has not been sufficient compelling evidence to support the hypothesis that bulimia is a form of seizure disorder.

antidepressants Drugs originally developed for the treatment of depression and now used for a variety of psychiatric and nonpsychiatric conditions, antidepressants are among the most commonly used psychotropic (affecting the mind) agents in the treatment of anorexia nervosa and bulimia in the United States. Three types of antidepressants have been commonly used in this country: tricyclics, MAO inhibitors and Selective Serotonin Reuptake Inhibitors (SSRIs). They all boost the action of the neurotransmitters SEROTONIN and norepinephrine, two of the chemicals that transmit impulses through the nervous system.

Although no antidepressants have been found to be effective in treating anorexia nervosa, each of the three classes of antidepressants has been regarded by some as successful in treatment of bulimic patients of normal body weight. However, there are a number of questions raised by others. First, there is no known way to determine which patients are likely to respond favorably. Most of the controlled trials of antidepressant medications have studied bulimia patients who are chronically and moderately to severely ill. It is not clear if the same success would be found in less severely ill patients. Of more concern to doctors is the fact that little is known about the long-term outcome of the drug treatment of bulimia or how best to combine drug treatment with other forms of therapy.

A 1985 study reported that most of the patients who participated in the original double-blind trial of IMIPRAMINE (a tricyclic) were doing well up to two years later. A majority of the patients were still on some antidepressant medication, and most of those who had attempted to discontinue medication had relapsed.

The longer-term effects of antidepressant medication for the treatment of bulimia nervosa and binge-eating disorder were reviewed by W. S. Agras in 1997. This study found that using a single antidepressant agent results in recovery about 25 percent of the time and that continued treatment leads to relapse in about one-third of these patients.

A new family of antidepressants that can regulate serotonin, chemically unrelated to tricyclics, MAO inhibitors and SSRIs, is now available. The first of these drugs to reach the market in the United States was fluoxetine, developed by Eli Lilly & Co. as PROZAC. Others are sertraline, fluvoxamine and femoxetime. These drugs have fewer or less severe side effects than other antidepressants, which can cause thirst, constipation and a CRAVING for carbohydrates.

Preliminary clinical investigations of these new antidepressants have yielded mixed results in the treatment of anorexia, bulimia nervosa, binge-eating disorder and obesity. A Columbia University study concluded that fluoxetine does not appear to add significant benefit to the inpatient treatment of anorexia nervosa.

Therapists have expressed concern that tricyclic antidepressants such as imipramine and AMITRIPTYLINE may actually increase the already high risk of suicide among eating-disorder patients. An additional risk is that MAO inhibitors require adherence to a strict diet and avoidance of a wide range of foods, so their use with eating disorders is considered to be a considerable risk. Some antidepressants stimulate APPETITE, which can be particularly difficult for the eating-disordered person, but the new serotonin-regulating drugs seem to spur weight loss instead. Prozac has been reported to lead to a weight loss of four pounds in six weeks for the average overweight depressed patient. A number of researchers say that it shows promise as a treatment of obesity. Although antidepressant medications, especially the SSRIs such as Prozac, seem to be effective in reducing binge eating, the problem is that there is a high rate of relapse once the drug is withdrawn. Plus, they may not target the preoccupation with weight and dieting that predispose the individual to further episodes of bulimia nervosa.

See also DEPRESSION.

Agras, W. S. "Pharmacotherapy of Bulimia Nervosa and Binge Eating Disorder: Longer-Term Outcomes." *Psychopharmacology Bulletin* 33 (1997).

Attica, E., et al. "Does Fluoxetine Augment the Inpatient Treatment of Anorexia Nervosa?" *American Journal of Psychiatry* 155 (April 1998).

Mayer, L. E., and B. T. Walsh. "The Use of Selective Serotonin Reuptake Inhibitors in Eating Disorders." *Journal of Clinical Psychiatry* 59 (1998).

Walsh, B. T., et al. "Medication and Psychotherapy in the Treatment of Bulimia Nervosa." *American Journal of Psychiatry* 154 (April 1997).

antipsychotic medication A group of drugs used to treat psychoses (mental disorders characterized by loss of contact with reality), antipsychotic medication was introduced into psychiatry during the early 1960s. Occasionally, anorexia patients, particularly agitated ones, have benefited from low doses of antipsychotic medications. Soon after their introduction, CHLORPROMAZINE began to be used along with insulin to produce weight gain among anorexics.

None of these medications have exhibited much overall success in controlled studies. In addition, the severity of potential side effects of antipsychotic medications, including grand mal seizures, hypertension and the long-term risk of tardive dyskinesia (involuntary movements of the face, mouth, etc., believed to be induced by prolonged use of certain tranquilizers), limits the use of these drugs in treating anorexia. Despite these limitations, they continue to be recommended in the management of particularly physically active or compulsive patients who respond to the sedative properties of antipsychotic drugs.

Although the distortion of body image (see BODY IMAGE DISTURBANCE) characteristic of anorexia nervosa at times approaches delusional proportions, there is no indication that antipsychotic medications reduce this disturbance.

anxiety Anxiety is described as a feeling of uneasiness, apprehension or dread that is often characterized by tension, increased pulse and sweating. Most persons find healthy ways to deal with their anxiety, such as social activities, hobbies, music, reading and sports. Anxiety can even be a positive signal that alerts the individual to a situation or event that requires preparation to overcome, such as the anxiety that motivates a student to study for an exam. Some people, however, respond in negative or inappropriate ways, such as having insomnia or recurrent headaches, overindulging in alcohol or drugs, overeating or experiencing a loss of appetite.

Instead of using anxiety as a signal to prepare to cope with some perceived stress, eating-disordered persons see anxiety as a signal of impending doom, a warning that whatever is coming will be emotionally overwhelming. They react to anxiety by trying to get rid of it rather than by heeding it. In them, anxiety is likely to set off a binge or, in anorexics, to further restrict eating.

Research has supported an anxiety model of bulimia nervosa, in which anxiety about gaining weight is the central feature of the disorder, and binge eating triggers an increase in such anxiety. The anxiety is then reduced by vomiting or some other purgative behavior.

The central theme of the PSYCHODYNAMIC APPROACH TO OBESITY is that anxiety precedes and triggers the overweight person's overeating response. The anxiety that results in overeating is produced by internal emotional conflicts rather than external stimuli. Eating often serves temporarily to make a person feel better. Because much internal conflict is believed to take place in the subconscious, an individual may often not be aware of the source of the anxiety. Studies have shown that uncontrollable anxiety increases eating in obese individuals, but controllable anxiety does not. Some therapists see the use of food as compensating for life's upsets, replacing what seems to be missing in life and soothing, calming and covering up daily stresses and anxiety. Theories in opposition to this include the EXTERNALITY APPROACH TO OBESITY.

appetite An emotional and physical impulse or desire or urge to eat, regardless of nutritional needs, appetite is psychological, dependent on memory and associations (social learning), unlike HUNGER, which is physiologically aroused by the body's need for food. Appetite is stimulated by the sight, smell or thought of food and is accompanied by the flow of saliva in the mouth and gastric juice in the stomach. Appetite may stimulate a person to eat when no hunger signals are present or to continue eating after he or she feels full. When appetite is disturbed, an individual consumes more calories than he uses up and thus gains weight.

For many years it was presumed that the stomach held the primary role in appetite control. As surgical techniques developed and gastrectomy (removal of the stomach) became possible, it became apparent that this is not so. Ultimate control of feeding lies in the brain. There are also several mechanisms by which the small intestine is thought to bring about SATIETY.

appetite-stimulating drugs Although patients with anorexia nervosa do not have a reduced appetite (they do get hungry; they simply choose not to eat), a number of researchers have tried appetite-stimulating drugs in the hope that they might induce anorexic patients to eat and gain weight. Only one of these drugs, an antihistamine called CYPROHEPTADINE, has actually been studied in detail, and it has been found generally to be useless.

appetite suppressants Appetite suppressants include drugs such as AMPHETAMINES, BULKING AGENTS and topical painkillers that lessen or eliminate appetite by slowing down the emptying of the stomach or by stimulating a "full" feeling following eating a smaller amount. They can also maintain a feeling of fullness long enough to help a patient limit the size of the next meal. One theory suggests that appetite suppressants temporarily lower the set point rather than suppress the appetite and that, because of this, any weight lost while using suppressants is usually rapidly regained once the dieter stops taking them. (See SET-POINT THEORY.) One popular appetite suppressant form is the "diet candy," but any lessening of appetite from eating the suggested small amount of these candies is not likely to last longer than an hour. Some appetite suppressants use the topical painkiller BENZOCAINE to reduce sensation in the mouth and make eating a less rewarding activity. Many clinicians strongly advise against the use of any appetite suppressant for bulimics or compulsive overeaters.

art therapy Also referred to as creative therapy, art therapy is an attempt to stimulate patients through the creation of art and design and then to transfer this creativity or expressiveness to the reshaping of the patient's life.

Work created during art therapy is not evaluated for aesthetic merit or artistic skill but for its value in opening up communication between patient and therapist. Artistic productions can be interpreted by experienced psychotherapists in the context of a therapy, as with free association or as is done in psychoanalysis with dreams.

Art therapy has existed in various forms since the 1940s. It has been used alone or along with other forms of treatment with both individuals and groups. Although the field has been gaining acceptance as a legitimate form of psychotherapy, critics say it has lagged behind other therapies in documenting and evaluating its effectiveness. Art therapy is thought to be especially helpful in the case of young children who may express in pictures what they cannot yet communicate verbally.

In the treatment of eating disorders, art therapy can provide anorexics with an opportunity to become more sensitive to their inner selves. They create artwork that originates within themselves and is not under the control of others. Anorexics convey their emotional needs through the use of "body language" (by starving themselves)—a nonverbal form of symbolic communication. Drawing and painting are also forms of nonverbal communication; through these forms they can express their emotional conflicts and enhance their self-awareness.

In art therapy, anorexics are encouraged to represent themselves, their families, their feelings, their view of treatment and so on. Interpretation of such work can provide an opportunity to begin more formal PSYCHOTHERAPY.

Allen, Pat. *Art Is a Way of Knowing,* Shambhala Publications, 1995.

Riley, Shirley, and Gerald D. Oster. *Contemporary Art Therapy With Adolescents,* Jessica Kingsley Publishers, London: 1999.

Skaife, Sally, and Val Huet, eds. *Art Psychotherapy in Groups: Between Picture and Words,* New York: 1998.

asthma link to obesity Several studies released in 1998 and 1999 link obesity to asthma, a medical condition occurring when the bronchial tubes swell up and go into a spasm, blocking the passage of air in and out of the lungs. In a presentation to the 1998 American Lung Association/American Thoracic Society International Conference, Carlos A. Camargo, Jr., an epidemiologist at Brigham and Women's Hospital in Boston and an instructor at Harvard Medical School, suggested that obese people are more susceptible to asthma than people of average weight. Prior to the study of more than 100,000 nurses, the general assumption was that asthma patients were prone to putting on weight because their breathing problems limited exercise. But Camargo's research showed that obesity preceded the diagnosis of asthma. Other experts described the study as good preliminary research but cautioned that more study needs to be done. Among the possible reasons for the link suggested by Camargo and others are that sedentary people may not take as many deep breaths as more active people, with the more frequent shallow breathing leading to the asthma symptoms, that the extra pounds that obese people carry may somehow affect their airways, or that there may be a genetic link between asthma and obesity.

In a study of 171 children between the ages of 4 and 16 at an urban community health center, pediatrician Jennifer Gennuso and her colleagues at the State University of New York at Buffalo reported that children and teenagers with asthma are significantly more likely than those without asthma to be obese.

In London, Dr. Sheif Shaheen and colleagues studied health histories of 9,000 people born during the same week in 1970 and then monitored throughout their lives. They found that the prevalence of asthma fell as birth weight increased.

Driscoll, Paul A. "Obesity May Increase Risk of Asthma." The Associated Press, April 25, 1998.

Gennuso, Jennifer, et al. "The Relationship Between Asthma and Obesity in Urban Minority Children and Adolescents." *Archives of Pediatrics and Adolescent Medicine* 152 (December 1998).

Shaheen, Sheif, et al. "Birth Weight, Body Mass Index and Asthma in Young Adults." *Thorax* 54 (May 1999).

atmospheric pressure and body fat As early as 1908, there were reports that the obese had a greater susceptibility than the lean to caisson disease, the decompression sickness now called the bends, suffered by underwater workers and caused by too-rapid decrease in atmospheric pressure. In 1935, it was confirmed that rapid changes in atmospheric pressure did result in more severe attacks of the bends among the obese than the lean. This held practical significance for deep-sea diving and aviation and led to the military's practice of rejecting people whose weight was more than 15 percent above that recommended by the standard body weight/height charts.

atypical anorexia nervosa *Atypical anorexia nervosa* is a term used by HILDE BRUCH to describe a condition in which weight loss occurs because of various symbolic misinterpretations of the eating function, rather than because of a preoccupation with weight. She classified as atypical those who refused to eat for fear of oral impregnation, for fear of abdominal pain or vomiting, because of feeling unworthy and in response to events in their lives. Bruch found such preoccupation only in exceptional cases and thus came to rate such patients as atypical.

This refusal to eat is decidedly different from the true anorexic's loss of appetite, but patients with atypical anorexia nervosa and those with the genuine disorder look deceptively alike, particularly after the condition has existed for some time. In contrast to genuine anorexics, however, in whom relentless pursuit of thinness and denial of their condition, even of acute emaciation, are key symptoms, atypical anorexics complain about weight loss and do not want to stay thin, or they value thinness only secondarily as a means of manipulating others. Inability to eat is the leading symptom in the atypical group. Often there is an unacknowledged desire to stay sick to remain in a dependent role, in contrast to the struggle for an independent identity that occurs in genuine, or primary, anorexics. Bruch described these patients as displaying various degrees of neurotic and hysterical symptoms.

Patients diagnosed as atypical do not display the peculiar features of the primary disorder: pursuit of thinness as a struggle for an independent identity, delusional denial of thinness, preoccupation with food, hyperactivity and striving for perfection.

Of 60 female patients on whom Bruch reported with the diagnosis of anorexia nervosa, there were 15 (25 percent) diagnosed as atypical. She found few if any differences in the descriptive data between the atypical and genuine group. Weight loss was of the same order of magnitude, age of onset in the atypical group was slightly higher and amenorrhea was not present as frequently with the atypical group. Both groups proved equally resistant to treatment.

Bruch found the one common characteristic among atypical anorexia patients to be a severe sense of inadequacy and discontent with their lives. Eating difficulties developed when the demands of reality became overpowering and their fragile sense of self was further undermined.

A 1995 study of eating-disordered children and adolescents during the previous three decades suggested that bulimia nervosa and atypical eating disorder are not replacing the traditional category of anorexia nervosa, but that eating disorders are becoming more widespread and dissimilar.

See also PSYCHOGENIC MALNUTRITION.

Ash, J. B., and E. Piazza. "Changing Symptomatology in Eating Disorders." *International Journal of Eating Disorders* 18 (July 1995).

Bruch, Hilde. "Psychogenic Malnutrition and Atypical Anorexia Nervosa." In *Eating Disorders: Obesity, Anorexia Nervosa, and the Person Within.* New York: Basic Books, 1985.

aversion therapy A type of behavioral therapy, aversion therapy is based on the experiments of Ivan Pavlov (1849–1936), a Russian scientist who worked extensively in the field of conditioned reflexes. Typically, an aversive experience (a foul odor, an electric shock) is administered to a patient at certain times to create a negative reaction toward certain foods or behaviors. This therapy was among the first techniques employed in the treatment of obesity. Repeated pairings of aversive experience with certain foods were assumed to result in decreasing palatability of those foods through a process of "Pavlovian" behavioral conditioning; this shift in preference was assumed to facilitate control over eating and, thus, weight reduction. Taste aversions develop most easily to novel and less-preferred foods and often persist for many years. One limitation of this therapy is the relative difficulty in establishing aversions to familiar, preferred foods, which are the very ones to which dieters may wish to develop aversions. Results with overweight patients have been poor, whether the unpleasant stimuli have been foul smells, electric shocks or unpleasant images.

In a 1996 study of 172 overweight women, those who received aversion therapy and HYPNOTIC THERAPY lost more weight than subjects receiving only hypnotic therapy, but the differences were not significant.

Although aversion therapy has been used quite frequently in the treatment of patients who are overweight because of compulsive eating, few reports deal specifically with patients identified as bulimic. It is now considered an outdated treatment.

Avicenna (A.D. 980–1037) An 11th-century Persian physician and philosopher, called the "Prince of Physicians," Avicenna was the first to write about anorexia nervosa. He described the case of a melancholic young prince who was successfully treated for the disorder. He was the author of more than 100 works, of which his *Canon of Medicine* was the most important and was used for centuries as a medical reference in both the Christian and Islamic worlds.

B

Bahamian Diet The Bahamian Diet is a controversial diet formula promoted by comedian Dick Gregory, who claims to have kept his weight down over the years via fasting and use of his formula, "a low-calorie, powdered, natural food supplement, taken in juice." Its original ingredients included soy protein, tricalcium, phosphate, lecithin, cellulose gel, guar gum, pectin, sesamum indicum seed, cucurbita pepo seed, salvia columbariae seed and sea vegetation.

In 1984 Gregory made an agreement with a Swiss-owned natural foods company and began to market the product, mainly to the black community. In 1987 he began to distribute his product through a Philadelphia-based marketing company called Correction Connection. Today the formula is marketed by Internet vitamin and health food sites at around $1 per ounce as a meal-replacement product. The National Association to Advance Fat Acceptance (NAAFA) organization has come out strongly against the Bahamian Diet. (See LIQUID FORMULAS; WALTER HUDSON.)

Banting, William (1797–1878) The "Father of Dieting," 19th-century English mortician William Banting's weight began to increase during his late thirties. When his doctor advised him to exercise to lose weight and suggested rowing, Banting bought a small boat, which he took out onto the Thames each morning. But all this exercise and the fresh air made him hungry; he went home and ate even more.

By age 50 he had become so obese that he couldn't bend to tie his shoes; he could hardly exert any energy without difficulty in breathing. He continued to eat and gain weight. As he wrote later, his body fell into a "low and impoverished state." When his doctor suggested that he sweat off some pounds in Turkish baths, he took 90 baths. They didn't work.

By this time, Banting was 65 years old, stood five feet five inches tall and weighed 230 pounds. Walking down stairs caused such strain on his legs that he had to navigate the stairs backward. Finally, in 1862, he consulted another physician, William Harvey.

Harvey was one of the few scientists and physicians of the day who studied the effects of dieting on general health. Until then, weight-control methods had included bleeding from the arm or jugular vein, applying leeches to the arms, eating vegetables with vinegar, taking hot baths or saltwater baths, staying awake most of the night, taking sea voyages, eating soap, pricking the flesh with needles, walking with naked feet and surgically removing fatty tissue with a scalpel.

Dr. Harvey put Banting on a high-protein, low-carbohydrate diet of 1,200 calories per day. Banting was willing to try anything, and it worked. The first week he lost two pounds, the next week three, and the third week four pounds. After a year he had lost a total of 46 pounds and 14 1/2 inches around his waist. Even his hearing and vision improved.

Banting was so pleased that he decided to tell others about his good fortune. In 1863 he wrote a pamphlet called *Letter on Corpulence, Addressed to the Public,* the first diet book. He gave away the first 2,500 copies, and it became the talk of London. The third edition sold 50,000 copies. By the fourth edition, it had grown from its original 25 pages to 100 pages with the addition of letters and testimonials praising Banting's success and his diet.

Banting became famous, frequently lecturing while wearing the clothes he had worn when he had weighed 230 pounds. The clothes would fall around him, and he would tell his audiences that this is what a proper diet should do for them.

Several doctors dismissed Banting as a fraud and as the "prototype hypochondriac." Some even started rumors that Banting was dying because of his diet. On two occasions in 1864, Banting found it necessary to write to the *Times* of London to deny that he was dying.

During Banting's lifetime *Bantingism* and *to bant* became household words. He lived to be 81, dying on March 16, 1878, slim and trim to the end.

bariatrics This branch of medicine deals with the causes, prevention and treatment of obesity and its associated conditions. There are 19,500 members of the American Society of Bariatric Physicians.

basal metabolic rate (BMR) This is the rate at which energy (fuel, fat and glucose obtained from food) is used by an individual at complete physical and mental rest for basic body functioning (breathing, heart activity, nervous system activity and various other essential organ functions). It is usually measured in the morning when a person is relaxed and has not eaten since the preceding evening. In an average person, this basic functioning accounts for approximately 70 percent of total energy expenditure. The remaining 30 percent is largely a reflection of one's level of physical activity. The BMR varies according to age, sex and weight. It is highest in children and begins to decline in young adults after age 24, dropping approximately 5 to 7 percent each decade after age 20, making it more difficult to lose weight as one gets older. BMR is also lower in hypothyroidism and higher in hyperthyroidism.

The wide variance in basal metabolic rate among individuals is one reason why different people respond differently to identical diet and exercise programs. People with high basal metabolic rates tend to remain slim even while eating large amounts of high-calorie food; those with lower BMRs seem to gain weight merely "looking at" food. The BMR actually decreases when caloric intake is severely restricted by starvation or stringent diet and increases when activity level increases.

See also SET-POINT THEORY.

benzocaine A crystalline compound used in ointments as a mild local anesthetic, benzocaine, when used in a diet pill, is supposed to deaden the taste buds and thereby lessen the craving for food. It is often used in "miracle" pills and weight-reducing candies in combination with methyl cellulose, which expands by absorbing water from the stomach to give a false sense of fullness. Researchers are divided over whether benzocaine in such small doses (7.5 mg per tablet) actually has a numbing effect on the salivary glands, but, as Edwin Bayrd wrote in *The Thin Game,* that argument "is quite beside the point, for the salivary glands are a part of the mouth and the pills are already in the stomach."

Beverly Hills Diet A diet promoted in a book of the same name (1980) by Judy Mazel and then updated in 1996, the Beverly Hills Diet stresses combinations of similar kinds of foods that are digested together. The first week allows only fruit; the second adds a few other items. The popularity of the book, which focuses on the reward of being "skinny" and "perfect," is viewed by the medical community as yet another symptom of "a weight-obsessed culture in which no price is too high for thinness, including health." P. Wright condemned the Beverly Hills Diet, writing in "The Psychology of Eating and Eating Disorders" (*Psychology Survey No. 6,* edited by H. Beloff and A. Colmon, 1987): "[It] actually advocates a form of bulimia in which dieters are advised to counteract an eating binge by consuming large amounts of raw fruit in order to produce diarrhea." Although readers have claimed successful—if temporary—weight loss, many have reported side effects, from anal fissures to general weakness to stomach cramps.

binge eating Binge eating is the rapid consumption of large amounts of food during a short period of time. A *binge* is usually defined as the consumption of 2,000 calories or more during the span of one to two hours. An average binge lasts from 60 to 75 minutes, with 3,400 calories consumed (an entire pecan pie, for instance).

Binge-Eating Scale (BES) The Binge-Eating Scale is a self-test developed in 1982 by Gormally, Black, Daston and Rardin to assess binge eating among the obese by measuring the feelings or perceptions that precede or follow a binge.

Sample items from the BES:

I don't think about food a great deal.
Most of my days seem to be preoccupied with thoughts about food. I feel like I live to eat.
Because I feel so helpless about controlling my eating, I have become very desperate about trying to get in control.

Binge Scale The Binge Scale is a self-test developed in 1980 by Hawkins and Clements to measure the frequency and duration of binge-eating behavior and attitudes associated with BULIMIA.

Sample item from the Binge Scale:

How often do you binge?
A. Seldom
B. Once or twice a month
C. Once a week
D. Almost every day

biofeedback Biofeedback is a technique that seeks to control certain emotional states, such as ANXIETY or DEPRESSION, by using electronic devices to modify involuntary body functions such as blood pressure or heartbeat.

This technique has been experimented with in the treatment of ANOREXIA NERVOSA, but it is not yet widely used. Its basic benefit is the teaching of relaxation techniques to counteract the typically high activity level of anorexics, who tend to deny fatigue and typically are unable to relax. They pursue their activities compulsively, producing excessive levels of autonomic arousal (heart, blood pressure and so on) that can lead to psychophysiological stress reactions.

Through connection to the biofeedback machines by muscle or temperature sensors, the patients learn to become active participants in the process of relaxation training. Patients find it difficult to deny their condition when the evidence can be seen on a sound or light monitor. Biofeedback may make it easier for the therapist to break through the denial process of anorexic patients.

biopsychosocial model of eating disorders This refers to the prevailing conceptualization of the causes of eating disorders and/or obesity. According to the model, rather than there being a single cause, these disorders/conditions are more likely the product of a complex combination of biological, psychological and social factors. The precise contribution of each of these factors may vary, depending on the disorder and the individual.

Johnson, C., and M. E. Connors. *The Etiology and Treatment of Bulimia Nervosa: A Biopsychosocial Perspective.* Northvale, N.J.: Jason Aronson Inc., Publishers, 1995.

body dysmorphic disorder (BDD) *BDD* is defined by DSM-IV as a preoccupation with some imagined defect in physical appearance or a gross exaggeration of a slight physical anomaly. This preoccupation with appearance is excessively time consuming and causes significant distress or impairment in functioning. Symptoms of dissatisfaction with body shape and size that are a function of an eating disorder do not come under BDD. The most common complaints are about features involving the head and body hair, facial features, skin blemishes, thighs, stomach, breasts, buttocks and genitals. It appears that a majority of patients have multiple dysmorphic symptoms. The exact connection between BDD and eating disorders is unclear, but Rosen has argued that both are basically disorders of body image.

Rosen, J. C. "Body Dysmorphic Disorder: Assessment and Treatment." In *Body Image, Eating Disorders, and Obesity,* edited by J. K. Thompson. Washington, D.C.: American Psychological Association, 1996, pp. 149–70.

body fat Body fat is a reservoir of available fuel for our energy needs. When we eat CALORIES in excess of our immediate needs, the body converts this fuel into a storable form (FAT). When we eat an insufficient number of calories, the body takes some of the stored fat and metabolizes it into available fuel. (See METABOLISM.)

Some body fat is desirable. For example, fat cushions the balls of our feet and protects the bony structure. Fat insulates our organs from cold during winter months and protects them against damage from outside the body. Too-low body fat reduces resistance to viral infection.

Excess body fat, however, is harmful. Excess fat requires the heart to pump harder and at higher pressures simply because the arterial circuit is longer. Fat also chokes down the available passageways, forcing the heart to pump still harder. This extra strain significantly increases the risk of heart attacks, strokes, hypertension and other cardiovascular diseases. In addition, excess fat puts undue strain on other body organs and has proven to increase significantly the risk of diabetes and even certain types of cancers.

A higher weight does not necessarily mean a higher amount of body fat, for example, a five-foot-seven-inch football player weighing 200 pounds may have 10 percent body fat (at the low end of the recommended range), while a desk-bound worker of the same height and weight who doesn't exercise much may have 25 percent body fat (more than the recommended maximum). (The theoretical maximum percentage of body fat is 68 percent.) What *is* recommended? According to the University of California *Wellness Letter* (January 1991), the ideal amount of body fat varies from person to person, depending on age, sex, fitness level and genetic makeup. It can also vary according to who sets the standards. Many researchers suggest a desirable range for men of between 11 and 18 percent; for women, between 16 and 23 percent. Others say that up to 23 percent is acceptable for men and up to 30 percent for women.

Research indicates that simple DIETING reduces lean body material (muscle) and predisposes the individual to regain lost weight with even higher percentages of body fat (see YO-YO DIETING). However, simultaneous dieting and exercise retains and even increases muscle, initially at the expense of water and then fatty tissue.

body-fat distribution The pattern of fat distribution on a person's body can have as direct a relationship to health and mortality as the total amount of body fat. For example, in women, upper-body fat may be associated with a higher risk of diabetes than lower-body fat accumulation. In both men and women, abdominal obesity is associated with an increased risk of heart disease.

A relative predominance of fat in the abdominal region (called the apple shape) as well as the shoulders and neck is found more often in men and is strongly related to metabolic disturbances such as diabetes mellitus, hypertriglyceridemia and hypertension. In women, gluteal-femoral (buttocks-hip-thigh) obesity is more common, but when they do have body fat concentrated in the stomach, they have a six-times-greater chance of developing breast cancer than women with flat stomachs.

People with beefy hips and trim waists (pear shaped) have higher levels of a protective form of cholesterol called HDL than do those who are apple shaped. This is believed to be a possible explanation of why people with fat posteriors tend to have healthier hearts than those with big bellies.

Body-fat distribution has been related not only to morbidity and mortality of obesity but also to adipose tissue cellularity; that is, in abdominal obesity fat cell size is relatively enlarged, whereas in glutealfemoral obesity the number of fat cells is increased.

Although gender differences are the most obvious influences of distribution of body fat, age is another significant factor; the body changes shape as it grows and ages. A National Institute on Aging study of 1,179 men and women age 17 to 96 showed progressive trends toward increased upper- and central-body fat deposits with age. In women there tends to be a postmenopausal acceleration of this trend.

A Yale University study determined the degree of weight preoccupation and body dissatisfaction in 77 women between the ages of 21 and 50. Women with the greatest distribution of their fat in the hips and buttocks, relative to the abdomen and waist, were the most eating disordered and saw attaining the "right" weight as more central to their sense of self.

Individual differences in fat distribution are largely determined by hereditary factors. Environmental factors, including diet and exercise habits, determine the extent to which individual genetic predispositions are fulfilled.

Weight loss does not guarantee that inches will be shed from desired areas. On the contrary, success as measured on the bathroom scale is often not translated into the reality of a more shapely body as visualized in the imagination. Recent studies have confirmed that some areas of the body tend to be resistant to slimming.

British researchers have documented the resistance of the thighs to weight loss regimens. Measurements of women's waists and thighs were used to compute a "fat-distribution score," a ratio between abdominal and thigh circumferences. Increasing thigh size relative to waist circumference yielded a lower ratio and vice versa. Following completion of a weight reduction regimen, fat distribution scores showed little change, indicating that fat was shed proportionately from both areas of the body without altering their proportions relative to each other. This study is consistent with the experiences and frustrations of many dieters who, despite weight loss, are unable to achieve their primary goal, improvement in body shape.

A Boston study reported in the May 1991 *American Journal of Clinical Nutrition* indicates that when smokers start putting on fat, they are slightly more likely than nonsmokers to deposit it around the abdomen. Because people with abdominal obesity are more likely to develop heart disease, this finding may offer one partial explanation for smokers' higher risk of this disease.

Jensen, Michael, Morey Haymond, Robert Rizza, Philip Cryer, and John Miles. "Influence of Body Fat Distribution on Free Fatty Acid Metabolism in Obesity." *Journal of Clinical Investigation* 83 (April 1989).

Mayo-Smith, W., C. W. Hayes, B. M. Biller, A. Klibanski, et al. "Body Fat Distribution Measured with CT: Correlations in Healthy Subjects, Patients with Anorexia Nervosa, and Patients with Cushing Syndrome." *Radiology* (February 1989).

Radke-Sharpe, Norean, Deborah Whitney-Saltiel, and Judith Rodin. "Fat Distribution as a Risk Factor for Weight and Eating Concerns." *International Journal of Eating Disorders* 9, no. 1 (1990).

Shimokata, H., J. D. Tobin, D. C. Muller, D. Elahi, et al. "Studies in the Distribution of Body Fat: Effects of Age, Sex, and Obesity." *Journal of Gerontology* (March 1989).

body image assessment (BIA) The BIA, originally developed by D. A. Williamson and colleagues, is a simple procedure for assessment of BODY IMAGE DISTURBANCE. The test consists of nine silhouettes ranging from very small to very large. A research participant or patient is asked to select the card that best represents her current body size and her ideal body size. The difference between the two is conceptualized as the degree of body dissatisfaction. Researchers demonstrated that, when compared with same-size controls, persons with anorexia and bulimia nervosa choose a larger current body size and smaller ideal body size.

Williamson, D. A., B. A. Cubic, and D. H. Gleaves. "Equivalence of Body Image Disturbance in Anorexia and Bulimia Nervosa." *Journal of Abnormal Psychology* 102 (1993), 177–80.

Williamson, D. A., C. J. Davis, S. M. Bennett, A. J. Goreczny, and D. H. Gleaves. "Development of a Simple Procedure for Assessing Body Image Disturbance." *Behavioral Assessment* 11 (1989) 433–46.

body image disturbance A term that has been used to describe numerous phenomena but generally refers to a disturbance in the way one thinks, feels or perceives one's body or how one behaves regarding such thoughts, feelings or perceptions. Experiencing body image disturbance (or distorted body image) is like looking into a funhouse mirror: you see yourself as fatter than you are. Body image disturbance is generally conceptualized as having several components or dimensions: (a) a perceptual component that refers to how accurately someone can estimate his/her own body size, (b) a subjective/attitudinal component that refers to attitudes, feelings and thoughts about one's body, and (c) a behavioral component that refers to avoidance of situations that may cause someone to experience dysphoria due to body image concerns. It has been found that body image disturbance and body dissatisfaction are associated with eating-disordered attitudes and behaviors and that body image disturbance likely plays a causal role in the development of eating-disorder symptoms.

Currently, some aspect of body image disturbance is included as a diagnostic criterion for both anorexia and bulimia nervosa. For anorexia nervosa, the criterion reads that there is a "disturbance in the way in which one's body weight or shape is experienced, undue influence of body weight or shape on self-evaluation, or denial of the seriousness of the current low body weight." For bulimia nervosa, the criterion simply reads that "self-evaluation is unduly influenced by body shape and weight." Both of these criteria have somewhat decreased the emphasis of perceptual body image and indeed much research suggests that the affective body image (i.e., how one feels about one's body) may be most important with regard to eating disorders. However, research by D. A. Williamson, David H. Gleaves and colleagues suggests that the perceptual component should not be abandoned because it may contribute to one's overall feelings about one's body and may be equally influential for anorexia and bulimia nervosa.

For the ANOREXIA NERVOSA patient, misperception reaches quasi-delusional proportions and is evident in the anorexic's lack of concern about, stubborn defense of or inability to recognize an emaciated condition. Some patients display a variation of this disturbance in which their misperception is restricted to a particular part or parts of the body. Stomach or thighs are magnified in a patient's mind and seem disproportionate to the rest of the body. These patients will acknowledge that in general they appear emaciated but believe that further dieting is necessary to eliminate a protruding belly or some other perceived unattractive feature. HILDE BRUCH first recognized body image disturbance to be an essential characteristic of anorexia nervosa, and she considered its correction necessary for recovery.

An analysis of multiple ethnic groups by the University of South Florida showed Caucasian and Hispanic Americans exhibiting more weight related body image disturbance than African Americans and Asian Americans. African Americans had the most positive general appearance body image.

Many obese individuals perceive themselves as larger than they are and have very negative attitudes toward their body. Patients who have been obese as children or adolescents and who subsequently lose weight often retain a distorted perception of themselves as very obese. (See OBESITY; CHILDHOOD OBESITY.)

In a 1996 study, obese individuals with binge-eating disorder reported significantly greater body image disturbance than obese nonbinge-eating participants.

Altabe, M. "Ethnicity and Body Image: Quantitive and Qualitative Analysis." *International Journal of Eating Disorders* 23, March 1998.

Gleaves, D. H., D. A. Williamson, K. P. Eberenz, S. B. Sebastian, and S. E. Barker. "Clarifying Body Image Disturbance: Testing a Multidimensional Model Using Structural Modeling." *Journal of Personality Assessment* 64, 1995; 478–93.

Mussell, M. P., et al. "Differences in Body Image and Depression Among Obese Women With and Without Binge Eating Disorder." *Obesity Research* 5 (September 1996).

Williamson, D. A., B. A. Cubic, and D. H. Gleaves. "Equivalence of Body Image Disturbance in Anorexia and Bulimia Nervosa." *Journal of Abnormal Psychology,* 102 (1993), 177–80.

body types Classifying human bodies by shape and size has been proposed since Hippocrates, who described the basic Greek physiques as phthisic (linear and vertical) and apoplectic (broad and horizontal). Ernst Kretschmer, a 19th-century psychiatrist, divided the population into pyknics (short and round) and asthenics (lean and long legged), with athletes falling somewhere in between. After analyzing thousands of specially posed photographs, William Sheldon devised a three-part classification of body types in 1940. He named them ENDOMORPHS (soft, round, fleshy, light boned, well padded), MESOMORPHS (muscular, square, broad shouldered, sturdy) and ECTOMORPHS (long legged, fragile, thin, skeletal, linear). Sheldon also claimed that body type is inherited and cannot be changed, demonstrating by his elaborate measurement system that people retained the same basic body type after weight changes of as much as 100 pounds. He demonstrated that even after subjects underwent semistarvation for six months and changed outward signs of body type, they all returned to their original shapes within two years. Forced-weight-gain tests produced similar results. Kretschmer's and Sheldon's studies are not considered scientifically sound today.

body wrapping This technique is claimed by hucksters on late-night television, in magazine ads and on the Internet to cause layers of fat to disappear without dieting. Common body-wrapping devices in the past have included sauna suits or heated belts strapped to the waist or stomach or whatever area needs reduction. The heat produced by such gadgets, either alone or when used in conjunction with exercise, supposedly melts away fat much as a hot stove burner melts lard or butter in a saucepan. The advertisements do not explain how the body can withstand temperatures high enough to melt deposited fat or how the melted fat will be eliminated from the body.

Other popular body wraps include plastic or cotton cloths soaked in herbal products. Sometimes the cream, gel or lotion is applied to the skin before the wrap is worn. Body wraps temporarily cause a loss of inches and sometimes pounds due to fluid loss or perspiration. The fluid, along with the inches or pounds, is soon replaced by drinking or eating. Experts consider body wraps to be potentially dangerous because they can bring about severe dehydration, personal injury from circulatory constriction or heart attack while exercising.

See also FRAUDULENT PRODUCTS.

borderline personality disorder (BPD) This personality disorder is characterized by instability in numerous areas of one's life, impulsiveness and fears of abandonment. Research suggests that BPD is the personality disorder most frequently associated with eating disorders, but its frequency may simply be an overlap in the criteria; for example, the binge eating of a person with bulimia nervosa would also meet the impulsiveness criteria for BPD.

brown fat This type of tissue is named for its brownish color, caused by the numerous blood vessels that course through it. In humans, thermogenesis takes place in brown fat tissue. Thermogenesis is a process, induced by food intake or by cold temperatures, whereby calories are converted to heat. Faulty thermogenesis can result in greater efficiency in energy storage, which could lead to excess fat. Abundant in newborn infants, brown fat can be found under the arms, across the back, near the kidneys and around large blood vessels in the chest. Research suggests that defective brown fat cells might be the cause of obesity in some people. Heavy people appear to have less brown fat than average-weight people, and what they do have seems to work inefficiently. All this is conjecture, with nothing proven scientifically.

Bruch, Hilde (1904–1984) A practicing psychiatrist and professor of psychiatry at Baylor College of Medicine in Houston, in the years following World War II, she was the most influential person in the United States in shaping the conception of eating disorders as psychiatric illnesses and in formulating psychotherapeutic approaches to their treatment. Throughout her work, Bruch stresses the formation of individual personality and factors within the family that precondition victims of these disorders to respond to certain kinds of problems by self-starvation or overeating.

Bruch did not regard obesity as a single condition but distinguished three main forms: in some individuals obesity is due to physical factors, and their weight has no association with emotional problems. Others have "reactive obesity," brought about by overeating in situations of psychological stress. The third type, "developmental obesity," has its onset in childhood and is associated with a disturbance in the maturation of the individual's personality.

Bruch was one of the first to stress that many cognitive defects in anorexics are directly related to starvation. Therefore, a meaningful psychiatric evaluation is possible only after the worst effects of malnutrition have been corrected.

Bruch's principal works include *Eating Disorders: Obesity, Anorexia Nervosa, and the Person Within* (New York: Basic Books, 1973, 1985); *The Golden Cage: The Enigma of Anorexia Nervosa* (Cambridge: Harvard University Press, 1978; New York: Vintage Books, 1979); *Conversations with Anorexics/Hilde Bruch,* edited by Danita Czyzewski and Melanie A. Sur (New York: Basic Books, 1988).

bruxism The habitual grinding of the teeth, either during sleep or as an unconscious habit while awake, bruxism's most common causes are said to be psychological factors such as fear, rage, rejection by others and emotional tension. The condition is sometimes seen in patients with eating disorders and results in loosening or drifting of the teeth. Bruxism causes even worse damage in bulimic patients, whose protective tooth enamel has been dissolved by bathings in gastric acid from VOMITING.

See also DENTAL CARIES.

bulimarexia *Bulimarexia* is a term coined in 1976 by Marlene Boskind-White to cover the compulsive practice of bingeing and purging; at the time BULIMIA was officially described as bingeing without purging (DSM-II). Bulimarexia was called a nomenclature atrocity by HILDE BRUCH. Though still used by some researchers and clinicians as interchangeable with "bulimia" or BULIMIA NERVOSA, in the current DSM, this term would be best captured under the diagnosis of anorexia nervosa, binge-eating/purging type.

Boskind-White, Marlene, and William C. White, Jr. *Bulimarexia: The Binge/Purge Cycle,* 2nd Edition. New York: W. W. Norton Co. Inc., 1991.

bulimia The word *bulimia* literally means "ox hunger" or gorging. It refers to the compulsive practice of binge eating. The term has been used in various ways by different medical authors, for example, to describe a subgroup of patients with anorexia nervosa who also binge eat. In DSM-

III, bulimia was an official diagnostic category. However, with DSM-III-R and DSM-IV, the criteria were refined and the name changed to BULIMIA NERVOSA. Although some people use the terms *bulimia* and *bulimia nervosa* interchangeably, it is more appropriate to use the term *bulimia* to refer to the symptom of binge eating and the term *bulimia nervosa* to refer to the current disorder as defined in DSM-IV.

bulimia nervosa This eating disorder is characterized by recurrent binge eating followed by some compensatory behavior (for example, vomiting or use of laxatives). Also characteristic of the disorder is an intense preoccupation with body size and shape. It is not known to be caused by any physical illness, although genetic and neurochemical factors have been suggested. It usually begins in adolescence or early adult life and is 10 times more common in females than in males.

A number of terms have been used to describe this disorder, but the term *bulimia nervosa,* introduced by GERALD F. M. RUSSELL, is the most widely accepted and frequently used because it implies a link to ANOREXIA NERVOSA and differentiates the syndrome from simple binge eating (bulimia).

Although it is common in most industrialized countries, bulimia nervosa is said to be epidemic in the United States. It is harder to detect than anorexia because there is no obvious physical evidence such as emaciation, and thus the extent of bulimia nervosa is less clear than that of anorexia, but medical experts estimate that as many as 16 to 30 percent of all women may have practiced bulimic behaviors to some degree. Bulimia nervosa initial symptoms usually appear between ages 13 and 20. According to DSM-IV, the prevalence of bulimia nervosa among adolescents and young adult females is 1 percent to 3 percent.

A study released in February 1999 adds evidence that bulimia nervosa springs at least in part from a chemical malfunction in the brain and not merely from an excessive desire to remain thin. Women who had suffered from bulimia nervosa and recovered were more affected psychologically than other women by being deprived of tryptophan, which plays an indirect role in appetite regulation. (See Chapter 7 for in-depth information on Bulimia Nervosa; and CHAPTER 8 for information on Males with Eating Disorders.)

bulking agents These APPETITE SUPPRESSANTS are made from food fiber, taken before meals because they swell up in the stomach, creating a sense of fullness that is supposed to inhibit excess eating. Some doctors dispute their effectiveness and discourage their use.

Bulk producers or fillers come in a number of forms: powders, capsules or pills. One such product is glucomannan, which is processed from the roots of the konjac plant. The Food and Drug Administration (FDA) has stated that the use of bulk producers are safe, but their value in reducing weight has not been established. At most, the FDA says, bulk producers absorb liquid and swell the stomach, thereby reducing HUNGER. There is no proof that they are any more effective than ordinary bulking foods such as whole grains, apples, carrots and sprouts, all of which can provide the same feeling of fullness.

bupropion SR This antidepressant is sold by Glaxo-Wellcome under the name Wellbutrin as an antidepressant and under the name Zyban as an aid to stop smoking. In 1999, Duke University researchers reported that it helped dieting obese women lose four times more weight than women who were given placebos. Although these results were promising, an official for the North American Association for the Study of Obesity cautioned that more definitive clinical trials are needed before bupropion SR can be recommended for treating obese patients. Prozac, another antidepressant, also initially looked like it might help people lose weight, but longer-term studies showed it did not work for weight loss.

C

caffeine Caffeine is an alkaloid, found naturally in coffee and tea, that is a central nervous system stimulant and a diuretic. About 100 to 150 milligrams (mg) are found in a strong cup of tea or coffee.

When researchers at King's College, University of London administered caffeine orally to human volunteers in single doses of 100 mg, it increased the resting metabolic rate of both lean and postobese subjects by 3 to 4 percent over a period of 150 minutes. (See METABOLISM.) Measurements of energy expenditure indicated that repeated caffeine administration at two-hour intervals over a 12-hour day increased the energy expenditure of both subject groups by 8 to 11 percent during that period but had no influence on the subsequent 12-hour night energy expenditure. The net effect was a significant increase in daily energy expenditure of 150 calories in the lean subjects and 79 calories in the postobese. The researchers feel that caffeine at commonly consumed doses can have a significant influence on energy balance and may promote thermogenesis in the treatment of obesity.

Authors have cautioned that regular use of 350 mg or more of caffeine a day results in a form of physical dependence. Regular use of more than 600 mg a day may cause chronic insomnia, breathlessness, persistent anxiety and depression, mild delirium and stomach upset. Heavy caffeine use is also suspected of association with heart disease and some forms of cancer.

Hamilton, Kim. "The Weight-Loss Perk." *Health,* July 1989.

calcium A Purdue University study presented in 1999 by Dorothy Teegarden, assistant professor of foods and nutrition, showed that increased levels of calcium appeared to help women lose body fat, but only if overall calorie consumption was limited. The study, which was partly financed by the National Dairy Council, tracked 54 women over two years; the women followed no particular diet. Those women who consumed fewer than 1,900 calories a day along with a daily calcium intake of at least 780 milligrams, either did not increase body fat or lost fat. Those women who took in 1,000 milligrams of calcium a day decreased body weight by up to seven pounds, all of which was in the form of body fat. Those who used dairy products as their calcium source lost more body fat than those who got their calcium from leafy vegetables or supplements. Those women with 500 or fewer milligrams of calcium intake per day actually showed an increase in body fat. Because of the high fat content in many dairy products, Teegarden suggested people needing to lower their body fat get calcium from yogurt or skim milk, which are both low fat and low calorie. Other sources of calcium include broccoli, cabbage and sardines.

Melville, Nancy A. "Get Calcium, Lose Weight." www.healthscout.com (May 4, 1999).

calorie A unit of measurement of heat, one large, or great, calorie (kilogram calorie) is the amount of heat required to raise the temperature of one kilogram (2.2046 pounds) of water by one degree Celsius (1.8 degrees Fahrenheit); this is the calorie commonly used in metabolic studies. One small calorie (gram calorie) is the amount of heat required to raise the temperature of one gram of water one degree Celsius. In writings on human nutrition the large or kilogram calorie is used. In medical literature, it is occasionally capitalized to distinguish it from a small calorie; sometimes it is abbreviated as kcal.

It is possible to calculate the amount of energy contained in a certain food by measuring the amount of heat units, or calories, in that food. (See CALORIMETRY.) Every bodily process—the building up of cells, motion of the muscles, the maintenance of body temperature—requires energy, and the body derives this energy from the food it consumes. Digestive processes reduce food to usable "fuel," which the body "burns" in the complex chemical reactions that sustain life.

From its daily intake of energy converted from food, the body uses only the amount it needs for current activity. The remainder is stored as FAT. If a person consumes more calories than necessary for daily bodily processes, he or she will gain weight. If he or she consumes less than necessary, the body will supplement it by drawing on energy stored as fat, and he or she will lose weight.

Bonnie Liebman, director of nutrition at the Center for Science in the Public Interest, Washington, D.C., told *Boardroom Reports* (May 15, 1989) that all calories are not alike:

"Nutritionists used to say that a calorie was a calorie no matter what kind of food it was—protein, fat or carbohydrate. It didn't matter whether one ate 3,000 calories of fat or 3,000 calories of carbohydrates, the calories the body didn't use were turned into fat. Thus, calorie-counting was the key to dieting. But a growing body of scientific evidence shows that, once inside the body, calories are not treated alike. Fat is handled very differently from protein and carbohydrates, with the fat calories being the most problematic."

Studies conducted by biochemist Jean-Pierre Flatt at the University of Massachusetts Medical School showed that fewer calories are required for the body to turn food fat into body fat than to turn PROTEINS and CARBOHYDRATES into body fat. In the case of food fat, only 3 percent of the calories taken in are burned off in the process of storing it as body fat. In the case of complex carbohydrates, 23 percent of the calories are used up in converting it to body fat.

It is also more difficult for the body to turn proteins and carbohydrates into fat, doing so only when massive amounts have been ingested and using a great amount of energy to do so. The body can store about 1,500 calories' worth of carbohydrates and protein (the rest are burned), but it can store 100,000 to 200,000 calories' worth of fat, according to Flatt. Whereas the normal body attempts to use food fat as energy before storing it in fat cells, the bodies of formerly obese people appear to put fat calories directly into storage, thereby contributing to their weight problem.

Researchers at Harvard Medical School studied 141 women age 34 to 59 and found no correlation between caloric intake and body weight. The fattest women did not necessarily eat the most. The researchers did find, however, that the women whose diets were highest in fat, particularly saturated fats from red meat and dairy products, were the most overweight regardless of the number of calories they consumed.

Americans today are heavier than ever but consume fewer calories than at the turn of the century. One of the reasons given for this is that we have become a more sedentary society. Another reason for our added weight is that although we may eat less than our ancestors did, the percentage of fats in our diet is 31 percent greater today than it used to be.

But experts agree that total calories do count, even those not derived from fat. They point to a National Health and Nutrition Examination Survey, which showed total caloric intake by adults increasing from 1,969 calories in 1978 to 2,200 in 1990.

Examples of estimated calories burned by engaging in various activities for 30 minutes:

- bicycling—340 calories
- digging—300 calories
- inline skating—238 calories
- mowing (push with motor)—182 calories
- mowing (push mower)—243 calories
- planting seedlings—162 calories
- planting trees—182 calories
- raking leaves—162 calories
- swimming—340 calories
- trimming shrubs—182 calories
- turning compost pile—250 calories
- walking uphill—204 calories
- weeding—182 calories

See also FAT CELLS; FATS; OBESITY.

calorimetry Calorimetry is a method of measuring the amount of energy (CALORIE) value in food via a burning process. First a small amount of food is weighed and placed in a sealed container, called a bomb calorimeter. Then the food is set on fire with an electric fuse. The calorimeter is then submerged in a premeasured amount of water. The rise in the temperature of the water when the food item is completely burned measures the calorie value of that amount and kind of food. This calorie value is then used to calculate the number of calories in a typical serving.

carbohydrate addict's diet A popular diet introduced in 1991 by Rachel and Richard Heller in a best-selling book series, the theory of the carbohydrate addict's diet is that some people are biologically predisposed to develop unmanageable cravings for carbohydrates and that when this occurs, it can often lead to weight gain. The authors believe that this condition results from an overproduction of insulin, impairing glucose metabolism, and an insufficient rise of brain serotonin, which is responsible for the feeling of satiety. The purpose of the diet is to control insulin release by minimizing the carbohydrate consumption that triggers it. The basic diet consists of two carbohydrate-restricted meals and one "reward" meal, which must be consumed within 60 minutes but at which the person may eat absolutely anything. Foods at the restricted meals include standard proportions of such foods as eggs, fish, meat, cheese, salads and most nonstarchy vegetables. Allowable foods contain no more than four grams of carbohydrate per standard serving. Although there is little or no scientific evidence for the theory behind the diet, some nutritionists accept the diet per se as healthy if the dieter selects appropriate foods.

carbohydrates Carbohydrates are a group of chemical substances that make up one of the three sources of nutrients (the others are proteins and fats) and contain only carbon, oxygen and hydrogen. Usually the ratio of hydrogen to oxygen is 2:1. The most common carbohydrates are sugar and starches; others include glycogen, dextrins and cellulose.

Carbohydrates are formed by green plants, which utilize sunlight energy to combine carbon dioxide and water in forming them. Carbohydrates are a basic source of energy. (See CALORIE). One gram yields approximately four calories. Carbohydrate is stored in the body as glycogen (a polysaccharide consisting of sugar molecules) in virtually all tissues, but principally in the liver and muscles, where it becomes a source of reserve energy. Whole grains, vegetables, legumes (peas and beans), tubers (potatoes), fruits, honey and refined sugar are all excellent sources of carbohydrates. Calories derived from sugar and candy, however, have been termed "empty" calories because these foods lack essential amino acids, vitamins and minerals.

Carpenter, Karen (1950–1983) A popular singer and recording star (with her brother Richard) during the 1970s, Carpenter died in 1983 at the age of 32 as a consequence of cardiomyopathy, secondary to the effects of the toxic substance emetine. She suffered from ANOREXIA NERVOSA, possibly with bulimic episodes, and abused syrup of IPECAC. Building up over time, the alkaloid emetine in the ipecac irreversibly damaged her heart muscle, eventually leading to her death by cardiac arrest. Because of her popularity, her death brought more attention to eating disorders than anything before or since. A TV movie, *The Karen Carpenter Story,* was first shown January 1, 1989.

cellulite The term *cellulite* was first used in the 1950s to refer to the tenacious FAT and fibrous tissue that forms bumps and ridges on thighs and buttocks, giving them a dimpled or "cottage cheese" look. It is especially common in women. According to Michael O'Shea, founder and chairman of the Sports Training Institute in New York City, the lumpiness is caused by fat deposits located directly beneath the skin pushing up between the tiny ligaments running from the skin's surface through the fat layer to the muscles underneath. When the fat cells increase in size, as they do during weight gain, they cause the fat deposits to bulge, giving the skin a dimpled look.

Edwin Bayrd, author of *The Thin Game,* wrote, however, that "this dimpling is a result of aging rather than overindulgence. It manifests itself when the subdermal connective tissue that forms a sort of honeycomb around the body's adipose cells begins to lose its elasticity and shrinks with age. When this happens, the overlying skin also contracts—and if the encased fat cells cannot shrink, they cannot help but pucker."

Early promoters of cellulite "therapy" claimed that cellulite is caused by a thickening of this connective tissue, which then traps fluids and "toxic materials" in that fat itself, causing the lumpy look. They promoted a variety of treatments and gimmicks to "melt" these fatty pockets, including balms, creams, lotions, injections, plastic wraps, massage, mineral baths, air hoses and wrappings of cheesecloth soaked in paraffin.

None of these "cures" proved consistently successful for a number of reasons. Primary among these is the very protective nature of the skin, which prevents penetration of most salves, ointments and other substances applied to its surface. Even if one of these "miracle extracts" were able to break through the skin and break down fat stores, this would not necessarily lead to the elimination of fat from the body. Fat cells constantly dispense fat into the bloodstream and simultaneously resynthesize triglyceride (storage fat) from circulating fatty acids. Circulating fat will be burned only if muscle or other tissue extracts it from the bloodstream. If the tissues do not need fuel, circulating fat is redeposited in fat cells.

Grapefruit diet pills have been promoted to "burn off cellulite" while allowing you to eat as much food as you want. Ingredients in these pills vary. In addition to grapefruit extract, some have contained a diuretic, and some, glucomannan (see BULKING AGENTS). Others may combine an appetite suppressant with herbs or other ingredients. The FDA has not approved any grapefruit pill for cellulite treatment.

More recently, Cellasene capsules have been marketed to combat cellulite. Cellasene is marketed as a dietary supplement, so it is not subject to FDA approval. Several alternative healers and herbal experts have called it "nonsense" and "just marketing." Various medical researchers are said to be testing it, but thus far no scientific studies of sufficient numbers of users to be valid have been published in peer-reviewed journals.

There is no scientific evidence to support cellulite therapies or the theories on which they are based. Studies have found no detectable difference between so-called cellulite and fat in other areas.

See also FRAUDULENT PRODUCTS.

Bayrd, Edwin. *The Thin Game.* New York: Newsweek Books, 1978.

Frey, Jennifer. "Lumpy, Bumpy, Dimpled: Living Off the Fat of the Land." *The Washington Post,* March 27, 1999.

Hellmich, Nanci. "A Big Fat Spat Over a New Way to Fight Cellulite." *USA Today,* May 25, 1999.

childhood obesity Obesity is affecting ever greater numbers of American youth and exacting a particularly harsh toll from low income minorities. The Third National Health and Nutrition Examination Survey (NHANES III) estimated that 13.7 percent of children and 11.5 percent of adolescents are overweight, while a number of smaller, ethnic-specific studies suggest that overweight and obesity may afflict up to 30 to 40 percent of children and youth from minority populations.

In 1999, the Centers for Disease Control and Prevention (CDC) said 8.6 percent of the low-income two- to four-year-olds it studied in 1997 were overweight, up from 7 percent in 1989. Among children under age two, the percentage rose from 10.8 to 11.3.

According to researcher Richard Strauss, the increasing prevalence of obesity over the last 20 years can only be explained by environmental factors. He adds that in most obese individuals, no measurable differences in metabolism can be detected and that few children today engage in regular, physical activity.

University of Michigan professor Charles Kuntzleman echoes these sentiments, stating that the most substantial factor in increased childhood obesity is the significant erosion of physical education and recreation programs in schools.

CDC researchers believe the increase in preschooler obesity is due to high-calorie convenience foods rather than lack of activity.

Bar-Or, O., et al. "Physical Activity, Genetics, and Nutritional Considerations in Childhood Weight Management." *Medicine And Science In Sports And Exercise* 30, January 1998.

Epstein, Leonard H. "Treatment of Childhood Obesity." In *Handbook of Eating Disorders,* edited by Kelly D. Brownell and John P. Foreyt. New York: Basic Books, 1986.

Mann, Roselyn. *Helping Obese Children: Weight Control Groups That Really Work.* Montreal and Holmes Beach, Fla.: Learning Publications, 1990.

Mei, Z., et al. "Increasing Prevalence of Overweight Among U.S. Low-Income Preschool Children." *Pediatrics* 101, January 1998.

Rotatori, Anthony F., and Robert A. Fox. *Obesity in Children and Youth: Measurement, Characteristics, Causes, and Treatment.* Springfield, Ill.: C. C. Thomas, 1990.

Shonkoff, Jack P., and Samuel J. Meisels, ed. *Handbook of Early Childhood Intervention, 2nd Edition.* Cambridge and New York: Cambridge University Press, 1999.

Strauss, Richard. "Childhood Obesity." *Current Problems in Pediatrics* 29 (January 1999).

Chipley, William Stout (1810–1880) Chief medical officer of the Eastern Lunatic Asylum of Kentucky, who published the first American description of SITOMANIA in 1859 in the *American Journal of Insanity,* Chipley's observations were based on his clinical experience at the asylum to which a number of young girls who would not eat were finally brought by their desperate families, always after treatment by their family doctors had failed. Chipley's commentary was significant because of his identification of a specific type of food refuser and because it called attention to the behavior of adolescent girls. He strongly believed that their refusal to eat was an intentional attempt to draw attention, elicit sympathy and exert power within a small circle of friends and family.

chlorpromazine Chlorpromazine is a tranquilizing drug used during the 1960s in conjunction with insulin to treat anorexia nervosa. Paul Garfinkel and David Garner wrote that it reduced a patient's initial anxiety and resistance to eating and weight gain. It also sometimes sedated the patient enough to help her tolerate bed rest or other enforced reduction of activity. Although this resulted in rapid weight gain, there were a number of serious problems, including lowered blood pressure and reduced body temperature.

In a comparison of two similar groups of hospitalized anorexic patients, one group treated with chlorpromazine and insulin and the other group treated without chlorpromazine, the patients treated with chlorpromazine gained weight substantially faster and left the hospital significantly sooner. After two years, 33 percent of each group required readmission. However, 45 percent of the patients treated with chlorpromazine had developed bulimia, compared with 12 percent of the patients treated without it. Furthermore, the chlorpromazine treatment was associated with significant side effects, including grand mal seizures.

Chlorpromazine was sometimes recommended only for patients who showed marked anxiety about food and an inability to eat after general supportive measures had been attempted. Insulin therapy with chlorpromazine is not used today.

cholecystokinin (CCK) This hormone is released from the intestine within five minutes after eating, which stimulates gallbladder contraction and pancreatic secretion. First isolated more than 60 years ago, it is now said also to send a signal from the stomach to the brain when the stomach is full. All mammals have CCK in varying amounts. In a U.S. Agriculture Department study, scientists discovered that they can block the hormone in pigs by injecting them with a vaccine that makes their appetite insatiable, in effect producing bigger pigs. In less than three months, the injected animals consumed an average of 22 more pounds of corn and soybean meal than untreated pigs, while putting on 11 pounds, of mostly meat rather than fat.

Medical researchers and psychiatrists are monitoring the animal experiments to see if the principle could help anorexics. Studies are also under way to develop drugs to block the CCK hormone in the hope of curbing food cravings.

In 1988, Thomas D. Geracioto, Jr., a clinical neuroendocrinologist at the National Institute of Mental Health, and Rodger A. Liddle of the University of California at San Francisco released results of a study on bulimia in which they compared several measurements of cholecystokinin in both bulimics and control subjects. They found that, on average, the bulimics secreted half as much cholecystokinin as the controls did, indicating that bulimics may not reach a reasonable satiety level. Some scientists speculate that lowered CCK may be an effect of disturbed eating behavior rather than its cause, others that CCK is but one of a group of hormones acting together in complex fashion. CCK can also cause nausea. Studies are now under way on infusing CCK in bulimics and normal volunteers and then exposing them to unlimited food. But results so far are inconclusive.

Because CCK is produced in the intestine and in the brain, scientists are searching to discover which parts of SATIETY are physiological, which are psychological and how they interconnect. Doctors have discovered that certain ANTIDEPRESSANT drugs that help bulimics to stop binge eating also raise their CCK levels.

In pill form, CCK has no effect because the chemical cannot survive in the digestive track. The Federal Drug Administration (FDA) considers CCK pills promoted for weight loss to be a drug requiring FDA premarket approval. The FDA has not yet received requested substantiation of weight-loss claims from CCK manufacturers.

Chase, Manilyn. "Pigs May Provide Hints for Humans on Not Being Hogs." *Wall Street Journal*, December 8, 1988.

Geracioti, Thomas D., Jr., and Rodger A. Liddle. "Impaired Cholecystokinin Secretion in Bulimia Nervosa." *New England Journal of Medicine*, September 15, 1988, 319: 11.
Moore, Beth O., and J. A. Deutsch. "An Anti-emetic Is Antidotal to the Satiety Effects of Cholecystokinin." *Nature*, May 23, 1985.

cholesterol A pearly white crystalline substance found in all foods derived from animals, cholesterol is an essential building block of our cells, but when present in high levels in the blood, it can lead to atherosclerosis (impeded blood flow due to thickening of the arteries). Cholesterol helps carry fats in the bloodstream to tissues throughout the body. Most cholesterol in the blood is made by the liver from saturated fats (see FATS, SATURATED); some is absorbed directly from cholesterol-rich foods such as egg yolks.

CLA (Conjugated Linoleic Acid) CLA is a recently discovered nutritional supplement that is being reported by scientists and researchers as having a positive impact on cancer prevention and preventive effects on diabetes. In addition, there is a large amount of data showing that CLA may cause fat loss and development of lean muscle mass. CLA is available under the brand name Tonalin and can be found in several product lines such as GNC, Natrol, Your Life, Nature's Way, Nature's Bounty and Nature's Plus. Scientists believe that we are getting much less CLA in our diets today than we were 30 years ago, which could be a contributing factor to the steady rise in obesity over the past 30 years, even as we have reduced our overall fat intake.

cognitive distortions Illogical, faulty thinking and irrational beliefs, which are numerous in anorexics, cognitive distortions include an inability to perceive one's own body shape and size accurately and may even affect one's understanding of the body's biological functions. For instance, anorexics often have strange ideas about what happens to the food they eat, imagining that it goes directly to their thighs, hips or abdomens. Among the irrational thinking common to anorexics: "If I gain *any* weight, I'll be fat." After a small lapse in the anorexic's eating regimen: "I'll never get better, my eating will never improve." Taking events and comments personally whether or not they are so intended. ("Two people laughed and whispered something to each other when I walked by. They were probably saying that I looked unattractive. I *have* gained three pounds.")

cognitive therapy Cognitive therapy is a treatment method for mental disorders founded on the premise that the way we think about the world and ourselves affects our emotions and behavior. Therapists work with patients' thoughts, senses, memories and perceptions, as expressed in their internal monologues about their behavior.

For example, internal monologues about weight reduction can play a critical role in the maintenance and control of obesity. An internal monologue may say, "It's taking me so long to lose the weight." A therapist will counsel the patient to replace that negative thought with the more positive, "But I am losing it. And this time I'm learning how to keep it off." Simple repetition of counterstatements over a period of time helps to change people's views of themselves, even if they do not completely believe them at the outset.

compulsive eating An eating pattern characterized by symptoms similar to those of bulimia nervosa, but without the purging, compulsive eating is also referred to as compulsive overeating or binge eating. (See BINGE-EATING DISORDER.) Much of the compulsive eater's life is centered on food, what she (most are women) can or cannot eat, what she will or will not eat, what she has or has not eaten and when she will or will not eat next. Typically, she eats continuously from morning until night, much of the time in secret. Her obsession with food is coupled with self-disgust, loathing and shame because of her total lack of self-control around food. Frequently, a compulsive eater thinks that if she does not have access to food, she will be all right, and she will therefore keep her home almost bare of food, except for the "health food" variety. But her compulsion will drive her out even in the night to look for food to satisfy her uncontrollable urges. Typically, she will continue to eat long after she is full. She eats not because she's hungry or even because she enjoys it but to satisfy an unacknowledged psychological need.

Not all compulsive eaters are obese; some control their weight by constant EXERCISE, FASTING for a few days at a time or even dieting. There are compulsive eaters at all levels of society, from shop floor to executive suite.

Because many compulsive eaters do have weight problems, they run a high risk of hypertension, heart disease and diabetes, and they usually ingest high levels of fat, cholesterol and sugar, which increase their risk of heart disease, cancer and iron-deficiency anemia.

So-called cures, ranging from hypnosis to hospitalization, do not help many compulsive eaters. Most helpful thus far have been clinics, both inpatient and outpatient, that address both physical and psychological aspects of the problem. Such treatment centers work on the premise that compulsive eating is an addiction similar to drug or alcohol addictions.

Unlike anorexia or bulimia, compulsive overeating generally has a more gradual beginning, according to Michele Siegel, Judith Brisman and Margot Weinshel. They explain that it often starts in early childhood when eating patterns are being formed. Sometimes a family focuses on food as a retreat from feelings, as a way to feel good or as an activity to fill otherwise empty time. Eating patterns that do not cause problems for growing children can cause them in adulthood. When compulsive overeating starts in young adulthood, it is often at times of stress when young people are ill prepared to handle certain kinds of frustration and emotion. Soon they begin to use food inappropriately (often against their better judgment) and eventually become addicted to it, losing control over the amounts of food they eat. HILDE BRUCH said that compulsive eaters often eat more when they feel worried or tense and that they feel less effective and competent when they try to control their food intake; she referred to their compulsion as a "neurotic need for food."

Bruch, Hilde. *Eating Disorders.* New York: Basic Books, 1985.

Ghiz, L., and J. C. Chrisler. "Compulsive Eating, Obsessive Thoughts of Food, and Their Relation to Assertiveness and Depression in Women." *Journal of Clinical Psychology* 51 no. 4 (July 1995).

Hirschmann, Jane R., and Carol H. Munter. *Overcoming Overeating.* New York: Fawcett Books, 1998.

Koontz, Katy. "Women Who Love Food Too Much." *Health,* February 1988.

Siegel, Michele, Judith Brisman, and Margot Weinshel. *Surviving an Eating Disorder, Revised Edition.* New York: HarperCollins, 1997.

conjugated linoleic acid See CLA.

control group A control group is used as a basis of comparison with an experimental group. In a study of the effectiveness of a drug, the experimental group would take the drug, and the control group would take either nothing or a PLACEBO.

See also DOUBLE-BLIND STUDY.

cosmetic surgery A surgical procedure, usually plastic surgery, performed for the sake of a patient's appearance is called cosmetic surgery. It may be intended to enhance a patient's looks, to disguise the effects of aging or to repair damage resulting from accident or injury, such as disfiguring scars or burns. Several weight- or fat-reduction surgeries can be considered cosmetic surgery. (See Chapter 5.)

Council on Size and Weight Discrimination, Inc. An organization formed in 1991 to influence public policy and opinion to fight discrimination based on body weight, size or shape, this nonprofit project-oriented advocacy group has a board of directors rather than a membership organization and depends on contributions and grants to support its efforts. Its projects include negotiations with architects' groups over the standard size of theater seats, testimony before regulatory agencies dealing with diet fraud and discussions with writers and editors of medical textbooks on what the next generation of doctors will be taught concerning weight and dieting.

couples therapy Couples therapy is a psychological therapy that involves both a patient and another person with whom the patient has a uniquely close relationship; those involved may be a patient's parent or his or her spouse or life partner. Couples therapy is used in a variety of settings and is recommended for treating eating disorders when there is significant conflict in a couple's relationship. The conflict may be caused by the personalities involved, the eating disorder itself or a combination. The purpose of couples therapy is to strengthen the relationship and to assist couples in problem solving and successfully resolving conflict.

Root, Maria, Patricia Fallon, and William Friedrich. *Bulimia: A Systems Approach to Treatment.* New York: W. W. Norton, 1986.

craving A craving is a frequent compulsive and uncontrollable desire to consume a particular food, such as chocolate, or foods from a specific group, such as starches. Consumption of this food gives both a physical and psychological sense of well-being and satisfaction. Research on both animals and humans has demonstrated that cravings can be caused by biochemical needs. A food craving may be the body's signal that something is out of balance. Although eating foods one craves makes one feel better for the moment, the resulting "high" eventually is followed by fatigue, depression, headaches, moodiness, unclear or confused thinking and the weight problems that frequently accompany the abuse of any food. Cravings have sometimes been found to be caused by nutritional deficiencies, food allergies or diseases.

Studies have shown that overweight people tend to crave fatty foods; the fatter people are, the more they prefer the taste of fat. In studies, when given a choice of milk shakes made with varying amounts of cream and sugar, overweight people have chosen fattier shakes than their lean counterparts. Overweight people report eating no more calories than others, but more of those calories come from fat.

The effect of fatty foods on the brain—and the way people think about fats—undermine Americans' attempts to stay trim, according to one school of thought. When the brain gets used to the sudden rush of fat/sugar mixtures, a physical craving develops similar to opiate drug addiction, according to research conducted at the University of Michigan. New research indicates that a drug for opiate overdoses can also block craving for such foods as cookies and candy, but it is not a practical or proven treatment.

Writing for *Scientific American* (January 1989), two researchers from the Massachusetts Institute of Technology, R. J. Wurtman and J. J. Wurtman, classified carbohydrate craving obesity as a distinct behavioral disorder. They named as symptoms depression, lethargy and an inability to concentrate, combined with episodic bouts of overeating and excessive weight gain. They also found these cravings to be cyclic, occurring usually in the late afternoons or evenings. They say it appears that this disorder is affected by biochemical disturbances in the neurotransmitter serotonin, which regulates appetite for carbohydrate-rich foods.

University of Arizona researchers reported in 1999 that chocolate cravings are real and should be considered in affected persons' diets, despite the downside of fat and sugar consumption. For some people, the authors found, chocolate represents "self-medication"—biogenic amines found naturally in chocolate are also produced in the brain and are important regulators of mood; they may even play a role in depression. The researchers also reported that chocolate's high concentration of magnesium may ease the effects of magnesium deficiency, a condition that research suggests may contribute to premenstrual syndrome. Thus, chocolate's long association with some women's monthly cravings may well have a hormonal basis.

Many women experience apparently physiological-based cravings during pregnancy and menstruation. Researchers note that appetite increases premenstrually, thus say it is possible (but not proven) that food cravings are a source of the extra appetite.

Cepeda-Benito and colleagues have developed a multidimensional assessment measure of food cravings.

Baker, Emily. "Food Cravings." Scripps Howard News Service, September 12, 1998.

Bruinsma, K., and D. L. Taren. "Chocolate: Food or Drug?" *Journal of the American Dietetic Association*, October 1999, 1249–56.

Cepeda-Benito, A., D. H. Gleaves, T. L. Williams, and S. A. Erath. "The Development and Validation of the State and Trait Food Cravings Questionnaires." *Behavior Therapy* (in press).

crystal methamphetamine Crystal methamphetamine is an illegal appetite-suppressing amphetamine. (See ICE.)

cultural influences on appearance Attitudes toward physical appearance and standards of beauty and desirability have varied over time and from culture to culture. In prerevolutionary China, for example, tiny feet represented the ideal for women of the upper classes, leading to widespread deformities caused by the practice of foot binding. In Greek and Roman representations of the ideal in the form of sculpted gods and goddesses, women often have ample thighs, hips and waists. During the Renaissance, full-bodied women were also the ideal. Plumpness was admired; in some cultures it was an appealing sexual characteristic. But in the 19th century, corsets were invented to enable women to achieve the then-ideal hourglass appearance.

It became rude, among the genteel, to eat heartily. It was even glamorous, in some quarters, to look sickly. Because tuberculosis was thought especially to afflict artists and other creative people, a tubercular appearance came to signify a romantic personality. Men preferred delicate, pale women, and women used whitening powders rather than rouge.

In Western society during the 20th century's early years, a buxom appearance was preferred. Then the "flat-chested" flappers became the ideal in the 1920s. Bustiness and the hourglass figure returned in the 1950s. This was followed once again by the still-current ideal of thinness. Researchers have documented recent shifts in our cultural image of women by using data from *Playboy* magazine centerfolds and statistics from Miss America Pageant contestants. The average weight of centerfold models in 1960 was approximately 90 percent of expected average weight, based on the Society of Actuaries 1959 norm; in 1978, it was approximately 83 percent. This decline occurred even while the expected averages of weight and height for young women were increasing. Today a thin look denotes self-control and success; the desire to conform to this slim physical model is one of the social variables that may lead to anorexia.

The culturally generated compulsion to be thin is also reflected in the proliferation of articles about dieting in magazines published principally for women. Fear of being fat, fear of losing control over eating and fear of not being as slim as possible are important social concerns. As far back as 1966, studies found that 70 percent of high school girls were unhappy with their bodies and wanted to lose weight. Particularly for women, thinness has become synonymous with attractiveness.

Studies examining changing standards of attractiveness for men and women portrayed in 20th-century media indicated that female television characters are more likely to be slim and less likely to be fat than male characters; that women receive more messages through magazine articles and advertisements to be slim and stay in shape than do men; that the prominence of curvaceous females portrayed in popular women's magazines has decreased dramatically since 1901; and that the standard of bodily attractiveness of movie actresses has become significantly thinner during the past 50 years.

A 1998 British study concurred with earlier research that mothers play a role in the transmission of cultural values regarding weight, shape and appearance of their daughters.

Brumberg, Joan Jacobs. *Fasting Girls*. New York: Plume, 1989.

Collins, M. Elizabeth. "Education for Healthy Body Weight: Helping Adolescents Balance the Cultural Pressure for Thinness." *Journal of School Health* 58, no. 6 (August 1988).

Hill, A. J., and J. A. Franklin. "Mothers, Daughters and Dieting." *British Journal of Clinical Psychology* 37 (February 1998).

Mazur, A. "U.S. Trends in Feminine Beauty and Overadaptation." *Journal of Sexual Research* 22 (1986).

cultural influences on eating disorders People with eating disorders have come mostly from white middle- or upper-class families, leading researchers to determine that higher socioeconomic status is an important risk factor. International studies offer further evidence to support this notion: eating disorders have increased dramatically in industrialized nations during the last 20 years but remain practically unheard of in the Third World countries. Thinness is not an ideal among people whose hunger is not a matter of choice. Concern over the shape of one's body is an indulgence of the affluent.

The shift toward a thinner ideal body shape in Western societies has been marked by the increasingly pervasive practice of dieting, especially among women. An estimated 90 percent of the customers of the "diet" industry are women. Though the benefits of slenderness have been extolled by health professionals, the potentially harmful side effects of dieting have received considerably less attention. Several researchers have connected the cultural pursuit of thinness with eating disorders:

- Data presented by Polivy and Herman indicate that dieting usually precedes binge eating; thus they speculated that dieting is the disorder in need of cure.
- Similarly, Garner stated that bulimia may become a problem in psychologically normal individuals after a period of intensive caloric restriction.
- Katz identified weight loss by itself as a precipitate for the appearance of anorexia nervosa in vulnerable individuals.
- Mazur identified anorexia nervosa and bulimia, as well as extreme diet and exercise regimens among "normal" women, as examples of often dangerous attempts to match the ever-changing ideal of feminine beauty.

In addition, Japanese researchers have reported that during the past 20 years, a slim body has become increasingly desirable for young women as a sign of beauty and success in Japan; dieting is now common among them. Research suggests that this dieting is a factor contributing to bulimia among young women in Japan.

Garner and his team reiterated that cultural influences do not cause eating disorders and that culture is mediated by the psychology of the individual as well as the social context of the family, but M. Elizabeth Collins cautioned in *Journal of School Health* that the potential impact of the media in establishing identifiable role models should not be underestimated.

Collins, M. Elizabeth. "Education for Healthy Body Weight: Helping Adolescents Balance the Cultural Pressure for Thinness." *Journal of School Health* 58, no. 6 (August 1988).

Feldman, W., E. Feldman, and J. Y. Goodman. "Culture versus Biology: Children's Attitudes toward Thinness and Fatness." *Pediatrics* 81 (February 1988).

Gamer, D. M., W. Rockert, N. P. Olmsted, et al. "Psychoeducational Principles in the Treatment of Bulimia and Anorexia." In *Handbook of Psychotherapy for Anorexia Nervosa and Bulimia*. New York: Guilford Press, 1985.

Katz, J. L. "Some Reflections on the Nature of the Eating Disorders: On the Need for Humility." *International Journal of Eating Disorders* 4 (1985).

Mazur, A. "U.S. Trends in Feminine Beauty and Overadaptation." *Journal of Sexual Research* 22 (1986).

Polivy, J., and C. P. Herman. "Dieting and Bingeing: A Causal Analysis." *American Psychology* 40 (1985).

Cushing's disease Cushing's disease is caused by overactivity of the pituitary gland, which influences growth, metabolism and other glands. The disease is characterized by a form of obesity and muscular weakness. It is much more common in women than in men. Obesity is confined almost exclusively to the trunk; any obesity involving the upper arms and the upper thighs is disproportionately small. Patients with Cushing's disease frequently have hypertension and are more susceptible to infection. There may be minor hirsutism in women, particularly on the upper lip and chin, and some in the periareolar region of the breast. Increased hair growth also often occurs over the lower abdomen, extending up from the pubic region.

cyproheptadine Cyproheptadine is an appetite-stimulating antihistamine used primarily for the treatment of allergic conditions. An early study in Peru found that cyproheptadine caused anorexics to gain significant weight, but two subsequent studies in the United States failed to replicate this result. In one, there was a differential drug effect related to the presence of bulimia, so that cyproheptadine significantly increased treatment efficiency in the nonbulimic patients and impaired treatment efficiency in the bulimic patients.

There are indications that cyproheptadine in relatively large doses may have some mild effect in promoting weight gain and relieving depression in anorexia nervosa. One major advantage of cyproheptadine is that it appears to have few side effects even in relatively large doses.

Cyproheptadine has been used to treat anorexia in the elderly.

D

dental caries (or cavities) Tooth decay and the progressive destruction of the hard tissues of the teeth through a process initiated by bacterially produced acids at the tooth surface, dental caries are seen extensively in patients with eating disorders. This is due to an excessive CARBOHYDRATE intake, poor oral hygiene and changes that occur in the saliva.

During binge periods (see BINGE EATING), huge amounts of sugar can be consumed, followed by sugar drinks, often used to relieve thirst after vomiting. Thus, bulimics tend to have a higher sugar intake than anorexics, whose diet is limited. But anorexics under the care of physicians also are susceptible to dental caries because some medications given to them, such as dextrose tablets, dietary supplements, and vitamin C drinks, contain sugar.

Neglect of oral hygiene can be seen in both anorexic and bulimic patients, due mainly to the upset in daily routine. Their eating habits get most of their attention. Meticulous oral hygiene is a necessity in these patients because of excess acid present in the oral cavity, excess sugar intake and disturbances in the saliva.

Dalin, Jeffrey B., D.D.S. "Oral Manifestations of Eating Disorders." In *Eating Disorders: Effective Care and Treatment.* St. Louis: Ishiyaku EuroAmerica, 1986.

depression A mental state characterized by sad mood, lack of hope and a general loss of interest in life, depression is distinguished from grief, which is a response to a real loss and generally proportionate to its importance. Symptoms vary with the severity of the illness. With mild depression, the main symptoms are anxiety, mood changes and sometimes inexplicable crying spells. Serious depression is usually accompanied by appetite and sleep disturbances; social withdrawal; increasingly poor performance in school, at home or at work; lack of energy and loss of concentration. Severely depressed persons may wish for death or even consider SUICIDE, exhibit phobias and dwell on thoughts of guilt or worthlessness.

In bulimics, depression may be obvious, evidenced by apathy, lethargy, joylessness, suicidal thoughts, sleep disturbances and general lack of pleasure in life. The severity of depressive symptoms in bulimics is similar to that of patients with mood disorders.

The relationship between depression and eating disorders has been under considerable study. Many people with eating disorders appear to also suffer from depression, and scientists have wondered whether depression could trigger an eating disorder. There are similarities in neurochemical abnormalities in both disorders. Low levels of SEROTONIN and norepinephrine are associated with depressive disorders as well as with eating disorders, and ANTIDEPRESSANT medications may help some people with eating disorders, particularly bulimics. In addition, both the depressed and the anorexic tend to have higher than normal levels of the hormone CORTISOL, which is released in response to stress. Depression is commonly seen in patients with bulimia; it is unclear, however, whether the depression leads to bulimia or vice versa.

Researchers have concluded that there is not enough support to prove a relationship between bulimia and depression: to date, they feel that properly designed tests and family history investigations have failed to find differences between bulimic and control samples, but it is generally agreed that it is possible that bulimic patients with family histories of depression are at greater risk of developing depression than bulimics without such a history. Hinz and Williamson concluded that it is more likely that the depression seen in bulimia is simply the result of living with a chronic condition.

HILDE BRUCH stated that people who use food to combat anxiety and loneliness are likely to become depressed when dieting is enforced. "Even without marked obesity, the secure knowledge that one's appetite and needs will be fulfilled is necessary for a sense of well-being. Mildly depressed patients are often concerned with the loss of satisfaction from ordinary activities. They often complain of having lost all interest, or of finding activities no longer worthwhile. The immediate enjoyment of food serves as reassurance that life still holds some satisfactions. People with this depressive mood are apt to eat between meals, often quite impulsively, as soon as the idea strikes them that something might be tasty or enjoyable."

One study of 5,600 high school students found that 500 of them suffered from depression, with girls more likely to be depressed than boys. Researchers have concluded that an important factor in adolescent depression is poor body image. In another study of 850 young women, age 12 to 23, more than two-thirds were unhappy with their weight and more than half with their shape.

Casper, R. C. "Depression and Eating Disorders." *Depression and Anxiety* 8 (suppl. 1, 1998).

"Great Bodies Come in Many Shapes." *University of California. Berkeley Wellness Letter* 7:5, February 1991.

Hinz, L. D., and D. A. Williamson. "Bulimia and Depression: A Review of the Affective Variant Hypothesis." *Psychological Bulletin* 102 (1987).

diabetes and eating disorders People who combine disordered eating with diabetes face significantly more health risks than nondiabetics with similar eating patterns in the general population.

Some studies have identified a higher incidence of eating disorders among diabetics. However, in a survey conducted at the International

Diabetes Center, of the 70 percent (385) of 550 females age 13 to 45 who returned their surveys, the number of individuals who met criteria for a clinical eating disorder was found to be similar to the number obtained in the general population.

But the diabetic's necessary focus on food, his deprivation of certain foods, his guilt over nonadherence to his diet, his unhealthy relationship with food and his rebelliousness toward dietary restrictions can all provoke a disordered eating pattern. The starvation of anorexia nervosa and the purging of bulimia can both lead to serious hypoglycemia (deficiency of sugar in the blood), and binge eating can lead to seriously elevated blood glucose levels and diabetic ketoacidosis.

Recent reports have cautioned health care providers to be aware of the possible association between eating disturbances and diabetes, and also the types of behavior, particularly insulin omission for weight loss, that are common in eating-disorder patients who also have diabetes.

If insulin-dependent patients develop anorexia, their extremely low weight may appear to control the diabetes for a while. Eventually, however, if they fail to take insulin and regain weight, these patients will die.

Birk, Randi. "Eating Disorders and Diabetes." *Diabetes Self-Management,* September/October 1988.

Crow, S. J. et al. "Eating Disorders and Insulin-dependent Diabetes Mellitus." *Psychosomatics* 39, no. 3 (May–June 1998).

Daneman, D., et al. "Eating Disorders in Young Women With Type 1 Diabetes." *Hormone Research* 50 (suppl. 1, 1998).

dichotomous thinking A faulty thinking pattern that occurs with numerous psychological disorders and commonly among eating disorders, dichotomous reasoning involves thinking in extreme, absolute, all-or-none terms and is typically applied to food, eating and weight. The patient divides food into good (low calorie) and bad (fattening) categories. A one-pound weight gain may be equated with incipient obesity. Breaking a rigid eating routine produces panic because it means a complete loss of control. Rigid attitudes and behaviors are not restricted to food and weight but extend to the pursuit of sports, studies and careers. (See also COGNITIVE DISTORTIONS.)

diet centers and programs The frustration of continuously striving to achieve the elusive "ideal" weight is a prime motivator for the overweight to turn to other "sufferers," seeking help, understanding, empathy, and when those other sufferers number about 97 million people, according to the National Institutes of Health, it is small wonder that an entire industry of diet centers, clubs and programs bringing these obsessive dieters together has flourished. Some, like TOPS (Take Off Pounds Sensibly) and OVEREATERS ANONYMOUS, are nonprofit organizations; others, like WEIGHT

WATCHERS, JENNY CRAIG and STOP THE INSANITY, are commercial enterprises. Diet centers provide dietary advice and social support and are especially helpful for those people who find that the only way to lose weight is to have others pushing and pulling them along toward their goals. Diet centers provide psychological motivation and "good examples" of others who have succeeded, as well as supervised diet programs with step-by-step daily routines, exercises, menus, weigh-ins and so on. One analysis of such diet centers found that short-term outcomes are at least equivalent to medically prescribed therapies. The average length of membership is about 26 weeks and the mean weight loss about 20 pounds. Little is known about long-term results. The reducing diet, group pressures, behavior modification techniques, a supportive group and financial commitments all play a part in accounting for the programs' success.

Despite numerous studies showing that most people regain weight after dieting, the market for diet products and programs is still booming. Many diet groups are now marketing themselves using new terms such as *nutritional programs.*

In the May/June 1989 issue of the *Walking Magazine,* author Madeline Chinnici described common-sense criteria for acceptable commercial diets: 1,000 or more calories per day; at least 50 percent carbohydrate, less than 30 percent fat and 15 to 20 percent protein; a variety of foods from the four basic food groups; promotion of a weight loss of not more than one to two pounds per week; promotion of permanent loss of fat, especially combined with regular exercise; no vitamin supplementation and no specialized medical supervision, for otherwise healthy people; no side effects in healthy people.

The Weight-control Information Network (WIN), a service through the National Institutes of Health, describes three types of weight-loss programs:

- Do-It-Yourself Programs—Any effort to lose weight by yourself or with a group of like-minded others through support groups or worksite or community-based programs fits in the "do-it-yourself" category. Individuals using such a program rely on their own judgment, group support and products such as diet books for advice.
- Nonclinical Programs—These programs may or may not be commercially operated, such as through a privately owned weight-loss chain. They often use books and pamphlets that are prepared by health-care providers. These programs use counselors (who usually are not health-care providers and may or may not have training) to provide services to you. Some programs require participants to use the program's food or supplements.
- Clinical Programs—This type of program may or may not be commercially owned. Services are provided in a health-care setting, such as a hospital, by licensed health professionals, such as physicians, nurses,

dietitians and/or psychologists. In some clinical programs, a health professional works alone; in others, a group of health professionals works together to provide services to patients. Clinical programs may offer you services such as nutrition education, medical care, behavior change therapy and physical activity. Clinical programs may also use other weight-loss methods, such as very low calorie diets, prescription weight-loss drugs and surgery, to treat severely overweight patients.

Progress in honesty In February 1999, a coalition of government, academic and commercial weight-loss organizations announced new guidelines to provide consumers with better information on the risks, costs and track records of commercial diet programs. Participants in the new agreement, including Weight Watchers International and Jenny Craig, agreed to abide by provisions aimed at helping dieters to comparison-shop among programs. Among these provisions: programs must disclose the qualifications of their staffs, and they must outline all costs of their regimens, including payments for proprietary diet foods.

See also FAD DIETS.

diet pills Commonly available over-the-counter diet pills contain the active appetite suppressor phenylpropanolamine (PPA) and are usually packaged and sold with a recommended daily dosage of 75 mg. Brand names include Acutrim, Control, Dexatrim, Dietac, Prolamine and Odrinex.

Although diet pills are commonly used by patients with ANOREXIA NERVOSA and BULIMIA, many bulimics experiment with diet pills but do not take them on an ongoing basis because of their side effects or because they find their use relatively ineffective as a weight-control technique.

These drugs have been shown to facilitate weight loss on a short-term basis in individuals with OBESITY. Studies suggest that diet pills are relatively safe but habit-forming. There have also been reports of side effects and toxicities for these drugs, including elevated blood pressure, renal failure, seizures, dehydration, anxiety and agitation, memory loss, transient neurological deficits and intracranial hemorrhage. For some allergic or hypersensitive individuals, the pills are dangerous even when taken according to directions.

In 1990 the Food and Drug Administration ruled that a diet pill known as Cal-Ban 3000 was potentially lethal and recommended that anyone using it stop immediately. The FDA recalled the product and blocked its sale after a man died when Cal-Ban tablets swelled in his throat. At least 50 other users experienced obstructions in the stomach, intestines and other parts of the digestive tract after taking the product. Cal-Ban 3000 diet tablets were advertised as creating a sense of fullness when they swell in the stomach. Their primary ingredient was guar gum, a dietary fiber that absorbs 5 to 10 times its weight in water. However, in some instances, the tablets began to swell in the digestive tract before reaching the stomach, causing injury. Under normal use, in small doses, as a laxative or food thickener, guar gum is harmless, but the suggested dosage with the Cal-Ban 3000 program was 15 grams a day, or about 30 tablets with each meal.

A 1990 congressional inquiry focused attention on the role diet pills play in eating disorders. It was brought out that many otherwise healthy teenagers think of pills as the standard way to diet. In a survey conducted by *Sassy* magazine, 49 percent of teenage girls responding reported using diet pills. A 1988 study by the National Institute of Drug Abuse revealed that 22 percent of high school seniors, boys and girls, currently use diet pills. Young people have no trouble buying diet pills, which are available throughout the country with no age restrictions.

The 1991/1992 Weight Loss Practices Survey, sponsored by FDA and the National Heart, Lung and Blood Institute, found that 5 percent of women and 2 percent of men trying to lose weight use diet pills.

In 1992, the FDA banned 111 ingredients in over-the-counter (OTC) diet pills—including amino acids, cellulose and grapefruit extract—after manufacturers were unable to prove that they worked.

See also FEN/PHEN REDUX.

"Better Dieting through Chemistry?" *U.S. News & World Report*, February 3, 1992.
"Diet Drug Ingredients Facing Ban by FDA." *Chemical Marketing Reporter*, November 5, 1990.
"FDA Bans 111 Diet Drug Ingredients." *Los Angeles Times*, August 8, 1991.
"FDA Wants Diet Pill Taken off Market." *Los Angeles Times*, July 28, 1–90.
Gillam, Jerry. "Bill to Limit Diet Pill Sales Moves Ahead." *Los Angeles Times*, May 3, 1991.
Larkin, Marilyn. "Ways To Win At Weight Loss." *FDA Consumer*, September 1997.
Papazian, Ruth. "Should You Go On a Diet?" *FDA Consumer*, May 1997.

dietary chaos syndrome *Dietary chaos syndrome* is a term used by British researcher R. L. Palmer to describe bulimia.

dietary fiber The edible but indigestible fibrous components of plants, fiber adds bulk to the diet and can aid normal bowel function by enabling the large intestine to work effectively and by helping regulate the absorption of nutrients in the small intestine. Dietary fiber is not a single substance, and there are significant differences in the physiological effects of the various fibers. A Recommended Dietary Allowance has not been established; however, an adequate amount can be obtained by eating several servings daily of whole-grain breads and cereals, fruits, root vegetables, legumes and nuts.

A report of the Council on Scientific Affairs of the American Medical Association stated that some scientists believe that excessive energy (caloric) intake may be inevitable when diets are low in fiber, with high-fiber diets possibly reducing energy intake, even when more food is eaten. Studies suggest that when people are allowed to eat unlimited amounts of high-fiber food but not foods containing sugar and other refined carbohydrates, the amount eaten decreases significantly, and appetites are satisfied. Although fiber has no magical effects in promoting weight loss, it can be an important part of a balanced but low-calorie diet. High-fiber diets are also beneficial because they help prevent constipation, a common result of reduced food intake. Limited data from clinical trials that suggest that fiber supplements or high-fiber diets are useful for weight reduction are contradictory. Dietary fiber may have a limited role as an adjunct in the treatment of obesity, but controlled, long-term trials are needed before this can be established.

dieter's teas Herbal teas sold through health food stores and mail-order catalogs, which are promoted as weight-loss aids based on the belief that the increased bowel movements they cause will prevent absorption of calories, dieter's teas contain senna, aloe, buckthorn and other plant-based laxatives that, when consumed in large amounts, can cause diarrhea, vomiting, nausea, stomach cramps and fainting. In recent years, the Food and Drug Administration (FDA) has received reports of several deaths in which dieter's teas may have been a contributing factor. As a result, FDA has issued consumer advisories. These teas, which are usually bought in health food stores, through mail-order catalogs and over the Internet, often are used for weight loss based on the belief that increased bowel movements will prevent absorption of calories. However, the FDA concluded in 1995 that laxative-induced diarrhea does not significantly reduce absorption of calories because the laxatives do not work on the small intestine, where calories are absorbed, but rather on the colon, the lower end of the bowel. Unless sweetened, dieter's teas provide essentially no nutrients and no calories.

Kurtzweil, Paula. "Dieter's Brews Make Tea Time A Dangerous Affair." *FDA Consumer,* July/August 1997.

dissociation A term generally referring to a disconnection of mental processes that are normally integrated, dissociation can be pathological and nonpathological. Nonpathological dissociation generally refers to daydreaming, absorption and imaginative involvement. Pathological dissociation generally refers to amnesia, depersonalization, derealization, identity confusion and identity alteration. The most extreme form of the dissociative disorders is dissociative identity disorder (formally known as multiple personality disorder).

For years, there has been a debate regarding the association between eating disorders and dissociative phenomena or disorders. Persons with eating disorders frequently describe a variety of dissociative experiences and some persons may have full-blown dissociative disorders. Some researchers and/or clinicians have hypothesized that there may be some sort of dissociative mechanism that is central to the eating disorders. However, the results of a recent study by Katz and Gleaves suggest that the elevated dissociative symptomatology sometimes seen in persons with eating disorders may simply be an artifact of a comorbid dissociative disorder. Regardless of this latter finding, dissociative experiences may be an important clinical variable to consider as part of treatment:

Katz, B. E., and D. H. Gleaves. "Dissociative symptoms among patients with eating disorders: Associated feature or artifact of a comorbid dissociative disorder." *Dissociation* 9, 1996.

Vanderlinden, J. and W. Vandereycken. *Trauma, Dissociation, and Impulse Dyscontrol in Eating Disorders.* Bristol, Pa.: Brunner/Mazel, 1997.

diuretic abuse Diuretics are usually drugs, but can also be common substances such as tea, coffee and water that help remove excess water from the body by stimulating the flow of urine. Diuretic drugs interfere with normal kidney action by changing the amount of water, potassium, sodium and waste products removed from the bloodstream. Normally, most of the potassium, sodium and water are returned to the bloodstream during the normal filtration process, but small amounts are expelled from the body along with waste products in the urine. Some diuretics reduce the amount of sodium and water taken back into the blood; others increase blood flow through the kidneys and thus the amount of water they filter and expel in the urine. They are often irresponsibly given by diet doctors so a patient can experience a quick weight loss. Any such weight loss is temporary and a consequence of the dehydrating effect.

Because diuretics are available in a wide variety of over-the-counter formulations as well as by prescription, the exact rate of diuretic use or abuse is unknown. Patients who abuse diuretics obtain them from several sources: over the counter; appropriate prescriptions for medical conditions; multiple prescriptions from two or more physicians, each unaware of the real amount of the drug the patient is using; prescriptions meant for another person; and misappropriation from workplaces including nursing homes, hospitals, pharmacies and pharmaceutical distributors.

The three groups of prescription diuretics most often abused by patients with eating disorders are the thiazides, loop diuretics and potassium-sparing diuretics.

Most bulimic patients who misuse or abuse diuretics use over-the-counter preparations. Commonly available over-the-counter diuretics include Premesyn-PMS, Sunril Premenstrual Capsules, Midol-PMS, Odrinil, Diurex-MPR, Pamprin Menstrual Relief, Aqua-Ban, Odrinil and

Diurex. Most of them contain one of three ingredients listed by the U.S. Food and Drug Administration as diuretics (Category I) effective in menstrual drug products: pamabrom, ammonium chloride and caffeine. In addition, the FDA has found that pyrilamine maleate (an antihistamine) is an appropriate adjunct to any of the Category I diuretics.

Ammonium chloride is the active diuretic ingredient in one of the most widely used over-the-counter formulations. It is considered safe in a dosage range of one to three grams daily in divided oral doses for periods of up to six days. Ammonium chloride results in formation of sodium chloride from sodium bicarbonate in the body, but the effect lasts only about four or five days. Nausea, vomiting and gastrointestinal distress are potential side effects.

CAFFEINE is considered by the FDA to be a safe and effective diuretic for over-the-counter use in doses of 100 to 200 mg every three to four hours. As a diuretic, caffeine acts by increasing the glomerular filtration rate in the kidneys. Sleeplessness is a potential side effect.

Pamabrom is considered by the FDA to be a safe and effective diuretic for relief of water accumulation during menstrual cycles. Recommended dosage is not more than 50 mg per dose and 200 mg in 24 hours.

The effects of these over-the-counter diuretics on individuals with eating disorders who may have other metabolic abnormalities owing to vomiting or LAXATIVE ABUSE can have severe consequences on renal function and fluid and electrolyte balance.

Killen, Joel, Barr C. Taylor, Michael J. Telch, Keith E. Saylor, David J. Maron, and Thomas N. Robinson. "Self-induced Vomiting and Laxative and Diuretic Abuse among Teenagers." *JAMA* 255, no. 11 (March 21, 1986).

Mitchell, J. E., C. Pomeroy, M. Seppala, and M. Huber. "Diuretic Use as a Marker for Eating Problems and Affective Disorders among Women." *Journal of Clinical Psychiatry* 49, no. 7 (July 1988).

Pomeroy, Claire, James E. Mitchell, Harold C. Seim, and Marvin Seppala. "Prescription Diuretic Abuse in Patients with Bulimia Nervosa." *Journal of Family Practice* 27, no. 5 (November 1988).

double-blind study A study in which neither the researchers nor the participants know which group is the experimental group and which the control group, the double-blind study's purpose is to eliminate any expectations, conscious or unconscious, that might affect the outcome of the study or trial.

DSM-IV The fourth and most recent edition of the *Diagnostic and Statistical Manual of Mental Disorders,* published by the American Psychiatric Association in 1994, DSM-IV provides criteria for classifying psychological disorders for physicians making diagnoses and researchers compiling statistics. This manual is considered the standard for the profession.

E

early satiety Bulimics who practice frequent vomiting often complain that they feel "full" following consumption of a relatively small amount of food, a characteristic referred to as early satiety.

eating attitudes test (EAT-26) This 26-question self-test was devised by researchers Paul E. Garfinkel and David M. Garner to measure the broad range of symptoms characteristic of anorexia nervosa. A high score on the EAT-26 does not necessarily reflect anorexia nervosa, nor does a low score invariably rule it out because people may not respond honestly on a self-report questionnaire. However, in practice, the EAT-26 has been shown to be quite accurate in discriminating anorexics from control subjects. It is most useful as a screening device; diagnoses of anorexia nervosa must be confirmed in clinical interviews. EAT-26 scores can also serve as an index of anorexic patients' improvement.

eating-disorders inventory (EDI) This 64-item self-test was designed in 1983 by Garner, Olmstead and Polivy to differentiate bulimics, extreme dieters and particular subgroups of anorexic patients. The EDI evaluates an individual on a number of different subscales including drive for thinness, body dissatisfaction, sense of ineffectiveness, perfectionism, interpersonal distrust and fears of maturity—psychological and behavioral components common to anorexia and bulimia. This test was intended to augment the EAT-26, which focuses primarily on dieting- and eating-related symptoms. It is one of very few tests for anorexia, bulimia and bulimia nervosa that measure not only symptoms but also psychological characteristics believed to be central in these disorders. The EDI has been used experimentally to discriminate individuals with eating disorders from nonpathological weight-preoccupied women.

The test has been revised (and is now called the EDI-2) with the addition of three new scales and 17 items. However, although recent research has continued to support the reliability and validity of the eight original subscales, the reliability and validity of the three new subscales appears questionable.

Eberenz, K. P., and D. H. Gleaves. "An Examination of the Internal Consistency and Factor Structure of the Eating Disorder Inventory-2 in a Clinical Sample." *International Journal of Eating Disorders* 16 (1994).

Welch, Garry, Anne Hall, and Claes Norring. "The Factor Structure of the Eating Disorder Inventory in a Patient Setting." *International Journal of Eating Disorders* 9:1, January 1988.

Welch, G., A. Hall, and F. Walkey. "The Factor Structure of the Eating Disorder Inventory." *Journal of Clinical Psychology,* January 1988, 44:1.

eating disorders awareness week (EDAW) In 1988 the last week of April was designated Eating Disorders Awareness Week by Congress. For several years, EDAW was held in late November. Currently, Eating Disorders Awareness Week is held each year during February. Its sevenfold purpose:

1. To increase efforts to prevent the development of eating disorders.
2. To educate the public and professional communities regarding warning signs and appropriate interventions.
3. To increase awareness of treatment programs and support services.
4. To encourage development of healthy attitudes toward psychological and physical development, body image and self-esteem by influential individuals (i.e., parents, educators and health professionals).
5. To challenge cultural attitudes regarding thinness, perfection, achievement and expression of emotion that contribute to the increasing incidence of eating disorders.
6. To improve the ability of professionals of all disciplines to provide effective treatment and support.
7. To promote a compassionate, nonjudgmental, public understanding of eating disorders.

ectomorph A person with a thin and skeletal or bony body type, an ectomorph is characterized by long, thin arms and legs and a narrow trunk, conveying a rather trim, thin appearance. Theories linking body types to emotional or psychological characteristics are not considered scientifically sound.

See also ENDOMORPH; MESOMORPH; BODY TYPES.

ego-state therapy Ego-state therapy is a treatment approach that applies various techniques from group and family therapy to the resolution of internal conflict in a single individual. In this therapy, the individual psyche is assumed to be made up of various parts that have different functions and constitute the whole.

Watkins, John G., and Helen H. Watkins. *Ego States: Theory and Therapy,* New York: W. W. Norton & Company, 1997.

employee health costs and obesity Obesity is closely related to employee health care costs, according to Northwestern University Medical School (Chicago) study. The study compared Body Mass Index (BMI) of 3,000 employees with their health care needs and its costs. Health care costs were lowest for workers with a BMI of 25–27, the equivalent to a body weight of approximately 155 pounds for a woman 5 feet 6 inches tall or 174 pounds for a man 5 feet 10 inches. The findings indicated that health costs rise with worker BMI. Workers with an "at risk" BMI used twice as many sick days as those with a lower BMI, with sick day costs over three years per employee of $1,500 for higher BMI employees and $700 for lower BMI employees. Three-year costs were $7,000 per employee for those with a BMI of 25 or higher, compared with $4,500 for those with a BMI below 25. Workers with a BMI of greater than 30 constituted only 19 percent of the population but accounted for 26 percent of total health care claims and 29 percent of total health care costs.

According to Wolf and Colditz, obesity-related health conditions total about $100 billion each year in the United States. About half that figure is attributable to indirect costs such as lost work time and premature death. Because of these numbers, employers are taking a closer look at how they can reverse the obesity trend in the workplace. In 1998, 93 percent of employers had programs that fostered employee health, up from 76 percent in 1992, according to a Chicago benefits consulting firm.

Burton, Wayne N. et al. "The Economic Costs Associated With Body Mass Index In a Workplace." *Journal of Occupational and Environmental Medicine* 40 (September 1998).

Freudenheim, Milt. "Employers Focus on Weight as Workplace Health Issue." *New York Times*, September 6, 1999.

"Weighty Matters: Obesity, Health and Productivity," a special report by *Business & Health* (August 1998).

Wolf, Anne, and Graham Colditz. "Current Estimates of the Economic Cost of Obesity in the United States." *Obesity Research* 6 (March 1998).

endocrine factors in obesity The endocrine glands produce hormones that regulate the body's rate of METABOLISM, growth and sexual development and functioning. "Glands" have often been blamed by individuals for their obesity, but obesity caused by endocrine alterations are uncommon, and the increase in body weight observed with acute endocrine disease is usually limited. Hypothyroidism, adrenal hyperplasia and hypogonadism are endocrine alterations that result in modest obesity.

endomorph An endomorph is a person with a body type characterized by a tendency toward roundness and substantial fat deposits. Endomorphs have wide trunks and shorter-than-average arms and legs, making them appear to be somewhat fat. People with significant endomorphy gradually fill out until late middle age, when they generally shrink a little.

Theories linking body types to emotional or psychological characteristics are not considered scientifically sound.

See also ECTOMORPH; MESOMORPH; BODY TYPES.

ephedrine This active chemical in the Chinese herbal MA HUANG is also known as ephedra. This stimulant is often used for weight loss. Combined with caffeine, ephedra is effective in promoting weight loss, but it is associated with cardiovascular side effects, including a potentially deadly irregular heartbeat.

exercise Exercise is physical exertion for improvement or maintenance of health and fitness, as well as weight loss.

Today's emphasis on fitness and athletics has had a negative as well as a positive effect on health, especially for adolescent girls. Encouraged to exercise for their looks rather than their health, girls are often told that exercise is "nature's best makeup." Researchers have found that slimness of hips is the most sought-after feature among adolescents aged 12 to 16. Dissatisfaction with hip measurement only increases during this period when hips show the most change from natural hormonal influences. Some adolescents are so intent on changing their appearance that they become obsessed with exercise.

Eating-disordered patients often use exercise as a means of purging themselves of unwanted calories—a practice that causes additional health problems, such as vitamin and mineral deficiencies that can cause damage to bones, AMENORRHEA and cardiac arrest from low potassium levels and electrolyte imbalances. Excessive exercising can become a dangerous habit and one that is difficult to break. One exercise machine maker advertises "No pain, no gain," but pain is a warning to the body that something is wrong. For anorexics and bulimics, exercise buffers some of the pain they should be feeling; they are numbing their bodies' warnings to stop their destructive behavior.

Breaking an exercise addiction can be as difficult as overcoming an eating disorder. Although the effects of anorexia can be measured on a bathroom scale, the "fitaholic's" problem is not so easily defined. Truly compulsive exercisers let their workouts dominate their existence to the detriment of family, job and social life. Obsessive runners may be taught relaxation techniques and other ways of coping with stress that can help them become less dependent on exercise for their sense of well-being.

exposure and response prevention (ERP) A treatment method originally used in treating phobic and obsessive-compulsive disorders, in which the patient is exposed to whatever is triggering his or her abnormal behavior, with the abnormal behavior then forcibly restrained.

In recent years, ERP has also been adapted to treatment of bulimia nervosa. For example, clinicians have described how a bulimic woman was made to wait increasing lengths of time between stages of the disordered behavior that culminated in vomiting. After eight weeks her vomiting, which had occurred roughly four times a day prior to treatment, ceased.

Explaining why ERP works, Rosen and Leitenberg explain in *Behavior Therapy* that "binge eating and self-induced vomiting seem linked in a vicious circle by anxiety." Eating (especially BINGE EATING) elicits the fear of weight gain; vomiting reduces it. "Once an individual has learned that vomiting following food intake leads to anxiety reduction, rational fears no longer inhibit overeating." Thus, if the end-result vomiting is delayed longer and longer after each binge-eating session, the binge eating needed to stimulate it is delayed until it no longer is needed (because the vomiting that counters it is no longer occurring). So "the driving force of this disorder may be vomiting, not bingeing."

Recent reviews of the treatment of bulimia nervosa do not conclude that ERP adds anything to the effectiveness of cognitive behavioral treatments.

externality approach to obesity One of two major types of treatment for obesity (the other is the PSYCHODYNAMIC APPROACH TO OBESITY), externality focuses on conspicuous food-related cues in patients' environments and attempts to control their responses to them. This approach developed from experiments at Columbia University performed in 1974 by social psychologist Stanley Schachter. Schachter's group found that obese people are more likely to eat when a clock says it's mealtime or when food is put onto a plate than when their bodies signal HUNGER.

This approach assumes that what obese people need is to change their responses to these external cues and that by allowing themselves to eat only when truly hungry, they will lose weight naturally. It has spawned a number of behavioral therapy techniques, such as putting food on smaller plates so the amount looks larger, eating only in a particular room and so on.

Some externalists' patients have achieved remarkable results (one group lost an average of 40 pounds each in a single year), but these results have not consistently been replicated by others. Not only have patients not lost 40 pounds, they have tended to gain back what they have lost.

extreme eating The term *extreme eating* was used by the International Food Information Council to describe the eating habits of many 1990s teens who seem to have lost their balance when it comes to choosing an appropriate diet. Going overboard in one or more areas of the diet, such as cutting out entire food groups, fervently following the latest fad diet or weight loss plan or regularly consuming a single type of food to excess could all be characterized as extreme eating behaviors.

"Extreme Eating: Are Teens Compromising Their Health?" *Food Insight*, November/December 1998.

F

fad diets Diets that achieve widespread, though short-lived, popularity, usually as a result of heavily promoted best-selling books and/or popular magazine or tabloid features, are termed *fad diets.*

Hardly a season goes by without at least one diet book high on the best-seller list. Some diets advocated by these books are simply variations of a basic, safe 1,000- to 2,000-calorie balanced diet. But others can do more harm than good because they advocate diets that are unbalanced. Many capitalize on well-known names or places; many are accompanied by testimonials of spectacular and effortless weight loss. Fad diets generally rely on some trick to give readers the appearance of novelty. They attract faithful followings by claiming "scientific breakthroughs" such as methods to lower METABOLISM. Many tell dieters to eat only certain foods and exclude others; some even restrict the diet to two or three foods such as grapefruit or eggs. Because one can eat only so much of one food in a day, caloric intake is lowered and weight is lost. The problem is that single-food diets become boring, eventually prompting dieters to "cheat." Soon the cheating increases, dieters are back to normal eating patterns and excess weight returns until another fad diet comes along.

In addition to being boring, many of these diets are nutritionally unbalanced and dangerous. If they stay on them long enough, dieters can experience irregular heartbeat, kidney stones, fatigue, nausea, dizziness, muscle loss and other serious side effects.

Fad diets can be classified into six basic types:

Low carbohydrate These diets (Dr. Cooper's, Dr. Atkins' Superenergy) typically produce rapid weight loss during their first week, primarily because of dehydration. This occurs because, to compensate for reduced carbohydrate intake, the body breaks down stored sugar and protein, a process that releases water. This begins several days after the dieting starts. Because carbohydrates are not available to use as a source of energy, the body is forced to use fats instead. This leads to fatty acids being released into the blood, where they are converted to ketones. The state of "ketosis" is purported to produce appetite suppression, resulting in accelerated weight loss. In actuality, however, there is no scientific evidence that ketosis does suppress the appetite. (See KETOGENIC DIET.)

High-protein These diets (Stillman, Scarsdale, Cambridge) are based on the assumption that because there is no storage form of protein as there is for carbohydrate and fat, high protein intake will result in excess protein being "burned off"; in other words, some calories ingested as protein will not enter the energy balance equation and therefore, according to this theory, don't really count. Unfortunately, there is no scientific evidence to support this theory. Excess amino acids (the building blocks of proteins) are converted into glucose or fat for storage. No food can "burn" fat. Body fat is "burned" or reduced only by the body's using more energy than is supplied by food eaten.

Especially popular in the 1970s, this is the type of diet that provides a quick and substantial, but only temporary, weight loss because fatty acids are incompletely broken down. The technical name for this process is *ketosis,* and it can lead to an acid and alkaline imbalance. Ketone bodies, formed when fat deposits are broken down for energy more quickly than the body can use them, must be excreted in the urine. The dieter thus loses water—and weight—in the process. But the loss is not of body fat and is quickly regained when normal eating is resumed.

Low-carbohydrate, high-fat Diets in this category (Dr. Atkins' Diet Revolution, Drinking Man's, Air Force, Mayo) hold that the ketotic state produced by increased fat consumption accelerates elimination of many "energy-rich" substances from the body. In addition, these programs induce water loss and dehydration and are usually low in certain vitamins and minerals. As these diets are generally unpleasant, they offer no hope of a permanent change in eating habits necessary for the maintenance of lower body weight. Another reason for quick weight loss with these ketogenic diets is that the body is getting energy from "lean body mass" (muscles and other organs) rather than fat. Although the body must expend 3,500 calories to burn off a pound of body fat, only about 480 calories are needed to get rid of a pound of lean body mass. Balanced diets contain enough carbohydrates to provide glucose (a form of sugar), the body's basic energy source. But when carbohydrates are lacking, the body must obtain glucose from protein in muscles and major organs such as the heart. Experts also warn that after a period of eating unlimited fats and protein, the body will begin to crave bread, pasta, rice, mashed potatoes and corn. Those high-carbohydrate dietary staples will become forbidden fruit and, therefore, the focus of attention.

High complex carbohydrate These diets (Pritikin, Macrobiotic, Duke University Rice, F-plan) are considered more nutritionally sound. In addition to stressing consumption of unrefined CARBOHYDRATES, they allow considerable amounts of fruits as well as protein in the form of nuts, beans, peas or fish, but because of the low fat content of these dishes, they tend to be bland, unappetizing and boring. In some, the high fiber content may produce bloating and flatulence. Because of the monotony of these programs, many dieters consume less than the recommended portions and thus may experience vitamin and mineral deficiencies, particularly of calcium. The nature of these diets may promote cheating and rarely motivates dieters to make a lifelong commitment to them.

Specific food Some diets are based on the theory that certain foods accelerate fat breakdown. The most commonly recommended foods include grapefruit and eggs. Other substances claimed to be "fatbusters" include bananas, a combination of bananas and skim milk, apple-cider vinegar, kelp, vitamin B-6 and lecithin. There is no evidence that these foods or combinations of foods accelerate fat breakdown. In addition, high fruit intake can cause diarrhea. These diets are nutritionally deficient and offer no hope of lifelong changes in eating habits.

Liquid protein diets These diets (Optifast, NaturSlim) are said to suppress appetite. They cause dehydration and can lead to headaches, nausea, muscle weakness and even death. One extreme form of this type of diet, containing fewer than 400 calories a day, was linked to 17 deaths in 1977 and 1978. Scientists who studied the deaths found that the dieters had died of irregular heart rhythms and cardiac arrest. The Food and Drug Administration now requires warning labels on weight reduction products when more than 50 percent of the product's calories come from protein. Other VERY LOW CALORIE liquid and powdered products have appeared on the market recently with lower proportions of protein. But any diet of fewer than 800 calories a day is potentially dangerous and should be undertaken only under medical supervision.

Willis, Judith Levine. "How to Take Weight Off (and Keep It Off) without Getting Ripped Off." *FDA Consumer,* DHHS Publication No. (FDA) 89-1116, U.S. Food and Drug Administration, 1989.

fake fat Fake fat is a popular name for all-natural FAT SUBSTITUTES.

family meal The family meal is a therapy technique in which an eating-disordered patient and family members eat meals together with a therapist who helps them identify dysfunctional communication patterns within the family that perpetuate the patient's disorder. Unsubstantiated claims of dramatic recovery have been made by proponents of this technique.

family therapy A form of GROUP THERAPY in which a therapist works with a patient and her family together, family therapy is sometimes called familization therapy. Generally, a family therapy group consists of one therapist and three or more family members. In working with a family, a therapist can assess the impact of the individual's behavior on the family and observe the handling of conflicts, family roles, family decision making and communication patterns and family values. This therapy is meant to teach all members of a family how to express and fulfill their needs and change old patterns that have been mutually unsatisfactory. It can help both patients and their families bring painful emotions to the surface and understand them. The duration of family therapy varies with individual cases. Family therapy can be especially useful in treating adolescents' eating disorders and may be helpful to young adults struggling with separation from their original families.

Ganley, Richard M. "Eating Disorders Are Family Affairs." *Renfrew Perspective* (spring 1988).
Karpell, Merrily. "The Fear of Stepping Out of Line." *Renfrew Perspective* (fall 1988).
Robin, A. L., et al. "Family Versus Individual Therapy for Anorexia: Impact on Family Conflict." *International Journal of Eating Disorders* 17 (May 1995).
Stierlin, Helm, and Gunthard Weber. *Unlocking the Family Door: A Systemic Approach to the Understanding and Treatment of Anorexia Nervosa.* New York: Brunner/Mazel, 1989.

fasting Fasting is the abstaining from food for a period of time. During the 1960s, several clinics began to use short-term fasts to bring about rapid weight reduction. One reason they became so popular is that fasters no longer feel hungry after the first few days of starvation. However, the severe consequences of the nutritional deficiencies and extensive loss of lean body mass that characterizes clinical starvation prompted investigators to find a safer and more effective dieting treatment. As a result, VERY LOW-CALORIE DIETS were developed.

Supervised fasting is one of the simplest methods of weight reduction, but it is best carried out in a medical setting because of the significant risk of complications and even of sudden death. Risks associated with fasting include hypoglycemia and impaired glucose tolerance, KETOSIS, loss of nitrogen and lean tissue, hair loss; loss of potassium, sodium, calcium, magnesium and phosphate; reduced kidney function, edema, anemia, alterations in liver function, gastrointestinal tract changes, nausea and vomiting and changes in metabolism.

In 15 studies, the mean length of treatment was 17 weeks, with mean weight loss of 77 pounds. Few studies report follow-up, and in those that do the results are poor. Supervised fasting is a very expensive technique with poor long-term results.

Female fasting, in the manner of ANOREXIA NERVOSA, is not a new behavior. There is a long history of food-refusing behavior and appetite control by women dating from medieval times, practiced for reasons of mystical piety rather than physical vanity, as in the life of St. Catherine of Siena (1347–80) and her imitators. A more recognizably modern version of the phenomenon became widespread in the 19th century (see FASTING GIRLS).

Duhamel, Denise. "Holding Fast." *American Health,* May 1990.
Graham, Janis. "Food File: Is Fasting Worth It?" *Health,* July 1991.
Segal, Marian. "A Sometime Solution to a Weighty Problem." *FDA Consumer,* April 1990.
Thompson, Trisha, and Laura Flynn McCarthy. "The Fasting Controversy." *Harper's Bazaar,* January 1992.

fasting girls The term *fasting girls* was used by Victorians on both sides of the Atlantic to describe cases of prolonged abstinence from food by girls or young women, in which there was uncertainty about the reasons for fasting and the intentions of the fasters. The term was used jokingly by some and disparagingly by others. Doctors generally spoke of fasting girls with skepticism. The controversy over fasting girls intensified the arguments about the relationship between mind and body that were central to the Victorian debate about religion and science. Reports of fasting girls appeared in the U.S. press as late as 1910. Sustained food refusal was still regarded by most as a religious or supernatural phenomenon rather than a psychological disorder; it fed on a strain of religious piety and supernatural belief more common then than now. The "fasting girls" phenomenon was of widespread interest, drawing the attention of the educated and the uneducated, the elite and the ordinary. But the character of society was changing, and during this time refusal of food changed from an act of personal piety to a symptom of a disorder; physicians changed their diagnoses from anorexia mirabilis to anorexia nervosa.

Brumberg, Joan Jacobs. *Fasting Girls.* New York: Plume (Reissue edition), 1989.
Vandereycken, Walter, and Ron van Deth. *From Fasting Saints to Anorexic Girls: The History of Self-Starvation.* Washington Square, N.Y.: New York University Press, 1996.

fat blockers Antiobesity drugs that work by blocking the absorption of some fat by the body are called fat blockers. See ORLISTAT.

fat cells Fat cells are the fatty or ADIPOSE TISSUE of the body. Evolving research suggests that the size and number of fat cells (adipocytes) may play a role in the predisposition to obesity. Obese individuals have slightly larger and significantly more fat cells than normal-weight individuals. A greater number of fat cells is particularly characteristic of juvenile-onset obesity.

There are two important periods of development when the number of fat cells is affected: infancy (up to two years of age) and the preadolescent years (from nine to 12). A correlation is believed to exist between the number of fat cells and the rapidity of weight gain. Once fat cells have formed, they do not die and they cannot be eliminated, so they must be shrunk—depleted of lipids—before an obese individual can reach normal weight.

When weight is lost by diminishing fat stores, existing fat cells shrink, but they are primed to manufacture and store fat more efficiently once a normal diet is resumed. This is the reason for the "yo-yo" effect of rapid weight loss and gain experienced by so many dieters (see YO-YO DIETING). Individuals who have been obese since childhood regain lost weight more rapidly after dieting.

The body can increase the amount of body fat in only two ways: by producing more fat cells or by storing more fat in the existing fat cells. But fat cells can expand just so far and then can reach their capacity of stored fat. At one time, researchers believed that a body's number of fat cells was set by puberty. It is now known that the number of fat cells can continue to increase, doing so when existing fat cells fill to their capacity.

The only way researchers have discovered to eliminate fat cells is through surgery. After years of removing fat surgically from various areas of the body, and after observing injuries in which fat tissue has been lost, doctors have determined that fat is usually not redeposited in the treated areas as long as diet and exercise are sufficient to keep the number of fat cells from increasing.

See also BODY FAT DISTRIBUTION; SET-POINT THEORY.

"Body Fat: The Hormone Factor." *Science News*, June 15, 1991.

Hirsch, J., S. K. Fried, N. K. Edens, and R. L. Leibel. "The Fat Cell." *Medical Clinics of North America* 73, January 1989.

fat phobia A fat phobia is a fear of eating fat caused by the avalanche of media stories and books during the 1990s that stressed the health dangers of too much fat in the diet. Nutritionist Ann C. Grandjean (Center for Human Nutrition, Omaha, Nebraska) was quoted in a *USA Today* article as saying, "Fat phobia is the biggest diet problem I see among young athletes. I'm talking about these young people who are eating only 6 percent of their calories from fat." She goes on to say that people are following horrendous diets in the name of low fat. Although many Americans do eat too much fat, some have cut their fat intake back way too far.

Hellmich, Nanci. "Get Fit, Stay Fit." *USA Today*, January 4, 1999.

fat power A term used by advocates of a movement toward greater social acceptance for the overweight, reflecting a nationwide trend of changing attitudes, *fat power* advocates point to the commercial success of products, services and media personalities as evidence of this shift. There are now dating services for overweight people, magazines such as *Big Beautiful Woman* and clothing being designed for the large-sized by such well-known names as Pierre Cardin. Among the euphemisms for obesity promoted by pro-fat groups are *size positive, fat-positive* and *plus–sized.*

See also CULTURAL INFLUENCES ON APPEARANCE.

fat recycling Also called fat grafting, fat recycling is the technique of removing fat cells from one part of the body and using them in another. It is a further refinement of liposuction.

Fat recycling is a relatively new and still-evolving cosmetic surgery technique in which fat removed during liposuction can be injected into the hollows between chin and cheek, for example, during face-lifts.

See also COSMETIC SURGERY.

fat substitutes Fat substitutes are artificial fat replacement substances developed by major food processing and manufacturing companies during the late 1980s and early 1990s. SIMPLESSE (NutraSweet), a low-calorie milk-protein-and-egg-white substance, was the first all-natural substitute to win approval from the Food and Drug Administration. Initial FDA approval for Simplesse was for use only in frozen dessert products. OLESTRA, a cooking-oil replacement developed by Procter & Gamble, is, on the other hand, heat resistant and can be used in baked goods, fried foods and snacks. According to the company, Olestra is "almost a carbon copy of regular fat, but with a molecule of sugar at its core instead of glycerine, and up to eight fatty acids attached to the core instead of the customary three."

Since these two products were introduced, the fat replacement field has become quite crowded; supermarket shelves are bulging with products aimed at what is anticipated to be a billion-dollar annual market. Among these additional fat substitutes have been Stellar, made from cornstarch by A. R. Staley Manufacturing, and Slendid, made from pectin extracted from citrus peels, developed by Hercules Inc. Procter & Gamble has developed Caprenin, a low-calorie fat that can replace cocoa butter in candy bars such as the new Milky Way II bar. Caprenin has only five calories per gram instead of the nine calories per gram in other fats. Its "secret" ingredient is behenic acid, a substance not easily metabolized by the body.

No one fat replacer is ideal for all uses—flavor, texture, lubrication, bulk or heat transfer. In some cases, a single fat replacer may do the job; in others, a combination of fat replacers may be necessary.

Some analysts say that the use of these low- or nonfat substitutes will revolutionize the food processing industry, dramatically increasing sales and consumption. But others feel that fat-substitute products will only take sales from existing processed food products.

The medical community has been cautious about the introduction of these fake fats. It will take some time before adequate studies are completed; to date, however, no data show that eating a fat substitute will help lower or even maintain body weight—unless overall calories are cut.

In fact, some concern is expressed that people will eat even more calories because of the fake fat; for example, a piece of fat-free cake that has 160 calories is more "fattening" than an apple that has only 65 calories and is also fat free. But nutritionists fear that a population addicted to sugar and chocolate will now feel that the fat-free cake gives them an excuse to indulge.

Segal, Marian. "Fat Substitutes: A Taste of the Future?" *FDA Consumer*, December 1990.

fats One of the three main classifications of nutrients (see CARBOHYDRATES and PROTEINS), fats belong to a class of compounds known as lipids. They are derived from both animal and plant foods, but they differ chemically from each. Those originating from animal sources are saturated fats; fats from plants are usually unsaturated fats (see FATS SATURATED; FATS, UNSATURATED). One exception is coconut oil, which is highly saturated and is widely used in food processing. Both saturated and unsaturated fats have the same caloric value, about nine calories per gram, more than twice that of carbohydrates and proteins (four calories per gram). (Some studies indicate that fat may have up to 11 calories per gram.)

Fat serves as the body's major store of energy, and METABOLISM of this substance supplies approximately 90 percent of energy requirements during prolonged EXERCISE. The higher caloric value of fat makes it a more efficiently convertible source of energy for storage than protein or carbohydrate.

The American Heart Association recommends limiting calories eaten as fat to the 20 to 30 percent range instead of the 40 to 50 percent typical of most Americans. Diets consisting of less than 20 percent fat generally lack sufficient taste and palatability for faithful adherence; much below 10 percent for a prolonged period could cause serious health problems or even death. Some fat must be included in a diet because fat serves as a carrier for several important vitamins including A, D, E and K. Very low fat diets may result in deficiency of these "fat-soluble" vitamins. Nevertheless, dedicated fat-free purists strive to eliminate all fats from their diets.

fats, saturated Fats whose chemical composition includes the maximum possible quantity of hydrogen, saturated fats come primarily from animals and are usually solid at room temperature. They tend to raise blood cholesterol levels. Examples of saturated fats are butter, fats in whole milk, cheese, cocoa butter; lard, meat fat, solid shortening, palm oil and coconut oil. From a nutritional standpoint, some saturated fat is essential for proper growth and metabolism; a deficiency can lead to eczema and other skin disorders.

See also CHOLESTEROL; FATS; FATS, UNSATURATED.

fats, unsaturated Unsaturated fats include fatty acids whose chemical composition includes some sites on the carbon atom unoccupied by hydrogen. When many sites are vacant, they are called polyunsaturated. Unsaturated fats are capable of absorbing additional hydrogen. They are also known as free fatty acids because of their free bonds that allow them to take on more hydrogen atoms. They usually come from plants and are liquid at room temperature. Examples of polyunsaturated fats are vegetable oils such as corn, cottonseed, sunflower, safflower and soybean.

Monounsaturated fats include olive, peanut and canola oil. Unsaturated fats tend to lower blood cholesterol levels.

See also CHOLESTEROL; FATS; FATS, SATURATED.

fear of fat syndrome Behavior resulting from an exaggerated concern about gaining weight but not classifiable as a serious disorder such as BULIMIA or ANOREXIA NERVOSA, fear of fat syndrome is much more common than anorexia nervosa and affects younger children.

There are both boys and girls as young as seven who experience fear of fat and on occasion diet and skip meals. They are not anorexic—they don't have an obsessive wish to be thinner—but they are obsessed with not gaining weight. This dieting before their bodies are fully formed can lead to stunted growth, a stunting of development of heart muscle and delaying of puberty. If children stop dieting, damage is usually temporary, but if they diet strenuously for more than six months, they are not likely to grow that year. Frequently this fear of fat is seen in children who are not fat to begin with.

See also CULTURAL INFLUENCES ON EATING DISORDERS; DIETING.

Moses, Nancy, Mansour-Max Banihvy, and Fima Lifshitz. "Fear of Obesity among Adolescent Girls." *Pediatrics* 83 (March 1989).

fen-phen/Redux Fen-phen refers to the use in combination of the drugs fenfluramine (brand name Pondimin) and phentermine; Redux is the brand name for dexfenfluramine. Phentermine was approved by the FDA in 1959 and fenfluramine in 1973, as appetite suppressants for the short-term (a few weeks) management of obesity. Dexfenfluramine was approved in 1996 for use as an appetite suppressant in the management of obesity. In recent years, based largely on a study by Weintraub, some physicians began to prescribe fenfluramine or dexfenfluramine in combination with phentermine, often for extended periods of time, for use in weight loss programs. In 1996 physicians had written 18 million prescriptions for fen-phen. Use of drugs in ways other than described in the FDA-approved label is called "off-label use." In the case of fen-phen and dexfen/phen, no studies were presented to the FDA to demonstrate either the effectiveness or safety of the drugs taken in combination.

When the Mayo Clinic and other treatment facilities reported more than 200 patients developing heart valve disease after taking fen-phen, the FDA notified doctors and drug makers on September 12, 1997, to withdraw fenfluramine and dexfenfluramine from the market. (There were also reports of cases of heart valve disease in patients taking only fenfluramine or dexfenfluramine but no cases meeting FDA's definition in patients taking phentermine alone.)

In October 1999, American Home Products, the maker of Pondimin and Redux, agreed to pay $3.75 billion to settle the more than 4,000 lawsuits filed by people claiming health problems due to the fen-phen diet drug combination. As many as 6 million Americans took the drugs until 1997, when they were withdrawn from the market.

Larkin, Marilynn. "Ways To Win At Weight Loss." *FDA Consumer,* September 1997.

Mundy, Alicia. "Weight-loss Wars." *U.S. News & World Report,* February 15, 1999.

Weintraub, M. "Synergistic Interactions Between Fenfluramine and Phentermine." *International Journal of Obesity* 23 (1999).

Weintraub, M., et al. "A Double-blind Clinical Trial in Weight Control." *Archives of Internal Medicine* 144 (1984).

fiber An edible, but indigestible, part of certain foods, fiber is important in the diet as roughage, or bulk. Fiber is found in starches, breads, vegetables and fruit.

See also DIETARY FIBER.

food addiction Some popular writings on the subject of food have proposed the existence of a disorder they call food addiction. Loosely construed, the concept of addiction might be said to apply to compulsive or disordered eating of certain foods, most commonly those high in sugar or starch content, but there is no scientific basis for believing that any ordinary food substance is literally physiologically addictive in the same sense as a narcotic drug. So-called food addiction is more plausibly understood as an expression of a psychological disorder, response to an unacceptably intense condition of emotional deprivation, anxiety or tension. The idea of food addiction is not medically or scientifically valid.

Some authors classify "addictive" foods as trigger foods that trigger cravings and compulsive eating or drinking.

See also ANOREXIA NERVOSA; BODY IMAGE DISTURBANCE; BODY WRAPPING; BULIMIA NERVOSA; COMPULSIVE EATING; DEPRESSION; DIET PILLS; DIETING; FAD DIETS; FAT DOCTORS; OBESITY; PERSONALITY DISORDERS; SELF-ESTEEM; SOCIAL FACTORS IN OBESITY; STRESS AND EATING DISORDERS.

food allergy A food allergy is a chronic condition in which there is a consistent physiological reaction to a certain food or foods. To be a true allergy, according to the American Academy of Allergy and Immunology, the condition must involve an *immunologic response* to a food protein by an allergy-specific immunoglobulin (antibody). Most food allergy symptoms are manifested on the skin (pruritus, erythema, hives, eczema, edema) or in the gastrointestinal tract (vomiting, diarrhea, abdominal pain).

Most adverse reactions to foods are nonimmunologic and therefore not allergic. Nonimmunologic responses, properly termed *food intolerances,* can usually be traced to toxicity, enzyme deficiencies or anaphylactoid, or pharmacologic or metabolic reactions. Headache, fatigue, muscle and joint pain and anxiety are symptoms that may be attributable to a reaction to food but not to an allergic reaction.

True allergic reactions occur most commonly in children, among whom the incidence is about 5 percent; in adults the figure is closer to 3 percent. Ninety percent of allergic reactions are caused by a relatively few foods, including milk, eggs, legumes, nuts, soy and wheat. Very severe reactions, which are called anaphylactic, are most often caused by fish, shellfish and, to a lesser extent, citrus fruits, melons, bananas, tomatoes, corn, rice and celery. Food allergy is difficult to diagnose by history and objective tests, such as skin or blood testing. It is an area of medicine in which much scientific work remains to be done by immunologists and others.

Anderson, J. "Introduction to Food Allergy, Science and Reason." *Allergy Proceedings* 7, no. 6 (1986).

Brody, Jane. "Food Allergies: A Growing Controversy." *The New York Times Magazine*, April 29, 1990.

Ferguson, Anne. "Food Sensitivity or Self-Deception?" *New England Journal of Medicine* 323, no. 7 (August 1990).

Hunter, J. O. "Food Allergy—or Enterometabolic Disorder?" *Lancet*, August 24, 1991.

forbidden foods *"Forbidden foods"* is a term used by clinicians and eating-disordered individuals to refer to foods that the person feels that he or she should not eat, usually because they are high in calories and because the person believes that he or she would not be able to stop eating them. Not coincidently, forbidden foods are also the foods on which persons with eating disorders usually binge. Although some approaches to treatment of eating disorders encourage the individual to abstain from these forbidden foods, the most effective treatments help the individual learn to eat the food without losing control (i.e., without bingeing and purging). Thus at the end of treatment for an eating disorder, a person would no longer have any forbidden foods.

forced feeding Feeding accomplished through invasive tubes in the nose or by a process called total parenteral nutrition is called forced feeding. See also HYPERALIMENTATION.

fraudulent products With so many people striving to lose weight and dealing with FEAR OF FAT SYNDROME, it is little wonder that unscrupulous promoters prey on those looking for "miracle" cures. The NATIONAL ASSOCIATION TO AID FAT ACCEPTANCE (NAAFA) takes an active interest in the battle against health frauds, including weight loss scams, and maintains a membership in the National Council Against Health Fraud.

One example reported in the *NAAFA Newsletter* was the widely promoted "Fat Magnet" diet pill that became the target of action by the U.S.

Postal Service. Placing a temporary restraining order on mail received by the Beverly Hills company promoting this product, the Postal Service alleged that the solicitations contained such false representations as "The substance in the Fat Magnet can attract, bind, and flush out body fat." In March 1990, NAAFA reported that the Federal Trade Commission had frozen the assets of Allied International, manufacturer of the "Fat Magnet." The U.S. District Court was to hear the case, based on false and misleading advertising. Advertisements for the product claimed that the pills "break into thousands of particles, each acting like a tiny magnet, attracting and trapping many times its size in undigested fat particles . . . then, all the trapped fat and calories are naturally flushed out of the body" (*NAAFA Newsletter,* March 1990). The FTC asked for an injunction to force the firm to cease sales and to issue $5 million in refunds. On April 11, 1991, the FTC announced that the manufacturer had agreed to establish an escrow fund for consumer redress.

Another example was Dream-Away and Advanced Dream-Away, the manufacturer of which was ordered to pay $1.1 million in refunds to consumers who bought their products. Promoters claimed that by simply taking their pills, one could lose weight while sleeping.

The Food and Drug Administration reports that one out of six people uses a fraudulent product in the course of a year. On the FDA's top 10 list of health frauds are instant weight loss schemes, often advertised in magazines or newspapers. This makes weight loss pretty much a wide-open market, according to FDA staffers, who cannot check or control every item being offered.

Another group of products being watched by both the FDA and the Better Business Bureau are anti-CELLULITE products, which proliferate during bathing suit season. Many of these "cures" are imports from France, where consumer protection is less stringent. Even the better-known cosmetics companies have recently been risking federal regulators' ire by entering the $20 million anticellulite market. The FDA's primary concern is whether marketers claim their products conceal or actually eliminate this fat (which would classify them as drugs). In 1987 the FDA filed complaints against 23 cosmetics companies for unapproved products that make such claims. Since then, at least 50 additional suits have been filed. Thus far, no product has received FDA approval to claim it will actually eliminate cellulite.

Darnton, Nina. "The Battle of the Bulges." *Newsweek,* March 2, 1992.
Diamond, S. J. "Public Is Aware of Diet Fraud." *Los Angeles Times,* November 1, 1991.
Toufexis, Anastasia. "Fountain of Youth in a Jar." *Tune,* October 14, 1991.

G

gamma butyrolactone (GBL) GBL is a chemical that is included in products sold as dietary supplements and is claimed to have such effects as building muscles, enhancing sexual performance and reducing stress. One of the products containing GBL, Revivarant, has been sold as a liquid in 32-ounce bottles and as Revivarant G in pill form and promoted as a diet drug. Because the Food and Drug Administration (FDA) received reports of serious health problems—some of them life threatening—associated with the use of products containing GBL, the FDA in January 1999 advised consumers to dispose of any products of this type in their possession and requested that sellers voluntarily withdraw the products from market.

gastric bubble A polyurethane device popular as an obesity control in the mid-1980s, the gastric bubble was inserted through a tube threaded down the esophagus and into the stomach and then inflated, thereby "filling" the stomach. The principle behind it was that limiting the stomach's capacity to store food would force the patient to eat smaller meals. It was mostly unsuccessful; at times the bubble slowly deflated, and at other times the bubble and the stomach walls retained enough flexibility to accommodate overeating. Plus, if the bubble seriously deflated, it could result in dire consequences if it snagged in the bowel.

Brink, Susan. "Pills, Balloons and Now Tapeworms." *U.S. News & World Report,* August 7, 1995.

genetic factors in eating disorders There is evidence that eating disorders run in families. Females are particularly vulnerable, and there have been a number of reports of identical twins both developing anorexia nervosa. In some cases, imitative behavior may be a factor. Comparisons of families of anorexics and bulimics with families without eating disorders have found some differences: families of bulimics report more hostile interactions; families of anorexics are as warm and supportive of their children as nondisordered families but have marital problems. Some mental health specialists theorize that anorexic children serve as "lightning rods" for families who cannot face or resolve their problems. However, most evidence is capable of other explanations, so until more scientifically controlled studies are carried out, a genetic factor in generating eating disorders must remain speculative.

genetic factors in obesity Obesity often follows family lines, and evidence from twin studies and other family studies, although not completely consistent, have for some time implied inheritance. Studies have shown that biochemical differences between obese people and those of normal weight are most likely genetic in origin.

Bouchard, C. "Genetic Factors in Obesity." *Medical Clinics of North America* 73, no. 1 (January 1989).

"Heritability of Weight Gain and Obesity" (letters). *New England Journal of Medicine* 323, no. 15 (October 1990).

Sorenson, Thorkild A., R. Arlen Price, Albert J. Stunkard, and Fini Schulsinger. "Genetics of Obesity in Adult Adoptees and Their Biological Siblings." *British Medical Journal* 298 (January 14, 1989).

Stunkard, Albert J., et al. "Energy Intake, Not Energy Output, Is a Determinant of Body Size in Infants." *American Journal of Clinical Nutrition* 69 (March 1999).

geophagia Geophagia is a condition in which the patient eats chalk or earth or clay; a type of PICA (the desire to eat inedible substances). After surveying the literature, Isolde Prince concluded that in many cultures geophagia is a common, acceptable, benign practice without psychological implications. In fact, geophagia occurring among nutritionally deprived populations is looked at differently than pica in the Western world, where nutrition is much more likely to be at a satisfactory level.

Although still subject to considerable debate, in nutritionally deprived populations geophagia probably fulfills nutritional needs for elements important for growth and development. These nutritional factors are particularly important during childhood and pregnancy. The main debatable point is whether clay eating provides elements such as iron, zinc and calcium and is a significant treatment for anemia or whether clays remove these elements from food and give rise to anemia.

See KAOLIN.

Prince, Isolde. "Pica and Geophagia in Cross-Cultural Perspective." *Transcultural Psychiatric Research Review* 26 (1989).

Rudavsky, Shari. "Dirt Eaters of the World, Unite." *Omni,* March 1989.

Simon, S. L. "Soil Ingestion By Humans: A Review of History, Data, and Etiology." *Health Physics* 74 (June 1998).

gonads obesity Gonads obesity is caused by hypogonadism (abnormally low functioning of the gonads, with consequences for growth and development); it is marked by a concentration of fat tissue in the pelvic and breast regions. Other features may include poor beard growth in men, decreased growth of pubic hair and lack of development of the genitalia. Many obese females with this disease have mild hirsutism, irregular menses or AMENORRHEA. Young obese girls sometimes have premature or early menarche (first menstrual period in puberty).

Gregory, Dick (October 12, 1932–) An entertainer, comedian and former fat man whose weight plummeted when he fasted as a protest against the Vietnam War and in favor of civil rights for blacks. Since that time he has repeatedly taken under his care massively obese persons to encourage them to lose weight on his BAHAMIAN DIET program using his own diet powder. Although he has treated these patients for free at his Bahamian facility, his exploitation of their plight on national talk shows and in print media to promote his products has stirred controversy in the medical profession and among activist groups such as the National Association to Advance Fat Acceptance. Allegations have also been made by former patients regarding the conditions and qualifications of the staff at another facility Gregory has operated in Florida.

See also LIQUID FORMULAS, WALTER HUDSON.

group therapy Group therapy is a form of psychotherapy in which discussion takes place among a therapist and a number of patients rather than between a therapist and a single individual. Group size may range as high as 40 people, but 8 to 10 people is more common. Members of the group usually meet for an hour or more once or twice a week to discuss their problems openly with one another, with the therapist offering guidance.

Since 1980, group therapy has become a common form of treatment for both anorexia and bulimia. Group treatment and support groups provide an arena for demystifying the eating disorder, diminishing feelings of isolation and secrecy, fostering realistic goal setting, sharing successful techniques, expressing feelings and obtaining feedback. PSYCHOTHERAPY groups are most effective in the treatment of bulimia. They may be open ended or have a time limit, membership may be closed or participants may join at any time and the duration and frequency of sessions may vary. The focus is on individual dynamics and group process.

One school of thought holds that group therapy is a good model for understanding female development issues. The theory behind this is that women are generally socialized to function cooperatively in groups and that, therefore, the social dynamics of group therapy mimic or parallel the processes of female socialization. Because the majority of eating-disorder patients are female, it is possible that the success of group therapy for such patients may be related to this.

A setting such as that found in group therapy or a self-help group provides eating-disordered women a social format in which they can express opinions differing from the social consensus yet remain a part of the group (and the larger culture). As group members feel increasingly confident expressing thoughts and concerns that do not support thinness as an ideal, they are practicing skills of autonomy within a framework of social relationships and minimizing their fear of rejection and isolation.

Many issues can thus be explored in group sessions, from "what if" questions to actual experiences ("What happened to you when you quit purging?"). Group therapy can also help an individual to initiate serious treatment. Many patients have a difficult time beginning individual psychotherapy but may be less defensive and resistant to recovery in a group setting. A patient may accept confrontation from peers in a group more readily and in a more positive light than from a therapist.

Group therapy does not, however, represent a panacea. Many eating-disorder patients will deny that they have problems or will deny any feelings about their condition. This can keep them from developing the openness toward the group that is essential to allow the group to function fully. The group format helps decrease this resistance to trust, but there is no guarantee of success.

In a review of the literature on the outcome of group therapy for bulimia nervosa, McKisack and Waller found no obvious advantage attached to any single therapeutic orientation or to the gender of therapists. However, they did determine that longer, more intensely scheduled groups realized greater success, as did the addition of other treatment components, such as individual work.

Goodner, Sherry. "Group Therapy for Eating Disorders." *BASH Magazine*, 1987.

McKisack, C., and G. Waller. "Factors Influencing the Outcome of Group Psychotherapy for Bulimia Nervosa." *International Journal of Eating Disorders* 22 (July 1997).

Piazza, Eugene U., and Catherine Steiner-Adair. "Recent Trends in Group Therapy for Anorexia Nervosa and Bulimia." In *Eating Disorders: Effective Care and Treatment*, edited by Felix E. F. Larocca. St. Louis: Ishiyaku EuroAmerica, 1986.

growth hormone in obesity Growth hormone (GH) is secreted by the pituitary gland and directly influences protein, carbohydrate and fat METABOLISM, plus controls growth. Compared with normal-weight persons, obese individuals have impaired growth hormone secretion, but the reason is not known. In obese subjects who have lost weight, growth hormone secretion becomes normal promptly. Conversely, overfed lean subjects have a weight-related impairment in growth hormone secretion. Other factors affecting growth hormone secretion include aging, nutritional status and exercise. In studies on calorie restriction, GH-treated subjects have lost more weight.

guided image therapy A treatment that uses visualization techniques to relax the patient and strengthen the patient's connection with his or her inner consciousness, the theory behind guided image therapy is that once relaxed and comforted, the patient will have less stress, which will enhance the healing process. In a study of 50 bulimia nervosa patients, guided imagery treatment substantially reduced bingeing and purging episodes. Guided imagery also demonstrated improvement on measures of attitudes concerning eating, dieting and body weight.

Esplen, M. J., P. E. Garfinkel, et al. "A Randomized Controlled Trail of Guided Imagery in Bulimia Nervosa." *Psychological Medicine* 28 (November 1998).

Gull, Sir William Withey (1816–1890) An eminent London physician of the 19th century who was one of the first to use the term *anorexia nervosa.* Gull worked and lived for many years at Guy's Hospital in London and treated Queen Victoria and her family. Gull described anorexia nervosa as a disease distinct from starvation among the insane and unrelated to organic diseases such as tuberculosis, diabetes or cancer. Most important, he observed that this disorder specifically affected young women between the ages of 16 and 23.

H

herbal fen-phen Herbal fen-phen refers to various dietary supplement-type products marketed over the Internet and through weight-loss clinics, print ads and retail outlets as "natural" alternatives to the prescription drugs phentermine and fenfluramine (commonly referred to as fen-phen—see FEN-PHEN/REDUX). The Food and Drug Administration (FDA) considers herbal fen-phen products to be unapproved drugs because their names reflect that they are intended for the same use as the antiobesity drugs. In November 1997, the FDA warned consumers that these unapproved drugs have not been shown to be safe or effective and may contain ingredients that have been associated with injuries.

The main ingredient of most herbal fen-phen products is ephedra, commonly known as Ma Huang. Ephedra is an amphetaminelike compound with potentially powerful stimulant effects on the nervous system and heart. FDA has received and investigated more than 800 reports of adverse events associated with the use of ephedrine alkaloid-containing products since 1994. These events ranged from episodes of high blood pressure, heart rate irregularities, insomnia, nervousness, tremors and headaches to seizures, heart attacks, strokes and death.

Many ephedra-containing herbal fen-phen products also contain Hypericum perforatum, an herb commonly known as St. John's Wort and sometimes referred to as "herbal Prozac." The actions and possible side effects of St. John's Wort have not been studied under carefully controlled trials either alone or in combination with ephedra.

Other herbal fen-phen products contain 5-hydroxy-tryptophan, a compound closely related to L-tryptophan, a dietary supplement widely used in this country until 1990. Used primarily as a sleep aid, L-tryptophan was pulled from the market after it was found to be linked to more than 1,500 cases, including about 38 deaths, of a rare blood disorder known as eosinophilia myalgia syndrome.

The FDA regards any over-the-counter product commercially promoted as an alternative to prescription antiobesity drugs to be a drug.

(See MA HUANG.)

hidden hunger In this phenomenon, messages between the brain and stomach are in error so that conscious feelings of HUNGER do not in any way correspond to actual bodily needs. Because they do not know when they really are hungry, it is difficult for overweight people, in whom this phenomenon occurs, to control their eating.

Hudson, Walter (1945–1991) Because of his immense bulk (nearly 1,200 pounds), Walter Hudson was bedridden in his Long Island home for some time. He had not been out of his home for 27 years, when, in 1987, he achieved sudden notoriety. When he became wedged in a door frame and had to be cut out by the local fire department, his story became news. DICK GREGORY publicly adopted him as a "cause," but after several months of dieting, when Hudson refused to leave his home for Gregory's weight loss facility in the Bahamas, Gregory withdrew his support.

Hudson next became a spokesperson for a commercial diet product, which Gregory then sued, claiming that Hudson's television commercial "deceptively misleads viewers into believing that Hudson lost his weight through [it] rather than through use of [Gregory's] products."

In commercials, Hudson claimed to have lost more than 900 pounds; in 1989 he weighed 520. He later formed his own company to sell clothing for large-size men, women and children. He died in 1991, apparently of heart failure.

hunger Hunger is an urge to eat prompted by an immediate physical need for food. In healthy people, hunger and APPETITE usually coincide. Opportunities to eat, however, may arouse appetite even in the absence of real hunger, and some experiences can be so unsettling or traumatic that they can cause loss of appetite even in the presence of hunger.

Some researchers have distinguished two kinds of hunger: stomach hunger and mouth hunger. Stomach, or physiological, hunger derives from the physiological need to refuel. Compulsive eaters rarely experience it; they eat from mouth hunger. Mouth, or psychological, hunger has nothing to do with sustaining life. Mouth-hungry people eat "just because it's there," "because you have to put something into your mouth," "because it tastes good," "because it looks so delicious," "because it's time for breakfast/lunch/dinner," "because someone went to the trouble to prepare it," "because it would be a shame to throw it away," "because I feel lonely/anxious/depressed" or "because I feel happy/excited/like celebrating." Mouth hunger is what you feel pulling you toward the refrigerator as soon as you sit down to work or what compels you to leave your house at 11:30 P.M. in search of an all-night ice cream stand. Mouth hunger is what continues to send spoon after spoon of ice cream to your mouth long after you've begun to feel ill. Mouth hunger is the hunger we attempt to control with diets.

HILDE BRUCH emphasized that the inability to recognize hunger is a trait that is of fundamental significance for the development of severe eating disturbances. Bruch also noted that obese children are routinely fed when they cry for reasons other than hunger. Consequently, their "real" hunger is responded to inappropriately, with under- or overfeeding.

Eventually, these children's ability to differentiate accurately between hunger and emotional states becomes undermined. Emotional distress is confused with hunger, and these potentially obese children may overeat in response to virtually any internal arousal state. As obese adults, they suffer from a deficit in hunger awareness. Studies have shown that obese subjects are relatively insensitive to stimuli typically associated with hunger and do not usually eat more in response to hunger cues.

Bruch, Hilde. *Eating Disorders: Obesity, Anorexia Nervosa, and the Person Within.* New York: Basic Books, 1973.

Hirschmann, Jane R., and Carol H. Munter. *Overcoming Overeating,* Reading, Mass.: Addison-Wesley, 1988.

hyperactivity Meaning increased or excessive activity, the term *hyperactivity* commonly refers to manifestations of disturbed behavior, mostly in children, characterized by constant movement, distraction, impulsiveness, inability to concentrate and aggressiveness. It is also characteristic of anorexics; many are usually active, with a tendency to exercise even when emaciated. Some rarely stay still; even when confined to bed, they have been known to perform isometric exercises under the blankets. This preoccupation with physical fitness is closely related to the consuming desire for thinness. The apparently unusual capacity for physical exertion is not evidence of special physical toughness; it is an indicator of a determination to be active despite the actual state of physical health. Sometimes anorexics will push themselves to the point of collapse, causing them finally to seek or be taken for medical treatment. Physical overactivity can also serve to distract attention from hunger.

HILDE BRUCH wrote that hyperactivity is rarely complained of, or even mentioned, by the parents of anorexics but that it will be found with great regularity if looked for. Hyperactivity usually develops before the noneating phase. It may take many forms. Sometimes an existing interest in athletics and sports becomes intensified. Sometimes anorexics may engage in activities that seem to be aimless, walking for miles, doing chinning and bending exercises, refusing to sit down or literally running around in circles. Some may roam around at night, too restless to sleep, or they will do housework, cooking and cleaning by the hour. They themselves do not feel that they exercise too much, and parents do not notice or are not alarmed. Anorexics, and their parents, can therefore deny hyperactivity.

The relationship between hyperactivity and disordered eating has been corroborated via animal research. One of the common findings in animal studies of the effect of restricting food intake is an increase in restlessness and spontaneous motion. When rats are placed on a limited feeding schedule, they increase the number of times they spin their exercise wheels. After a few days of increased activity, however, adult rats will alter their cycles so that most of their activity occurs during the hour or two before feeding; then the total number of revolutions of the wheels per day will be somewhat lower than during times when they are feeding at their own pleasure. Prepubertal rats, on the other hand, do not adjust their activity in this way and will literally run themselves to death if feeding is not increased. This suggests that the heightened energy output that frequently accompanies dieting may be biologically determined.

Recent clinical studies with eating-disordered patients suggest that physical activity plays a more central role in the development and maintenance of eating disorders than had previously been thought.

Davis, C. "Eating Disorders and Hyperactivity: A Psychobiological Perspective." *Canadian Journal of Psychiatry* 42 (March 1997).

Kron, L., J. L. Katz, and G. Gorsynski. "Hyperactivity in Anorexia Nervosa: A Fundamental Clinical Feature." *Comprehensive Psychiatry* 5 (May 1978).

hyperalimentation Intravenous feeding, hyperalimentation involves the infusion of a protein solution made up of hydrolysate, glucose, electrolytes, minerals and vitamins at a constant rate through a catheter that has been surgically placed in a major blood vessel such as the subclavian or jugular vein. Helpful in the treatment of anorexia nervosa, it avoids the arguments about FORCED FEEDING. Although it prevents patients' surreptitiously disposing of food, vomiting and other tricks, inventive anorexics find ways of interfering with the flow; they even manage to turn the machinery off. But by bringing about a rapid correction of poor nutrition, hyperalimentation makes patients more accessible to psychotherapy. Hyperalimentation is considered to be a drastic treatment measure and is regarded negatively by many who cite possible infections and overhydration, as well as unwise control over patients who are already struggling to escape feelings of powerlessness.

hypercellularity The condition of having too many cells is termed *hypercellularity.*

It appears that the number of fat cells in the body cannot be decreased. However, during periods of rapid growth, a proliferation of cells can be slowed or stopped. Thus it is believed that changing nutrition at the proper time may modify the rate of cell development. This is especially important in treating obesity-prone children.

See also FAT CELLS.

hypergymnasia The term *hypergymnasia* was used by Adel Eldahmy, medical director of the Long Beach (California) Eating Disorders Clinic, to describe the excessive exercising an increasing number of bulimic patients turn to once they have stopped PURGING. Instead of vomiting or using laxatives, they go to a gym seven days a week, two or three hours a day, to burn off calories. They've been scared sufficiently to stop purging, but they don't see anything wrong with exercising until they're dangerously dehydrated.

See also EXERCISE; HYPERACTIVITY.

hyperplastic obesity A severe, lifelong type of obesity that is anatomically generalized (not concentrated in any area or areas of the body) and is resistant to therapy, hyperplastic obesity is further characterized by an increased number of fat cells of normal or of increased size.

See also HYPERTROPHIC OBESITY.

hypertension Chronic high blood pressure (excessive pressure of the blood against the arterial walls), hypertension is usually defined as a condition in which resting systolic pressure is consistently greater than 160 millimeters of mercury and diastolic pressure is over 90 millimeters.

Because a number of studies have demonstrated that blood pressure falls during periods of caloric restriction, weight reduction is an accepted treatment for hypertension. Some clinicians, however, have failed to detect significant blood pressure lowering in cases of substantial weight loss. In clinical studies in which obese rats were fed, fasted and refed, blood pressure did not correlate directly with varying body weight but appeared instead to be regulated by nutritional conditions. These findings conflict with the traditional view that weight loss or gain per se triggers changes in blood pressure.

In these studies, repeated cycles of weight loss and gain induced hypertension in the obese rats. Because there is also evidence that humans develop hypertension during rapid regaining of weight, some clinicians suggest that more emphasis should be placed on long-term maintenance of weight loss in obese hypertensive patients because caloric restriction may actually exacerbate hypertension if followed by rapid regaining of weight.

Hypertension tends to occur in patients with greater lean body mass and thus greater weight, but these people are not necessarily fatter than those people with normal blood pressure.

hypertrophic obesity Adult-onset obesity, or hypertrophic obesity, is more amenable to therapy than childhood obesity or obesity caused by or associated with a pathological condition. Physiologically, it is characterized by the increased size, but not the increased number, of fat cells.

See also HYPERPLASTIC OBESITY.

hypnotherapy The use of hypnosis in the treatment of psychological disorders, hypnotherapy is intended to help patients remember and come to terms with disturbing memories or emotions that they have repressed from consciousness.

According to the American Medical Association, scientific studies regarding the effectiveness of hypnotherapy are lacking. Hypnosis has been used effectively as part of a therapeutic strategy for anorexia nervosa. Hypnotherapeutic intervention is most effective when symptoms such as hyperactivity, distorted body image, feelings of inadequacy and perfectionistic tendencies are present. It may also help patients to overcome resistance to therapy.

Hypnotic suggestion has been used to increase patients' awareness of hunger by associating it with the pleasure of eating. Hypnoanalysis has been used for uncovering psychodynamic conflicts behind anorexic symptoms. A combination of behavior therapy and hypnosis has been used to associate food and appetite with pleasant memories and to help patients ventilate feelings of aggression and hostility.

Hypnosis has also been used in treatment programs for weight loss but with mixed results. According to reviews of weight-loss studies, the addition of hypnosis to other treatment has not affected outcome to any significant degree.

hypokalemia A potassium deficiency often resulting from chronic vomiting because of the loss of salt, minerals and other nutrients, hypokalemia commonly results in heart irregularity and, if severe, may lead to sudden death. When accompanying malnutrition, hypokalemia also adversely affects the renal and gastrointestinal systems. Hypokalemia also results in specific injury to the kidney tubules, affecting their ability to concentrate urine, resulting in frequent urination and increased thirst. Its effects on the gastrointestinal system include gastric fullness, regurgitation of food, heartburn, constipation and exacerbation of external hemorrhoids.

hypothalamic disease This disease, trauma or tumor affects the APPETITE center located in the hypothalamus (a part of the brain that controls functions of the autonomic nervous system), resulting in obesity. Individuals suffering from this condition usually have an insatiable appetite, eating compulsively day and night. Their obesity advances relentlessly, and eventually they become massive in size. In some instances there is a decrease in normal brain function.

Patients diagnosed as having hypothalamic disease often have a history of brain damage caused by trauma or inflammation. Such cases show a generalized type of obesity with no areas of the body being spared. Excess ADIPOSE TISSUE tends to concentrate in the face and neck region as well as in the upper arms, upper legs and pelvis. In men there may be a retraction of the testes, and in young women development of secondary sexual characteristics may be delayed. Diagnosis is based on these physical findings, as well as on brain scans and thyroid function tests. The prescribed treatment for this disease is weight reduction as well as treatment of brain lesions. Early death may result from extreme obesity and complications of pneumonia or blood poisoning from infected skin sites.

I

iatrogenesis in eating disorders An iatrogenic disorder is an abnormal mental or physical condition produced inadvertently as a result of treatment by a physician for some other disorder.

In the treatment of eating disorders, various practices and mistakes in treatment can result in iatrogenic disorders:

- Failure to attend to food and weight issues in PSYCHOTHERAPY. A study of normal volunteers has shown that semistarvation can produce an overall dampening of emotions or lead to the experience of severe DEPRESSION, ANXIETY, mood changes, feelings of inadequacy and social withdrawal. Semistarvation is responsible for food preoccupations, radically altered eating habits and BINGE EATING in some individuals.
- Establishment of unrealistic goals in treatment. Although arriving at an ideal normal weight for a patient is difficult, iatrogenesis occurs when the goal weight established is so low as virtually to preclude recovery; for example, a bulimic patient may have a higher-than-average set point (see SET-POINT THEORY), and therefore her weight goal should be higher than that on a standard height/weight chart. Most bulimic patients have weights greater than those of the average population, and between one-third and one-half have weight consistent with obesity.
- Inappropriate application of BEHAVIOR MODIFICATION techniques grounded in insensitivity to a particular patient's responses; for example, if coercion or punishment is used to encourage or discourage an eating behavior, the patient may eat to avoid the negative reinforcement and then purge—thus developing bulimia. The difference between successful and unsuccessful treatment depends on the way the program is applied; too-rigid application may only perpetuate, or complicate, the disorder.
- Unnecessary TUBE FEEDING. The greatest problems associated with tube feeding derive from its use as a punishment. In a psychologically vulnerable patient, this may cause confusion about bodily functions, confirm an already existing sense of worthlessness or cause mistrust; it may also lead to physiological complications.
- Inappropriate treatment with medication. Five different types of medication are sometimes misused: diuretics, laxatives, emetics, thyroxine and "diet pills." Misuse of drugs serves to aggravate eating disorders as well as distort diagnosis.

The danger of iatrogenic effects also exists in the abstinence and addiction models of bulimia; for example, OVEREATERS ANONYMOUS (a group whose practices are based on those of Alcoholics Anonymous) views bulimia as a progressive and lifelong illness, controllable only by abstinence from the "addictive" substance. But abstaining from food is much more difficult than abstaining from alcohol. Several main principles of Overeaters Anonymous could be iatrogenic for the bulimic patient:

- The belief that overweight or obesity is the result of "compulsive overeating." Most studies of the obese indicate that they do not eat more than individuals of normal weight. People who are compulsive overeaters are also compulsive dieters and may be responding to a sense of hunger in their bodies. This sense of hunger could be responsible for the food preoccupations and cravings that are often reported.
- The idea that bulimics are suffering from a "progressive illness which cannot be cured, only arrested." Bulimic patients can be treated successfully and cured.
- The principle of controlling overeating through abstinence from "the addiction." This principle encourages DICHOTOMOUS THINKING in a bulimic patient, with the bulimic patient adopting a self-defeating "all-or-nothing" attitude.
- Participation in self-help and support groups. Association with others who have an eating disorder may foster a group identity pleasurable or satisfying to a patient. Difficulty can develop in relinquishing a support group and moving beyond the "sick role" into greater recovery. The association of several popular stars with eating disorders has also somewhat glamorized them. The goals of a self-help group should be to provide mutual support without reinforcing the disorder.

ice The slang term for an appetite-suppressing drug sold illegally on the streets, ice is 98 percent pure crystal methamphetamine. Its appearance resembles frozen ice water. It is as addictive and dangerous as crack cocaine. Many users are women, some of them using it for weight loss. Although it does cause weight loss for a short time, addiction and toxic problems soon set in. Ice can be smoked, snorted or injected; is domestically produced; is comparable in price to crack; and gives the user a high—and suppresses appetite—for 8 to 24 hours. A crack high lasts an average of 15 minutes.

imipramine The first true ANTIDEPRESSANT, imipramine has been in use since the 1950s under the commercial name Tofranil. A tricyclic antidepressant, it has been used by millions of people and has an established record of long-term safety when used as prescribed. Imipramine has some side effects, among them dry mouth, light-headedness on standing up (which usually disappears after a week or two) and sleepiness—many more side effects than the newer selective serotonin reuptake inhibitors (e.g., Prozac). It has been used successfully in the treatment of bulimia, with patients receiving it reducing their binge frequency about 75 percent. However, long-term maintenance is a problem as there is a high probability of relapse after the drugs are discontinued.

inpatient programs Residential treatment centers for eating disordered patients, inpatient programs are found by therapists to be worthwhile for those individuals who are truly motivated to help themselves overcome their condition. However, when patients are "sent there" by doctors or family against their wishes, they frequently look at them as simply another phase they have to put up with until its over. Sometimes, insurance does not cover a long enough stay to make their treatment effective.

insomnia Chronic inability to sleep or consistent interruption of sleep by periods of wakefulness, insomnia is not a disease but may be a symptom of many diseases. Bulimics frequently report troubled sleep patterns and insomnia and use BINGE EATING as a kind of sleeping pill. Sleep disturbance is a regular complication of starvation. Insomnia, especially premature early morning awakening, affects many anorexics and depressed people.

insurance Treatment for eating disorders is frequently either not covered or only partially covered by hospitalization policies. In *Simon v. Blue Cross and Blue Shield of Greater New York,* a New York State appeals court in 1988 held that hospitalization of a person for anorexia nervosa is medical, not psychiatric, care and therefore is not subject to insurance policy limitations on psychiatric coverage. The physician who examined the patient at the time of her first hospitalization asserted that because of rapid weight loss the patient was "emaciated, malnourished, dehydrated, and hypotensive. She required immediate medical treatment for these conditions." This case is covered in *Hospital and Community Psychiatry,* June 1989, page 662.

Another problem clinicians have with insurance companies is that different companies allow different frequencies of treatment or different amounts of therapy, meaning that some patients can be "cut off" just as their treatment is beginning to be effective.

International No Diet Day (INDD) No Diet Day was started in 1992 by Mary Evans Young, director of the British antidiet campaign Diet Breakers, and author of *Diet Breaking: Having It All Without Having To Diet* (Hodder & Stoughton, 1995). The following year and each year since then, No Diet Day has been celebrated internationally. Its major thrust is to challenge the cultural attitudes and values that contribute to chronic dieting, weight preoccupation, eating disorders and size discrimination.

Internet obesity therapy Researchers at Brown University School of Medicine used Web sites to help people lose weight. They assigned 91 people who were at least 20 pounds overweight to two groups—Internet behavior therapy and controls. Each group had access to the study Web site and access to diet, exercise and behavior information on the Internet. The behavior therapy group also participated in online diaries and exercise activities. Three months into the study, the Internet therapy group had lost an average of 9 pounds and reduced their waist measurement by an average of 2.5 inches. Those not enrolled in the therapy program lost an average of 3 pounds and 1 inch from their waists.

interoceptive disturbance An interoceptive disturbance is an inability to identify accurately internal sensations such as HUNGER, SATIETY, fatigue, cold and sexual feelings. HILDE BRUCH suggested that both anorexia nervosa and juvenile obesity are fundamentally related to this disturbed awareness. Anorexic patients often describe extreme confusion about their bodily sensations; sometimes they appear devoid of thoughts and feelings reflecting personal experiences. Rarely can they focus on and accurately describe their emotional and physical states.

interpersonal psychotherapy (IPT) A form of psychotherapy that has been found to be an effective treatment for bulimia nervosa, interpersonal psychotherapy focuses on resolving relationship issues and problems rather than on eating problems per se. That IPT has been found to be an effective treatment for bulimia nervosa is an interesting and important finding because it demonstrates that a treatment that does not directly target eating behavior can be effective in altering such behavior.

Fairburn, C. G., R. Jones, R. C. Peveler, R. A. Hope, and M. O'Connor. "Psychotherapy and bulimia nervosa: The longer-term effects of interpersonal psychotherapy, behaviour therapy, and cognitive behaviour therapy." *Archives of General Psychiatry* 50 (1993).

ipecac A dried root of the plant ipecacuanha grown in Brazil, ipecac is the source of emetine, a powdered white alkaloid emetic used to induce vomiting and the active ingredient in ipecac syrup, abused by some eating-disordered patients.

Ipecac syrup is sold over the counter in the United States in 30-cubic-centimeter bottles, equivalent to 21 milligrams of emetine base. The long persistence of emetine in the body is the basis for cumulative toxicity. The effects of emetine toxicosis are gastrointestinal, neuromuscular and cardiovascular. Gastrointestinal symptoms include diarrhea, nausea, vomiting and dysphagia (difficulty in swallowing). The neuromuscular manifestations include weakness, aching, tenderness and stiffness of muscles, especially those of the neck and the extremities. There have been case reports of myopathies, including fatal cardiomyopathy, associated with the use of ipecac syrup. The most serious toxic effects are cardiovascular and include hypotension, precordial path, tachycardia and dyspnea. It is estimated that an accumulated dose of 1.25 grams of emetine base can produce death in an adult. The drug is used commonly in emergency situations involving overdoses.

The AMERICAN ANOREXIA/BULIMIA ASSOCIATION (AABA) has lobbied the U.S. Food and Drug Administration against over-the-counter sales of ipecac. Because of the wide availability of the drug and its speedy emetic action, ipecac was abused, according to AABA sources, by an estimated 30,000 young women in 1987.

J

Janet, Pierre (1859–1947) A French psychiatrist and researcher specializing in the study of hysteria, Pierre Janet was the first to describe in modern medical terms the symptoms of BULIMIA. In his book *Les Obsessions et la psychasthenie* (1903), he wrote about a young woman who developed compulsive eating binges, many of them in secret.

jaw wiring Wiring the jaws together prevents the eating of solid foods and allows only liquid nutrition, directly restricting calorie intake. Weight reduction usually occurs during this time; as much as 70 and 80 pounds have been lost when jaws have been left wired for long periods of time. However, much of this is regained once they are unwired. Some patients find the conspicuousness and the claustrophobic qualities of jaw wiring to be rather unpleasant.

This procedure has been used primarily to help compulsive eaters. Once a week the braces are loosened so the teeth can be brushed.

jejunocolonic bypass An intestinal bypass procedure developed in the 1960s that was intended to aid weight loss, jejunocolonic bypass is no longer performed, however, because of detrimental side effects (severe diarrhea, uncontrolled weight loss, malnutrition, liver dysfunction) during the postoperative months. Patients did lose much weight, but as side effects worsened, surgeons had to reconnect their intestines. Subsequently, all lost weight was regained. Regained weight proved that the bypass was the cause of weight reduction, however, and this experience provided the impetus for continued investigation into surgical weight control.

jejunoileal bypass The most frequently performed small intestine bypass operation in the treatment of patients with morbid obesity until it was replaced by gastric bypass in the late 1970s, the jejunolineal bypass was effective in producing weight loss (an average of 100 pounds five years after surgery), but side effects and complications were substantial.

Jenny Craig Program The Jenny Craig diet program combines frozen and prepackaged shelf foods with one-on-one counseling, independent homework and group classes on behavior modification. In the beginning, participants buy most of their foods from the Jenny Craig company. As the diet progresses, more and more regular foods are incorporated into the diet, with the Jenny Craig food use lessening. The idea behind the plan is to teach portion control and how to make healthy food choices and to encourage exercise.

K

kaolin The ingestion of kaolin (also known as white dirt, chalk or white clay) is a relatively common type of PICA found in the central Georgia Piedmont area. Although geophagia (earth eating) has been observed and documented in many areas of the world, the specific preference for consuming kaolin is less well known. After reviewing the literature, researchers determined that kaolin ingestion appears to be a culturally transmitted form of pica, not selectively associated with other psychopathology, and appears to meet the DSM-IV criteria for a "culture-bound" syndrome.

ketogenic diet A ketogenic diet produces elevated levels of acetone or ketone bodies, accompanied by mild acidosis or ketoacidosis. In this kind of diet, the ratio of calories derived from fat to those from carbohydrates is three or four to one.

The combustion of fatty acids in the bloodstream produces ketones, which eventually are broken down into carbon dioxide and water by the liver and other tissues of the body. Under abnormal conditions such as diabetes mellitus, starvation or a diet composed almost entirely of fat, the breakdown of fatty acids may be halted at the ketone stage, causing increasing levels of ketone bodies in the blood and body tissues. Ketones are powerful appetite suppressants that account for the loss of HUNGER occurring on the second day of any rigorous fast.

Ketone-producing diets have been around for more than 100 years. William Harvey, an English surgeon, first experimented with high-protein, low-carbohydrate, ketone-producing diets in the mid-1800s. The diet he developed is generally known as the Banting Diet (see BANTING, WILLIAM), after an early patient of Harvey's who was so delighted by the effects of the doctor's weight loss program that he published a pamphlet in praise of it. Since that time versions of the Banting Diet, with minor modifications, have appeared at regular intervals: as the Pennington or Dupont Diet in 1953, the Air Force Diet in 1960, the Drinking Man's Diet in 1965 and the Stillman and Atkins diets in the 1970s.

Elevated levels of ketones are potentially dangerous (see KETOSIS).

ketosis Ketosis is a condition in which excessive amounts of ketones accumulate in the body. Ketones are chemicals the body makes when there is not enough glucose in the blood and it must break down fat for its energy. When this occurs, fatty acids are released into the blood; these fatty acids are then converted to ketones. Ketones can poison and even kill body cells. Ketones that build up in the body for a long time can lead to serious illness and coma. Symptoms include a "fruity" odor to the breath, loss of appetite, nausea, vomiting and abdominal pain. Ketosis can be diagnosed by a test to detect ketones in the urine. FASTING can cause ketosis. Treatment in this case is a gradual reintroduction of a nutritious diet.

Ketosis also occurs in uncontrolled diabetes mellitus because carbohydrates are not properly utilized. In these cases, it is treated with either diet change or insulin.

kleptomania A psychological compulsion to steal, kleptomania in the form of shoplifting is a bulimia-associated symptom affecting many bulimic patients. This stealing is invariably compulsive, and the patients experience the same guilt feelings as they do when BINGE EATING. Other than food or laxatives stolen for the purpose of binge eating or purging, bulimics rarely steal to get something they cannot afford to buy. This symptom occurs even in persons who have no history of shoplifting prior to the onset of bulimia. Patients have been known to feel so guilty after stealing something that they attempt surreptitiously to return it the next day, only to find themselves compulsively stealing something else.

An increasing number of shoplifting bulimics are entering therapy through the courts, as an alternative to prosecution or sentencing. In fact, some therapists see shoplifting as, in effect, a cry for help.

L

Lasègue, Charles (1816–1883) A French psychiatrist who was one of the first to publish a detailed description of anorexia nervosa, in 1873 Lasègue described the disorder as a variant of hysteria. His contemporary, Englishman SIR WILLIAM WITHEY GULL, concentrated on the medical aspects of anorexia, but Lasègue emphasized its psychological aspects. He confirmed what Gull had suggested, that anorexic women came from families willing and able to spend emotional and financial resources on them. He was the first physician to suggest that refusal of food constitutes a form of conflict between a maturing girl and her parents.

Last Chance Diet This fad diet became prominent in 1976 when the *Last Chance Diet Book* became a best-seller and led to the widespread use of liquid protein products without medical supervision. These products provided 300–400 calories per day in the form of collagen hydrolysate, a protein low in biological value. Some 100,000 people had used these products by the end of 1977, and 60 deaths had been reported to the Centers for Disease Control. Seventeen of these were attributed to the diet; in the next year the Food and Drug Administration issued warnings about it.

See also FAD DIETS.

laxative abuse Misuse of laxatives is a fairly common problem among bulimic women, and laxatives appear to be the type of drug most commonly abused by anorexic patients. This misuse usually involves the ingestion of many times the amounts recommended by the manufacturer.

In a University of Kansas study of women with eating disorders, more than one-half of the women had abused laxatives at some point, and in a survey of 2,400 North Carolina middle school students, nearly 10 percent of the girls and 4 percent of the boys reported vomiting or using laxatives to lose weight.

Researchers have found that patients who use self-induced VOMITING for weight control tend to eat significantly more during binges and yet weigh less than those who use laxatives, suggesting that laxative abuse is relatively ineffective for this purpose and that dietary restraint is responsible for any weight loss among laxative abusers. One study found that the weight loss experienced by patients following ingestion of laxatives resulted from temporary fluid loss; the amount of caloric absorption prevented by laxative use was minimal.

Laxatives containing stimulant compounds are favored by those with eating disorders because these agents will reliably produce a watery diarrhea fairly promptly and a sense of weight loss if sufficient amounts are ingested. Most laxative abuse is practiced independently, but laxatives are often prescribed by diet doctors in an effort to speed food through the intestines so nutrients are not absorbed and turned to fat.

Complications of laxative abuse include constipation, bleeding and dehydration.

leptin The hormone leptin, produced by adipocytes (fat cells), was discovered in the mid-1990s in mice and was subsequently mapped in humans. Leptin is thought to act as a lipostat: as the amount of fat stored in adipocytes rises, leptin is released into the blood and signals to the brain that the body has enough to eat. Early experiments on mice showed that the more leptin they had circulating, the less they would eat. Experiments on humans have had mixed results. Although some people have lost weight with leptin hormone injections, others have not been affected by it at all. In a small clinical trial, obese people injected with the hormone lost 1 1/2 to 16 pounds over six months. Researchers question whether leptin will become a drug because of the need for daily injections over several months, as well as the high doses needed. But scientists do agree that the discovery of leptin is exciting because it opens a new area for obesity research.

lipoprotein lipase The enzyme lipoprotein lipase aids in the storage of body fat. Studies have shown that obese people may have difficulty achieving a normal level of lipoprotein lipase. A University of Colorado study reported that obese people, in comparison with people of normal weight, produce too much of the enzyme and that even after weight loss their enzyme activity had not fully returned to normal.

Levels of lipoprotein lipase in ADIPOSE TISSUES affect the maintenance of fat-cell size, body weight and obesity. Genetic and diet-induced obesity have been found to be associated with increases in lipoprotein lipase levels in the adipose tissue of humans and rodents after overnight fasting. Progressive increases in body mass index in humans are associated with increases in adipose tissue lipoprotein lipase. Most evidence suggests that an increase in levels of lipoprotein lipase in adipose tissue preserves rather than causes obesity.

One study found that people who had maintained a large weight loss for eight or more years still produced too much of the enzyme. But as soon as those obese people who have lost weight start regaining it, their enzyme level drops.

Eckel, Robert H. "Lipoprotein Lipase." *New England Journal of Medicine* 320, no. 16 (April 20, 1989).

liquid formulas A number of commercial diet supplement drinks promoted since the 1970s, the earliest and most highly publicized of which was

Robert Linn's "Prolinn," described as "a formula composed of all the amino acids needed to form a protein molecule." Such liquids have been used by hospitals for years to feed seriously ill patients. Once Linn's formula was published, other brands, such as Winmill, GroLean, Ran-Tein, T-Amino, LPP, E.M.F., Pro-Fast, Nu-Trim/20 and Multi-Protein Slim, appeared.

The first liquid protein supplements were withdrawn when the Centers for Disease Control attributed 60 deaths to their use. The protein in these early supplements was collagen based; their inadequate amino acid composition led to dangerous loss of lean muscle mass, including heart muscle. In addition, these early diets did not provide adequate potassium, which may have resulted in serious disturbances of heart rhythm.

Then, during the mid-1980s, a new generation of liquid protein diets was developed. Made from high-quality protein, with adequate vitamins, minerals and electrolytes to maintain health, some of them are even intended for use in programs of medical monitoring, nutrition education, behavior modification, exercise and support groups sponsored by the manufacturers. Three widely used programs are Optifast (Sandoz Nutrition), Medifast (Jason Pharmaceuticals) and Ultrafast (National Center for Nutrition). In November 1988 these reformatted liquid protein diet programs received a commercial boost when the popular TV talk-show host Oprah Winfrey revealed that the loss of nearly 70 pounds that she had experienced was the result of following the Optifast liquid diet program.

Formula diets come in dry form as mixtures of essential nutrients; water must be added before use. Prepared in two to six servings, most of these diets provide milk or egg (not vegetable) protein and varying proportions of carbohydrate and fat. The addition of carbohydrate decreases ketosis, hyperuricemia, electrolyte depletion and loss of lean tissue proteins. Fat improves palatability and provides essential fatty acids.

Users who stay with the program usually lose four to 10 pounds during the first week of the formula diet and two to five pounds per week thereafter. Twelve-week programs usually result in a loss of 22 to 33 pounds. One study evaluated 4,026 morbidly obese patients who showed interest in the Optifast diet program. Ten percent failed to join or did not meet entry criteria; one-fourth of those remaining left the program within the first three weeks; among the 2,717 remaining patients, one-third reached the desired weight during treatment, but fewer than half of these remained within 10 pounds of that weight when examined 18 months later. In other words, 80 to 90 percent of patients who wanted to lose weight were ultimately unsuccessful.

These programs are recommended only for those people who are at least 30 percent or 50 pounds above desired body weight. Liquid diets may cause gingivitis and other dental problems, along with the normal adverse effects of rapid weight loss. According to the Federal Trade Commission (FTC), these programs require professional supervision because there is evidence that patients on liquid diets risk developing gallstones. Also to be considered are the high costs (generally between $1,400 and $2,800), time needed for medical monitoring and group support and social restrictions when dinnertime comes. Episodes of sudden death (sometimes associated with myocardial abnormalities) like those that occurred with older liquid protein preparations have not been reported with current diet formulas.

However, even these new liquid formulas have come under attack. In October 1991 the FTC charged marketers of Optifast 70, Medifast 70 and Ultrafast with making deceptive claims that their programs are safe and effective over the long term. As a result, liquid formula diet promoters must back up their claims of weight loss with more substantial studies over a longer duration.

See also DIETING; FAD DIETS.

low-fat diet Whether or not dietary fat intake plays an important role in the rising prevalence of overweight and obesity has long been a matter of controversy among weight loss experts. According to a review of 28 studies investigating the relationship between fat intake and weight, people who switch to a low-fat diet but eat as much else as they like still decrease their calorie intake by 11 percent to 30 percent. Findings suggest that the incidence of obesity has increased in nations where fat intake has risen but remained steady in countries where the population has continued to follow a low-fat diet.

From these findings, Bray and Popkin contend that because low-fat diets pack comparatively fewer calories in the same amount of food and are thus more satisfying, they can fill people up before they eat too many calories. Because these diets are more satisfying, people are more likely to stick with them for the long-term and not only lose weight, but keep it off.

The researchers estimate that the average person could expect to lose a pound or more a month simply by lowering their fat intake by 10 percent. They add that by combining lowered-fat intake with increased exercise, people can lose considerably more weight.

But not all experts agree with this review and conclusion, criticizing the researchers' choice of studies and their analysis. They argue that the degree of effect of dietary fat intake on body fat needs long-term trials to be determined.

Bray, George A., and Barry Popkin. "Dietary Fat Intake Does Affect Obesity!" *American Journal of Clinical Nutrition* 68 (December 1998).

M

ma huang A popular herbal remedy that contains ephedrine, ma huang is a stimulant that can raise heart rate and increase blood pressure. More than 50 products containing ma huang are sold in health food stores to enhance energy and lose weight, as well as in body building. Because most of them have the word *natural* on the label, people assume they are safe, but taken in large enough doses without medical supervision, ephedrine can cause strokes, heart attacks, rapid heart beat, even sudden death. Ephedrine directly stimulates receptors on the heart, which increase heart rate and the amount of work the heart must do to pump blood throughout the body. Ma huang is usually sold in capsule or powder form. Experts advise staying away from ma huang altogether unless your doctor approves of your taking it.

malnutrition Malnutrition is poor nourishment that results from improper diet or from some defect in metabolism that prevents the body from digesting or absorbing food properly. Extreme malnutrition may lead to starvation.

Eating disorders sometimes result in malnutrition. Intentional malnutrition is the hallmark of anorexia nervosa, but it also represents a significant medical complication of bulimia in 20 percent of cases. Principal manifestations of malnutrition involve five body organ systems: endocrine (amenorrhea and estrogen deficiency), cardiovascular (lowered blood pressure and reduced heart rate), neuromuscular (osteoporosis), renal (kidney stones and renal failure) and gastrointestinal (gastritis and decreased acid secretion).

Mediterranean Diet A popular diet developed in 1995 by a team that included the Harvard School of Public Health and the United Nations World Health Organization, the Mediterranean Diet emphasizes whole-grain breads, pasta, rice, fruits, beans, nuts and vegetables, with some fish and poultry and very little red meat. Study results announced at the 1999 Experimental Biology annual meeting in Washington, D.C. reported that almost three times as many people were able to stick to a higher fat "Mediterranean-style" diet that included peanuts and peanut butter during an 18-month weight-loss study. The high-fat group lost an average of 11 pounds each, while the low-fat group lost an average of six pounds each. In addition, more than 80 percent of the subjects on the low-fat diet dropped out of the study compared to less than half (46 percent) of the subjects on the Mediterranean-style diet.

menstrual dysfunction Abnormal functioning of the menstrual cycle in females, menstrual dysfunction is a common condition accompanying ANOREXIA NERVOSA and BULIMIA NERVOSA. Early studies emphasized the role of weight loss and lean/fat ratio in AMENORRHEA. But later studies conducted at the University of Rochester Medical Center, Rochester, New York, to determine the incidence of menstrual abnormalities in a group of women with abnormal eating attitudes but without obvious eating disorder symptoms found that 93.4 percent (compared with 15.0 percent of the CONTROL GROUP) reported an abnormal menstrual history. These data suggest that menstrual dysfunction often occurs in women with abnormal eating behavior but without weight loss or diagnosable eating pathology.

menus for dieters Research has indicated that the order in which a person eats different foods during a meal can help him reach SATIETY at strategic moments and maintain a feeling of fullness for a longer period of time. Starchy or sugary foods contribute substantially after 10–20 minutes and continue as long as glucose is being absorbed rapidly. Thus, to be satisfying, a main meal should start with potatoes, pasta, rice or bread and even sugars in sauces and dressings, to the extent that such items can be included in a nutritionally balanced reduced-calorie diet. Soups are customarily a first course, but because of their low concentration of CARBOHYDRATES they may not "spoil" the appetite at the right time later in a meal. However, they may be useful to dieters as a main course because their low average calorie density and slowly digesting particles will help to slow the rate of gastric emptying after the meal. Thus, such foods may spread out satiety, helping to fight the temptation to snack or take the next meal early.

Gibbs, J., and G. P. Smith. "The Neuroendocrinology of Postprandial Satiety." *Frontiers in Neuroendocrinology* 8 (August 1984).

Woods, Stephen C., et al. "Peptides and the Control of Meal Size." *Diabetologia* 20 (1981).

Meridia Meridia is a brand name for sibutramine, a weight-loss drug. (See Chapter 5.)

mesomorph A person whose body type is square and muscular, a mesomorph has an athletic physique characterized by a broad trunk and shoulder with well-proportioned muscular arms and legs.

Theories linking body types to emotional or psychological characteristics are not considered scientifically sound.

See also ECTOMORPH, ENDOMORPH; BODY TYPES.

metabolism The sum of all chemical and physical processes by which the body transforms food and keeps itself alive, metabolism is a two-phase process: catabolic and anabolic. In the catabolic, or destructive, phase, the body breaks down foods into simpler chemical substances. During this process, energy is released in the form of heat. The anabolic, or constructive, phase uses these substances to create new cells or mend damage.

Obese patients with the lowest metabolic rates prior to a diet lose the least amount of weight. It has been estimated that a dieter can expect to lose an average of 1.5 ounces per day for the first month if calories are cut from 2,000 to 1,500 per day. During the second month, expected weight loss would be half that amount, during the third month, half the second month; after that, no loss at all. Such evidence indicates that the metabolism adapts to caloric restriction by becoming more efficient.

In a 1989 news item, *Insight* magazine reported that new studies "seem to show that a metabolic difference may be the precursor to psychological problems that lead to such eating disorders as bulimia and anorexia nervosa." The article cited a recent study conducted at the Western Psychiatric Institute and Clinic in Pittsburgh, which found that recovering bulimics needed only 10 calories per pound of body weight daily to maintain their normal weight. That is less than 73 percent of the 13.8 daily calories per pound that the average woman needed. Anorexics who had returned to a normal weight needed about 60 percent more calories than the average female to maintain their healthy weight.

Although a disrupted metabolism and other physical changes resulting from an eating disorder could trigger changes in the body's need for calories, Walter Kaye, director of the inpatient eating-disorder clinic at Western Psychiatric, said that an inborn difference in metabolism could explain some people's vulnerability to eating disorders and why post-treatment relapse rates are so high.

metoclopramide A drug that increases the speed with which fluid and food pass from the stomach, metoclopramide is often used prior to surgery and has also been prescribed to relieve the bloating complained of by many ANOREXIA NERVOSA patients after meals. However, the use of metoclopramide has been associated with significant depression and with hormonal changes, limiting its potential use in treating anorexia nervosa.

Mirasol A residential treatment center in Tucson, Arizona, that stresses natural healing along with traditional methods to treat eating disorders, Mirasol's program is based on biofeedback, clinical hypnosis, Qigong (an ancient Chinese holistic system of self-healing exercise and meditation), Jungian mandala and dream work, group process, body image work and traditional cognitive behavioral methods.

mood disorders and eating disorders Mood disorders (formerly referred to as affective disorders) are disorders of feelings or emotions, usually involving depression or elation or mood swings between those emotions. They are sometimes related directly to another physical or mental illness. The mood disorders of depression, premenstrual syndrome (PMS) and seasonal affective disorder (SAD) share similar features with eating disorders, including symptoms and development, a genetic or familial tie, and receive similar treatments.

One symptom common to all these disorders is weight fluctuation. Depressed patients and SAD patients usually gain or lose weight as a result of increased or decreased appetite; PMS patients may retain water, causing weight gain, or they may crave foods high in CARBOHYDRATES as their snacking increases. So does their weight. Marked weight gain or loss is also often a key symptom to diagnosing eating disorders.

Additional evidence that mood and eating disorders are related is that 20 to 30 percent of all eating-disorder patients are also depressed, and many of them have a family history of depression as well. Patients with anorexia nervosa may also show signs of mania such as euphoria and hyperactivity, as well as feelings of sadness, thoughts of suicide and suicidal behavior. In one study, 27 out of 94 anorexic patients were depressed following treatment; three others had committed suicide. Several other studies have reported incidence of depression among former anorexic patients in the 40 to 45 percent range.

Researchers have also found a biological link between eating and mood disorders. APPETITE is controlled by the same endorphins (hormones secreted in the brain) that control the sense of well-being, pain tolerance levels, irritability, memory, ability to concentrate and other feelings and functions. The hormone melatonin, which affects appetite, aggression and sex drive, may be one culprit in the cases of SAD, PMS and bulimia. Both exposure to light and darkness and premenstrual changes in the body determine the levels of melatonin produced. Disproportionate levels of melatonin seem to be a problem in bulimics and compulsive overeaters, causing them to eat more at certain times of the day. In women with premenstrual syndrome, melatonin may cause heavier eating before the period; in SAD patients it may cause them to eat more at other times. Victims of these disorders often find that after ingesting carbohydrates, they are in a better mood, can concentrate more easily and are less irritable. This theory is being studied more thoroughly because a craving for carbohydrates, which bring melatonin to more normal levels, is common to all these disorders.

Another problem area may be SEROTONIN, a NEUROTRANSMITTER that also affects frame of mind, appetite and sex drive. Low levels of serotonin can also cause craving for carbohydrates.

One study that investigated the incidence of mood and anxiety disorders in women who had been diagnosed with anorexia nervosa several years earlier indicated that these disorders developed frequently, regardless of the outcome of the anorexia nervosa. Major depression and anxiety disorders developed before the eating disorder in more than half of these cases.

A genetic or familial tie between eating and mood disorders has also been noted in several studies. In one, a group of 26 anorexic patients had two fathers, 15 mothers and six siblings diagnosed as having mood disorders. In another study, 25 anorexia nervosa patients were compared with 25 nonanorexics. The relatives of those with anorexia had a 22 percent incidence of mood disorder, whereas only 10 percent of the relatives of the control group had such histories. Finally, a University of Minnesota study reported that among patients with bulimia, 34 to 60 percent had first-degree relatives with mood disorders. As with the relatives of the patients with anorexia nervosa, the predominant type of mood disorder among them was major depressive disorder.

Evidence against a connection between eating disorders and mood disorders is that eating disorders and mood disorders have different patterns of recovery; treatments that work for depression do not always work for eating disorders, and treatments specifically for eating disorders have been found to alleviate depression. Plus, according to a University of Illinois at Chicago study, only 3 percent of depressed adolescents are eating disordered after five years, and their chances of developing an eating disorder in their lifetime is only 2 percent. The chances of their developing another mood disorder are 6 to 10 percent.

movement therapy This psychotherapeutic treatment method is based on the premise that the way we move is intrinsically connected to our thoughts and feelings. Dance, as spontaneous body movement, has been used almost from the beginning of history to express feelings and attitudes. The American Dance Therapy Association defines movement/dance therapy as "the psychotherapeutic use of movement to further the physical and emotional integration of the individual." It is a technique that uses nonverbal interaction between people as the primary means for accomplishing therapeutic goals.

According to RENFREW CENTER movement therapist Ziona Brotleit:

> The relationship established between patients and therapists by sharing a movement activity supports and enables behavioral change. The movement therapist helps patients learn about themselves from the way in which they move and assists them in bringing about desired changes.
>
> The tendency of women with eating disorders to block their emotions and to fear loss of control is seen in blocked, split, rigid and restricted movement styles. Their self-esteem problems are demonstrated primarily in significant body image distortions. They seem to lack healthy

boundaries in relationships and have either a rigid or an unclear sense of their kinesphere (personal body space). They tend to use more gestural than postural movements and lack the natural fluidity of movement.

At the end of movement therapy, eating disordered patients seem more comfortable watching themselves in the mirror and their body image is less distorted and more acceptable to them. They generally seem more self-accepting and sure of themselves.

Brotleit, Ziona. "Moving Forward." *Renfrew Perspective* (summer 1989).

Silk, Geraldine. "Creative Movement for People Who Are Developmentally Disabled." *Journal of Physical Education* 60, no. 9 (November 1989).

Stark, Arlynne. "American Dance Therapy Association, a Kinesthetic Approach." *Dance Magazine,* November 1987.

Stern, Ricky. "Many Ways to Grow: Creative Art Therapies." *Pediatric Annals* 18, no. 10 (October 1989).

multicompulsive Also referred to as multiimpulsive, multicompulsive refers to having more than one compulsion simultaneously. Ten percent of bulimics are reported to display compulsive behavior in other areas, such as alcohol, drugs, stealing and sex. Multicompulsive behavior is very difficult to treat.

Bulimics and anorexics sometimes become involved with drugs such as cocaine, methamphetamine, CAFFEINE and over-the-counter DIET PILLS as they learn about and experiment with their appetite-suppressing qualities. As their eating disorders worsen, substances such as alcohol, marijuana, barbiturates and so on become an enticing anodyne for painful reality.

Eating-disordered women may actually convince themselves that their substance abuse in some way helps lessen the severity of their eating disorders, but in reality, substance abuse tends only to exacerbate their effects. For example, a bulimic woman who also abuses cocaine will extol the drug's tendency to offset food binges and decrease her appetite; on further discussion, however, she will be less enthusiastic about addressing her BINGE EATING and PURGING as she copes with the DEPRESSION and despair that set in after the cocaine has worn off. An eating-disordered marijuana abuser may insist that her use of the drug is not a problem, emphasizing its relaxing effect, but she may neglect to mention the subsequent "killer munchies" that trigger marathon binges.

Eating-disordered women may be particularly vulnerable to substance abuse when they are attempting to break away from bulimic or anorexic behavior. As uncomfortable feelings and memories begin to surface, they may seek intoxication as a means to numb their feelings without resorting to compulsive behavior toward food. Richard L. Pyle, a clinician with the Department of Psychiatry of the University of Minnesota, reports that at least 2 percent of the women coming to his clinic for evaluation are currently abusing alcohol and that one in five has had previous treatment for chemical dependency.

Bulimic women who abuse alcohol present special problems. Perhaps the most significant problem is the high frequency of SUICIDE attempts. In one study, 32 percent of bulimic women who had a history of alcohol abuse reported suicide attempts, compared with none by non-alcohol-abusing bulimics and with 26 percent by a third group of bulimic women who had a history of major depression. In addition, bulimic women who had a history of chemical dependency had an older age of onset; significantly more DIURETIC ABUSE and LAXATIVE ABUSE; worse functioning in social, financial and work areas; a higher incidence of stealing both before and after the onset of their eating disorder; and, more often, a history of previous inpatient treatment for bulimia (56 percent versus 4 percent).

Daily substance abuse produces sufficient loss of control that outpatient treatment of bulimia nervosa is often unsuccessful. Inpatient care may be required to treat the chemical dependency, either concurrently with or preceding outpatient care for bulimia nervosa. Many clinicians also believe that a history of substance abuse in bulimia nervosa is associated with negative treatment outcome.

However, a two- to five-year follow-up study by Dr. Pyle's clinic indicated that, after treatment in an intensive outpatient group psychotherapy program, 24 patients who had a history of chemical abuse did as well as 65 who did not. In both groups 67 percent of the patients were symptom free at follow-up, and 25 percent were virtually unchanged. Only one of the 24 women with a history of chemical dependency required chemical dependency treatment during the follow-up, which averaged three-and-a-half years, and three of 65 bulimic women without a history of chemical abuse required chemical dependency treatment. Therefore, Dr. Pyle summarized, a history of chemical abuse does not necessarily influence outcome negatively; and following successful treatment, patients with a history of alcohol abuse are no more at risk for chemical dependency than those with no history of alcohol abuse.

Doctors are also reporting a new trend of girls and young women using highly addictive cocaine and crack to lose weight. Drug dealers even promote these drugs with weight loss in mind, telling girls as young as 10 years of age that boys like only thin girls and that crack (or cocaine) will help them lose weight. Crack, which is cheaper, is used mainly by poorer users, whereas cocaine is the drug of choice for the wealthier. Crack and cocaine suppress HUNGER by stimulating the central nervous system. Users feel no need to eat or sleep.

In a potentially important recent study by Gleaves and Eberenz, the authors found that a large proportion of bulimic patients who displayed multiimpulsive characteristics also reported a history of sexual abuse. The authors speculated that many of the behaviors observed among this subgroup of patients may be part of a chronic post-traumatic stress reaction. The authors also noted that treatments may need to address the post-traumatic condition before directly attempting to change eating behavior.

Gleaves, D. H., and K. P. Eberenz. "Sexual Abuse Histories Among Treatment-Resistant Bulimia Nervosa Patients." *International Journal of Eating Disorders* 15 (1994).
Mitchell, James E., Richard L. Pyle, et al. "A 2–5 Year Follow-up Study of Patients Treated for Bulimia." *International Journal of Eating Disorders* 8, no. 2 (March 1989).
Morrison, Beckie. "Learning to Overcome Addictions." *Renfrew Perspective* (winter 1989).

multidimensional/multifactorial models Currently, the psychopathology of eating disorders is believed to be multidimensional in nature, and a series of factor analytic studies have identified what the various dimensions are for both anorexia and bulimia nervosa. Generally consistent across studies, the dimensions or features appear to be (1) bulimic behaviors (i.e., bingeing and purging); (2) restrictive eating; (3) body dissatisfaction/fear of fatness; (4) affective disturbance; and (5) personality disturbance. Some studies have found the latter two dimensions to be a single dimension.

Gleaves, D. H., and K. P. Eberenz. "The Psychopathology of Anorexia Nervosa: A Factor Analytic Investigation." *Journal of Psychopathology and Behavioral Assessment* 15 (1993).
———. "Validating a Multidimensional Model of the Psychopathology of Bulimia Nervosa." *Journal of Clinical Psychology* 51 (1995).
Gleaves, D. H., D. A. Williamson, and S. E. Barker. "Confirmatory Factor Analysis of a Multidimensional Model of Bulimia Naervosa." *Journal of Abnormal Psychology* 102 (1993).

Multifactorial Assessment of Eating Disorder Symptoms (MAEDS) The MAEDS is a brief self-report instrument designed to be used to evaluate treatment outcome for anorexia and bulimia nervosa. The instrument has six scales empirically and theoretically related to eating disorders: depression, binge eating, purgative behavior, fear of fatness, restrictive eating, and avoidance of forbidden foods.

Anderson, D. A., D. A. Williamson, E. G. Duchmann, D. H. Gleaves, and J. S. Barbin. "Development and Validation of a Multiaxial Treatment Outcome Measure for Eating Disorders." *Assessment* 6 (1999).

music Slow music reduces APPETITE, according to Johns Hopkins University research reported in 1991 in *McCall's, Tufts University Diet and Nutrition Letter* and *Small Business Reports*. Researchers counted the number of bites people took during meals while listening to music. Subjects who listened to no music took 3.9 bites per minute, with a third asking for second helpings. Those who listened to lively music ate an average of 5.1 bites per minute, with almost half requesting second helpings. But subjects listening to soothing flute instrumentals ate only 3.2 bites per minute, and none requested seconds. Most of the slow-music diners left about a quarter of the food on their plates and said they were full. They also had fewer digestive complaints and said their food tasted better. Researchers speculated that heightened taste occurred because chewing forces air from the throat to the nose, allowing the nose to smell the food. Because odor is an important element in the sense of taste, slower chewing gives a heightened sense of flavor.

See also TASTE.

N

NAAFA (National Association to Advance Fat Acceptance) Formerly known as the National Association to Aid Fat Americans, this nonprofit, tax-exempt organization formed in 1969 seeks to increase the happiness and well-being of fat people.

Its basic purposes are to assist the large number of people regarded by the medical profession as "persistently or incurably overweight" to adapt to themselves and increase their self-confidence; to promote social tolerance toward fat people; to serve as a forum in which important problems affecting heavy people can be openly discussed; to disseminate knowledge pertaining to the sociological, psychological, medical and physiological aspects of obesity; and to sponsor research concerning these aspects of obesity. NAAFA is concerned with the general issues of fat people's lives, such as job discrimination, individual psychological problems and difficulties with respect to social acceptance and mobility. Its goal is to remedy these difficulties rather than to make members leaner. Its monthly publication is the *NAAFA Newsletter.*

narcissistic personality disorder As defined in DSM-IV, the essential feature of narcissistic personality disorder is a pervasive pattern of grandiosity, a need for admiration and a lack of empathy that begins by early adulthood and is present in a variety of contexts. Many theories attribute anorexia and bulimia nervosa to "pathological narcissism." To evaluate this conception, Steiger et al. compared narcissism scores of 90 eating-disorder sufferers with 90 control subjects. Narcissism scores of eating-disordered patients consistently exceeded those of the control cases.

Steiger, H., et al. "A Controlled Study of Trait Narcissism in Anorexia and Bulimia Nervosa." *International Journal of Eating Disorders* 22 (September 1997).

neurogenic binge eating This pattern of binge eating seems to result from a neurological problem. Neurogenic binge eating was extensively studied during the 1970s.

Researchers speculated that an epilepsylike seizure may cause some binge eating. They concluded provisionally that two categories of BULIMIA should be distinguished: psychogenic (psychologically caused) and neurogenic (neurologically caused) binge eating. The overwhelming majority of bulimics are psychogenic bingers. Bulimics who binge eat as a result of anger and frustration and claim that they "can't help it" may be out of control, but they usually come to understand that they are using food to ease psychological pain.

Neurogenic binge eating is an entirely different experience, one that resembles a sudden possession or an eating seizure. The victim may be going about her business and suddenly be overwhelmed by an intense, insatiable desire to eat. She feels as if not she herself but forces outside her were making her eat—episodically, unpredictably and uncontrollably. She feels disoriented and strangely unlike herself during her binge, as if in an altered state of consciousness, and if she sleeps afterward, she is likely to be confused momentarily when she awakens.

The original researchers suspected that this mysterious disorder may have been an electrical disturbance in the brain similar to epilepsy, because patients stopped binge eating while taking Dilantin, an anticonvulsant drug.

These patients are described as generally in good physical health and may be underweight, normal weight or overweight. However, unlike other binge eaters, they experience an "aura" prior to bingeing (flashes of light, unusual smells, increased tension or fear); perceptual disturbances (feelings of depersonalization) while bingeing; occurrence afterward of a phenomenon of a kind typical of postconvulsive states (extended sleep, loss of consciousness, confusion, memory loss, loss of bladder control); rage attacks (temper tantrums, headaches, dizziness, stomachaches or nausea and a numbness or tingling in the upper or lower extremities); and neurological "*soft* signs," such as occurrence during a binge of an abnormal electroencephalographic (EEG) pattern, more typically seen in drowsiness or sleep. However, James E. Mitchell, in "Medical and Physiological Aspects of Bulimia" in *Handbook of Eating Disorders,* notes that "this pattern is also present in some normal subjects. The question of EEG abnormalities in bulimia deserves further study."

Although Rau and Green report a positive treatment outcome for patients with neurological signs and a weight deviation of greater or less than 25 percent from normal body weight, other studies have reported less-promising results with anticonvulsants.

Mitchell, James E. "Bulimia: Medical and Physiological Aspects." In *Handbook of Eating Disorders,* edited by Kelly D. Brownell and John P. Foreyt. New York: Basic Books, 1986.

Rau, J., and R. Green. "Neurological Factors Affecting Binge Eating: Body over Mind." In *The Binge-Purge Syndrome: Diagnosis, Treatment, and Research,* edited by R. Hawkins, W. Fremouw, and P. Clement. New York: Springer, 1984.

neurotransmitters Neurotransmitters are chemicals that transmit electrical impulses or "messages" from one neuron (nerve cell) to another or to a muscle cell.

Much scientific study has been directed at key chemical messengers in the brain that play a major role in regulating hormone production. Researchers have found anorexics and bulimics to have abnormal levels of certain neurotransmitters; for example, low levels of the neurotransmitter SEROTONIN are linked to bulimia, as well as the mood disorders, depression and impulsive behavior associated with bulimia. Low serotonin levels may contribute to bulimics' binge eating of food high in carbohydrates.

In anorexia, lower-than-normal levels of neurotransmitter norepinephrine are found in the spinal fluid. Because the norepinephrine levels are low in anorexic patients who have regained weight, it is possible that this neurotransmitter abnormality precedes weight loss and may, in fact, indicate a genetic connection to the eating disorder. But the same biochemical condition also could result from anorexics' starvation practices.

Fava, Maurizio, Paul M. Copeland, Ulrich Schweiger, and David B. Herzog. "Neurochemical Abnormalities of Anorexia Nervosa and Bulimia Nervosa." *American Journal of Psychiatry* 146, no. 8 (August 1989).

nutrients Substances in food necessary for life, nutrients include carbohydrates, fats, proteins, vitamins, minerals and water. Carbohydrates, fats and proteins provide energy, and vitamins and minerals are essential for the METABOLISM that uses this energy. Water, composing 60 percent of our total body weight, provides the medium in which chemical reactions take place.

nutrition The combination of processes by which the body takes in and uses the foods necessary for maintenance, energy, growth and renewal, nutrition includes digestion and METABOLISM.

nutritional counseling Nutritional counseling is frequently recommended in the treatment of eating disorders. As physicians Michele Siegel, Judith Brisman and Margot Weinshel explain in their book *Surviving an Eating Disorder,* "Some people with eating disorders have extremely chaotic eating patterns or have not eaten a 'meal' in years. Nutritionists, who are trained to assess nutritional imbalances and develop dietary programs, can help recovering clients correct nutritional deficits and develop healthy eating habits, perhaps for the first time." The authors say that counseling is most successful after binge eating, purging or starving behaviors have decreased, when food is no longer used as a coping mechanism and eating is a response to physiological, not psychological, hungers.

Sometimes, nutritional counseling is recommended to provide an appropriate diet, but a diet is not always the answer to an eating disorder. Many eating-disordered people are actually experts on diet and nutrition—they know what they should be eating. Eating disturbances are not due to lack of knowledge or information but to the psychological disorders that keep people from using them. Thus nutritional counseling works best, some experts feel, after psychological treatment has progressed.

Beumont, P. J. V. "Diet Guide for Bulimics." *BASH Magazine,* June 1989.
Siegel, Michele, Judith Brisman, and Margot Weinshel. *Surviving an Eating Disorder.* New York: HarperCollins, 1997.

O

obesity Body weight in excess of biological needs; excessive fatness—these describe obesity.

The first federal guidelines on the identification, evaluation, and treatment of overweight and obesity in adults were released on June 17, 1998, by the National Heart, Lung, and Blood Institute (NHLBI), in cooperation with the National Institute of Diabetes and Digestive and Kidney Diseases (NIDDK), both part of the National Institutes of Health (NIH).

These clinical practice guidelines were designed to help physicians in their care of overweight and obesity, a growing public health problem that affects 97 million U.S. adults—55 percent of the population. (See Chapter 5—MEDICAL AND SURGICAL TREATMENT OF OBESITY.)

Booth, D. A. "Holding Weight Down: Physiological and Psychological Considerations." From "A View of Obesity," *Medicographia* 7, no. 3 (1985).

Bray, George A. "Effects of Obesity on Health and Happiness." In *Handbook of Eating Disorders,* edited by Kelly D. Brownell and John Foreyt. New York: Basic Books, 1986.

Brownell, Kelly D., and Thomas A. Wadden. "Behavior Therapy for Obesity: Modern Approaches and Better Results." In *Handbook of Eating Disorders,* edited by Kelly D. Brownell and John P. Foreyt. New York: Basic Books, 1986.

Clinical Guidelines on the Identification of Overweight and Obesity in Adults—The Evidence Report, National Institutes of Health, 1998.

Jeffrey, D. Balfour, Brenda Dawson, and Gregory L. Wilson. "Behavioral and Cognitive-Behavioral Assessment." In *Assessment of Addictive Behaviors,* edited by Dennis Donovan and G. Alan Marlatt. New York: Guilford Press, 1988.

Kornhaber, Arthur, and Elaine Kornhaber. "Psychological Types of Obesity and Their Treatment." In *Childhood Obesity,* edited by Platon J. Collipp. New York: Warner Books, 1986.

Polivy, Jane. "Psychological Consequences of Food Restriction." *Journal of the American Dietetic Association* 96, June 1996.

Stunkard, Albert J. "Obesity: Risk Factors, Consequences and Control." *Medical Journal of Australia* 148 (February 1, 1988).

obesophobic Having a fear of being fat, *obesophobic* is a term used by some clinicians to describe people judged underweight by standard measurements but who still think they are too fat and who are preoccupied with their weight.

See also FEAR OF FAT SYNDROME.

olestra Trade or proprietary name for a no-calorie fat substitute developed by Procter & Gamble in 1989 after nearly 20 years of research, olestra is intended for use in shortenings and oils and in the preparation of certain fried snacks, like potato chips. It tastes, feels and, in cooking, functions like fat but is not in any sense a food and is not found naturally in any food.

Also known as sucrose polyester (SPE), olestra is not absorbed into the bloodstream and therefore, according to Procter & Gamble, should likely produce fewer complications than other food substitutes such as aspartame, a sugar substitute known to cross into the bloodstream. In one study by the company, 10 fat people were fed with up to 60 grams of SPE in their diet for 20 days, so that their caloric intake was reduced by 23 percent and fat intake by 50 percent. On average, the patients lost eight pounds each. Patients on the SPE diet did not crave additional food to make up for their calorie loss. SPE satiates the desire to gorge, as does food made with conventional fats.

Olestra has remained under review by the Food and Drug Administration since 1987. Although Procter & Gamble maintains that olestra is safe for humans, some scientists have questioned it. Rats in some tests have developed tumors and leukemia, among other diseases, according to the Center for Science in the Public Interest, a consumer advocacy group. Nutrition activists say that the nutrient-depleting characteristic of olestra could contribute to serious health problems if people consume small amounts of it throughout the day.

FDA concluded in January 1996 that olestra was safe for use in savory snacks (potato chips, corn chips), but required that fat-soluble vitamins lost through absorption be added back to olestra.

Although Procter & Gamble did pull in $347 million during 1998 by adding olestra to several of its chip products and calling them Wow snacks, the numbers fell far short of its projections. Reasons given: Regulatory approval was so long in coming that the fickle cycle of consumer taste had edged away from low-fat food; because Procter & Gamble had exclusive rights to olestra, other players had not entered the market, with the resultant competition sparking promotion and lower pricing; and numerous complaints arose over stomach upset problems. Eventually, Procter & Gamble hopes to get FDA approval to use olestra in other products, from ice cream to french fries.

See also FAT SUBSTITUTES.

Canedy, Dana. "Low Fat's Lowered Expectations: America's Olestra Craving Was Overestimated." *The New York Times*, July 21, 1999.

Sherrid, Pamela. "It's Crunch Time for P & G's Olestra." *U.S. News & World Report*, May 11, 1999.

Optifast A commercial PROTEIN-SPARING MODIFIED FAST program, intended for use under medical supervision, the Optifast program achieved prominence when television talk-show hostess Oprah Winfrey announced in 1988 that she had lost 67 pounds on the Optifast program. After this announcement, the Optifast company received hundreds of thousands of calls from consumers desperate to lose weight. Sales boomed as people paid $3,000 to $5,000 each to participate in the program. But 18 months later, as reports surfaced about the dangers of VERY LOW CALORIE DIETS, both Oprah and the majority of the Optifast users had regained much of their lost weight (plus added poundage), and the company had cut back on satellite clinics. Today, company promotions focus more on the fact that Optifast is a physician-supervised program and less on the weight loss results.

oral fixation and obesity Some psychoanalytic theorists relate obesity to a developmental fixation during the earliest, or oral, stage of development. Because the first and most central love attachment to develop is that between mother and infant, and because much of the infant's contact with the mother occurs during feeding, the infant naturally associates eating with maternal care. During normal development, the infant's world expands, and the focus on oral needs becomes integrated with other sensory experiences. If, however, either outside events or internal processes affect development negatively during this oral phase, the child may not easily relinquish the need for oral gratification, and that same child may continue in adulthood to relate to food as the primary symbol of emotional care, turning to it whenever there is a need or desire to recapture the security and comfort experienced in infancy.

According to other researchers, this attempt to link a psychiatric disorder or personality type to obesity has not been successful, even though there is some evidence that this theory of oral fixations holds true for some individuals.

oral nutritional supplements Nutrients in liquid form, these supplements are the least invasive way of supplementing an anorexic patient's food intake during hospitalization.

Because a nutritional supplement is considered a medication, its use is charted in a patient's files and the patient is required to drink it in the presence of a nurse. Not considering it food helps avoid conflicts with the patient over eating or not eating.

oral soft tissues Periodontal tissues; gingival tissues; the lining of the mouth, the pharynx and the esophagus; the lips and tongue and the salivary glands—all are areas of the oral cavity that can be affected by anorexia nervosa and bulimia. Tissue health is impaired by dry mouth and the resulting reduction of the saliva's membrane-lubricating effects. As a result of dryness and poor oral hygiene, gingivitis, or inflammation of the gums, is quite common in eating-disordered patients. If untreated, this inflammation spreads into the supporting structures of the teeth, causes bone loss and eventually results in loss of the teeth. Vitamin deficiencies from poor diets have very marked effects on soft tissues, including scurvy, inflammation of the tongue and a burning sensation in the tongue. Salivary gland enlargement is not an uncommon occurrence in patients with eating disorders.

See also DENTAL CARIES; PERIMYLOLYSIS.

osteopenia *Osteopenia* is general term referring to loss of bone, regardless of cause. Bone loss may be due to a number of disorders, the most common of which are osteoporosis, osteomalacia and osteitis fibrosa. There are various causes for these conditions, and treatment and prevention strategies vary accordingly.

Osteoporosis is a condition in which bone mass becomes demineralized, less dense and brittle. It is associated with aging. This is the most common form of osteopenia and has received the most publicity. It accounts for the fragility of the bones in elderly women. A progressive condition, it generally begins at menopause or when there is any loss of hormones. Women are more susceptible to osteoporosis than men for a number of reasons, including their smaller size and lower dietary calcium intake. Other hormones and certain drugs also contribute to the development of osteoporosis.

Osteomalacia is the softening of the bones, characterized by an accumulation of newly created bone mass that has not become mineralized. Hardening of bone mass requires both calcium and phosphorus and will be affected negatively by a deficiency of these minerals or by the presence of certain hormones or drugs. Persons with osteomalacia frequently suffer from generalized bone pain even in the absence of fractures.

Osteitis fibrosa is a condition in which bone degenerates, or is resorbed, very rapidly. It usually results from excessive production of certain substances such as parathyroid hormone or thyroid hormone. In these cases, bone is diminished faster than new bone mass can be formed.

Osteopenia has been recognized as a serious complication of anorexia nervosa within the last 15 years. In 1983, E. R. McAnarney and her colleagues reported a case of pathological rib fracture in a 25-year-old anorexic. Since then there have been at least 10 other reports documenting pathological fractures in anorexics including ribs, vertebrae and hips. In one instance, successful treatment of anorexia nervosa resulted in improvement of the patients' bone density, although she continued to have mild osteopenia.

Reduced bone densities are found in some anorexics, caused by reduced calcium intake and a drop in estrogen levels from self-starvation. Although, in general, a certain level of activity is necessary to promote adequate bone growth, the kind of excessive activity that characterizes some anorexics (such as 1,000 sit-ups a night) may overstress already-weakened bone and lead to fractures.

Insufficient calcium for bone growth may result from a number of factors besides poor dietary intake. Production of high levels of serum cortisol during FASTING may increase the loss of calcium from the body. PURGING practices such as self-induced VOMITING and LAXATIVE ABUSE can also cause unnecessary elimination by the kidney of essential chemicals required in bone formation. Consequently, eating-disordered patients may have reduced bone mass or may predispose themselves to the future development of osteoporosis through their restrictive dietary practices and purging behaviors.

One study of anorexic women who had been given either calcium or estrogen and who had gained weight showed that bone loss was halted but not reversed. Physical exercise and calcium and estrogen treatments did not affect bone restoration. From this, it was concluded that a period of severe weight loss in young women may be a risk factor for premature osteoporosis.

The few reports on recovery have been conflicting: some studies suggest restoration of normal bone mass with recovery from anorexia nervosa; others suggest that the improvement may only be partial.

Brotman, A. W., and T. A. Stern. "Osteoporosis and Pathological Fractures in Anorexia Nervosa." *American Journal of Psychiatry* 142 (1985).

Grinspoon, S., et al. "Mechanisms and Treatment Options for Bone Loss in Anorexia Nervosa." *Psychopharmacology Bulletin* 33 (1997).

Kaplan, F. S, M. Pertschuk, M. D. Fallon, and J. G. Haddad. "Osteoporosis and Hip Fracture in a Young Woman with Anorexia Nervosa." *Clinical Orthopaedics and Related Research* 212 (1986).

McAnarney, E. R., D. E. Greydanus, V. A. Campanella, and R. A. Hoekelman. "Rib Fractures and Anorexia Nervosa." *Journal of Adolescent Health Care* 4 (1983).

Rigotti, N. A., S. R. Nussbaum, D. B. Herzog, and R. M. Neer. "Osteoporosis in Women with Anorexia Nervosa." *New England Journal of Medicine* 311 (1984).

Ward, A., et al. "Persistent Osteopenia After Recovery from Anorexia Nervosa." *International Journal of Eating Disorders* 22, July 1997.

Overeaters Anonymous (OA) OA is a nonprofit self-help group formed in 1960 that follows many of the principles of Alcoholics Anonymous; membership is based on freewill donations. OA promotes the belief that "compulsive eating is a progressive illness that can't be cured but can be arrested." Like Alcoholics Anonymous, this group has a 12-step recovery program, based on acceptance of the premise that an overeater is powerless over food and that only a power greater than oneself can restore one to sanity.

P

pagophagia The craving to eat ice is termed *pagophagia.*

pathophysiology The study of abnormal function as related to body structure is termed *pathophysiology.*

The late physiologist William Sheldon speculated that a genetic trait common to the overweight is a long intestinal tract. He estimated that in long, thin body types, ECTOMORPHS, the length is about 20 feet; thus food reaches the colon in a matter of hours, before many calories can be absorbed. Heavy ENDOMORPHS, however, might have up to 40 feet of intestine, which gives them additional absorptive surface and more time to absorb and store every bit of fat and sugar. Sheldon believed that MESOMORPHS have about 30 feet of bowel and tend to be neither fat nor thin. Sheldon's theories are not considered valid, although the terms associated with them frequently appear in books and articles.

perfectionism Extreme or obsessive striving for perfection, perfectionism is a trait often exhibited by young people with eating disorders. One definition of perfectionistic thinking is that it involves the setting of unrealistic standards, rigid and indiscriminate adherence to these standards and the equating of self-worth and performance. Others go a step further and argue for a distinction between "normal" perfectionism, a useful characteristic, and neurotic perfectionism, a dysfunctional or self-defeating one. The latter is characteristic of those who are predisposed toward developing an eating disorder, according to Peter Slade, reader in clinical psychology at the New Medical School, University of Liverpool, England.

For perfectionists, eating disorders are another side of the "all-or-nothing" mind set. The more they focus on being perfect, the more aware they become of their faults. Feelings of worthlessness set in. Especially if they think they are being dominated in other areas of their life—family, school, work—they may decide to take charge of at least one area: eating. Controlling and monitoring their food intake is something within their power. Other areas of perfectionistic tendencies have also been documented. In one study of 20 anorexics, school achievement was found to be significantly greater than would be predicted by standard tests. Many women with eating disorders also admit to feeling pressured to be "the perfect person." Often they share low SELF-ESTEEM and a deep fear of making mistakes.

See also DICHOTOMOUS THINKING.

perimylolysis Perymylolysis is a loss of enamel and dentin from the surfaces of the teeth as a result of repeated contact with regurgitated gastric acids, rubbed in by movements of the tongue. Destruction can range from slight (smooth and polished surface of the teeth) to extremely severe (the complete dissolution of tooth structure through to the nerve). In more severe cases, all surfaces of the teeth are affected by acid erosion. This decay can be caused by a number of factors, but once other problems are ruled out, the patient can be assumed to have an eating disorder.

Perimylolysis is generally seen in the bulimic or bulimic/anorexic patient and not in the patient exhibiting restrictive anorexia alone because the latter does not usually vomit to purge. The chronic vomiting characteristic of bulimics (sometimes five to 10 or more times daily) brings gastric acids into the oral cavity; these acids dissolve tooth structure. Enamel will not usually erode until repeated regurgitation has occurred for two years. The surfaces most commonly affected are the lingual, or tongue-side parts of the upper teeth. The other teeth are protected by the position of the tongue, the lips and the cheeks. It has been suggested that acidic gastric juices accumulate among the papillae of the tongue and that tongue movement continually deposits the acid on the lingual surfaces of the teeth.

See also DENTAL CARIES; ORAL SOFT TISSUES.

personality disorder According to the DSM-IV, personality disorders are enduring patterns of inner experience and behaviors that deviate markedly from the expectations of the individual's culture, are pervasive and inflexible, have an onset in adolescence or early childhood, are stable over time and lead to distress or impairment. Research has found personality disorder to be a possible risk factor for bulimia.

pharmacotherapy The use of drugs in the treatment of psychological disorders, pharmacotherapy, an outgrowth of research in the neurobiological sciences, has made great inroads in the treatment of psychological disorders and psychiatric illness. By studying medications used in the treatment of depression, researchers have found clues to the potential role of drugs in the treatment of eating disorders.

Pharmacologic treatment of anorexia is problematic. There is some concern about the use of tricyclic antidepressants, which have anticholinergic side effects, in patients already at risk of arrhythmia. A variety of medications have proven effective, including fluoxetine; however, the preferred medication to use in the treatment of anorexia is unclear.

More studies have been done on medication treatments for bulimics; ANTIDEPRESSANTS, anticonvulsants (see ANTICONVULSANT TREATMENT) and others have been tested. Studies have shown that antidepressants do cause short-term improvements of bulimic behaviors. Even bulimic patients without symptoms of depression show improvement on antidepressants.

Although research demonstrates the effectiveness of serotonergic agents in the treatment of bulimia, high doses must be used to reliably obtain the desired result. The effects of such medications as PROZAC appear to be independent of their effect on depression. However, Goldbloom and colleagues recently found that the combination of pharmacotherapy (Prozac) and psychotherapy was superior to pharmacotherapy alone but not superior to psychotherapy alone.

In two studies published during 1999, drug therapy had significant impact on severe binge eaters. The University of Florida reported that patients who used the anticonvulsant topiramate decreased their incidence of binge-eating episodes for as long as two years (the length of the study). One-third of the patients ended uncontrolled consumption completely. In an Albany Medical College, New York, study, severe binge eaters improved their eating pattern, depression scores, and achieved weight loss similar to non-binge eaters after 24 weeks of pharmacologic treatment (phentermine resin and dl-fenfluramine).

Goldbloom, D. S., M. Olmsted, R. Davis, J. Clewes, M. Heinmaa, W. Rockert, and B. Shaw. "A Randomized Controlled Trial of Fluoxetine and Cognitive Behavioral Therapy for Bulimia Nervosa: Short-term Outcome." *Behavior Research & Therapy* 35, (1997).

Goldstein, D. J., M. C. Wilson, R. C. Ascroft, and M. Al-Banna. "Effectiveness of Fluoxetine Therapy in Bulimia Nervosa Regardless of Comorbid Depression." *International Journal of Eating Disorders* 25 (1999).

Sobel, Stephen V. "What's New in the Treatment of Anorexia and Bulimia?" *Medscape Women's Health* (September 1996).

Phen-Pro Phen-Pro is a combination of the diet drug phentermine and Prozac. Phentermine has been used as a diet drug since 1959, but only recently has it been coupled with Prozac. The combination works by stimulating noradrenaline and serotonin, which makes the body feel full. In a Georgetown University study, 28 percent of patients taking Phen-Pro reached their ideal body weight, 50 percent lost a lot of weight but then plateaued, and 1 percent gained weight. Possible side effects include sleep disturbance, agitation, dry mouth and constipation—typical side effects of some antidepressants. Experts also say it may take several weeks to start working. Prozac's maker, Eli Lilly & Co., said in 1998 that it did not support combining Prozac with phentermine, but obesity experts say some doctors are prescribing the combination.

phenylpropanolamine (PPA) An AMPHETAMINE-like agent available without prescription and approved for sale as an APPETITE SUPPRESSANT, PPA is used in over-the-counter diet products such as Dietac and Dexatrim. PPA is also the decongestant in such cold remedies as Contac, Robitussin CF and Vicks Formula 44D. It is potentially harmful for those with high blood pressure.

PPA works by stimulating a type of adrenaline receptor to fool the body into thinking it's full. According to the FDA, even the best studies show only about a half-pound greater weight loss per week using PPA combined with diet and exercise.

physical activity and obesity Cardiologist James Rippe, considered the father of the walking movement in the United States, says the United States is facing two major lifestyle-related epidemics that are intricately linked: an epidemic of obesity and an epidemic of inactivity. Among his points: "Multiple interactions exist between lack of physical activity and obesity. Increased physical activity lowers the risk of obesity, may favorably influence distribution of body weight, and confers a variety of health-related benefits even in the absence of weight loss. Physical activity is important for achieving proper energy balance, which is needed to prevent or reverse obesity. Not only is energy expended during physical activity, physical activity also has a positive effect on resting metabolic rate. Regular physical activity can improve body composition. Properly designed programs of physical activity may preserve or even increase lean muscle mass during weight loss. Physical activity has also been strongly associated with maintenance of weight loss. Physical activity that expends 1,500 to 2,000 kcal a week appears necessary to maintain weight loss. Numerous studies have shown that the combination of proper nutrition and regular physical activity is the most effective intervention for weight loss and maintenance of weight loss. Walking is the most convenient and logical way most obese persons can increase their physical activity."

Rippe, James M., and S. Hess. "The Role of Physical Activity in the Prevention and Management of Obesity." *Journal of the American Dietetic Association* 98 no. 10, suppl 2 (October 1998).

physiological arousal Physical response to stimuli, for instance, the development of a feeling of hunger in response to the sight of food, is termed *physiological arousal.*

Although several studies have suggested that physiological arousal is an important factor in overeating by obese persons, a 1988 University of Southern Colorado study found no differences in arousal between weight groups. They examined differences in arousal between obese and normal-weight persons while exposed to food stimuli during eating and during exposure to visual imagery of both food and nonfood stimuli. Although the presentation and eating of pizza did produce significant changes in arousal, there was no differential arousal between the obese and normal-weight persons.

pica Pica is the ingestion of strange or repulsive substances not normally considered suitable for food. The phenomenon occurs throughout the world and has been recorded for centuries. The most common explanation is that those who evidence pica are seeking trace minerals or inorganic minerals missing from their diet and desperately needed by their bodies. However, there is a lack of evidence for this explanation. Pica is seen most often in young children, in children and adults with mental retardation or in persons with severe psychiatric disorders.

pimozide Pimozide is an antipsychotic medication. In a Dutch study, anorexia nervosa patients treated with pimozide gained weight faster than another group that was administered PLACEBO, but overall the difference from placebo was not statistically significant. There was also no significant difference in the pimozide patients' attitudes.

pituitary obesity The pituitary gland influences most body functions and is particularly important in growth, sexual maturity and reproduction. It does this through the release of hormones (thyroid, adrenals and gonads). Pituitary obesity may result from a disorder of the pituitary, including the loss of more than one of these pituitary hormones.

The major cause of pituitary obesity is CUSHING'S DISEASE, caused by an excess of ACTH (which stimulates the adrenal glands to secrete hormones, with multiple effects on metabolism); it is also associated with hypothyroidism. Pituitary obesity is slow to develop, is of a generalized type and can be diagnosed by a dryness of the skin, shortened growth of the eyebrows and diminished function of the reflexes. Other characteristics that suggest a pituitary disorder include pallor, a generalized obesity and, in both sexes, lack of fully developed sexual characteristics. In men with this disorder, there is a tendency for the adipose tissue to concentrate in the pelvic region. Secretion of the growth hormone becomes sluggish in the obese, compared with people of normal weight. Yet it returns to normal with weight reduction, indicating that this is the result rather than the cause of the obesity. When pituitary obesity is treated by correcting the basic disorder, it is possible for the patient to lose weight by restricting calories.

placebo A Harmless inactive substance (or ineffective procedure), a placebo is given to a CONTROL GROUP in a study as if it were an effective treatment, used as a comparison for the substance or procedure being tested. A placebo substance is made to look and taste identical to the active preparation; subjects are not told which they are taking.

polyphagia Excessive craving for all types of food, polyphagia is a very great HUNGER.

ponderosity Ponderosity is body weight relative to height. Individual differences in ponderosity are important determinants of health status. In a family study by Trudy L. Burns, P. P. Moll and R. M. Lauer reported in *American Journal of Epidemiology* (May 1989), the researchers determined that if the specific environmental exposure associated with differences in ponderosity could be identified, strategies could be devised to prevent the development of excess ponderosity in high-risk children and to reduce the risk of development of chronic diseases associated with obesity in adulthood.

post-traumatic effect This is a specific form of ANXIETY that appears following a stressful or frightening event. There have been numerous cases recorded of anorexia nervosa and bulimia apparently precipitated by physical trauma such as surgery, automobile accident, rape or sexual abuse. Trauma resulting in either temporary or permanent body disfigurement may in turn bring on or make worse DEPRESSION, BODY IMAGE DISTURBANCE and family or social stresses and may possibly affect hypothalamic function, thereby contributing to the onset of eating disorders.

See also STRESS AND EATING DISORDERS.

Prader-Willi syndrome Prader-Willi syndrome is a birth defect whose victims are always hungry and do not know how to stop gorging. About one child in 10,000 to 15,000 is born with this incurable syndrome, identified in 1956 by Swiss doctors. Characteristics include short stature, unusually small hands and feet, hyperphasia (excessive talkativeness), hypo gonadism (retarded sexual development) and some degree of learning disability or mental retardation. Unless people with this syndrome are strictly supervised, their compulsion to gorge (hyperphagia) can cause them to swell to two or three times their ideal weight. That can lead to heart or respiratory problems and early death. Specialists have noted that hyperphagia is first manifested between ages one and six, and that while victims do reach SATIETY, it is only after consuming three times more calories than controls. Their hunger also returns more quickly. Many patients develop diabetes during adult life.

pregnancy and eating disorders In a study of 66 women who had a history of anorexia nervosa and 98 randomly selected community controls, neither group differed on rate of pregnancy, mean number of pregnancies per woman or age at first pregnancy. But the women with anorexia nervosa had significantly more miscarriages and cesarean deliveries, and their offspring were significantly more likely to be born prematurely and were of lower birth weight than offspring of controls. There were no differences between women with active versus remitted anorexia nervosa on any of these measures; however, offspring of anorexic women with no history of bulimia nervosa had significantly lower body weight than offspring of anorexic women with a lifetime history of bulimia nervosa.

In another study of women with current or past anorexia and/or bulimia nervosa, children of women with eating disorders also had significantly lower birth weights and lengths than control children. There were no differences observed in childhood temperament or mothers' satisfaction with children's appearance. But mothers with eating disorders did have more difficulty maintaining breast-feeding and they made significantly fewer positive comments about food and eating than control mothers during mealtime observations.

Yet, a 1998 Australian study of 88 women delivering low-birth-weight infants determined that women with a past history of an eating disorder had no greater risk of delivering a low-birth-weight infant. Women delivering small-for-gestational-age infants did report elevated eating-disorder psychopathology after delivery and more eating disturbances before and during pregnancy.

Benton-Hardy and Lock suggested that pregnancy could be a possible contributor to the development of anorexia in a predisposed person. They wrote that "although (the subject, a 17-year-old girl) has other factors associated with the development of anorexia, the psychological and physical changes of pregnancy appear to be the crucial changes which precipitated anorexia nervosa."

In a study of 48 women 10 or more years following initial treatment for bulimia nervosa, short-term episodes of bulimic-free behavior were associated with pregnancy and breast feeding on some pregnancies. The prevalence of miscarriage and postnatal depression was greater among women who had not recovered from their eating disorder at the time of their pregnancy.

Abraham, S. "Sexuality and Reproduction in Bulimia Nervosa Patients Over 10 Years." *Journal of Psychosomatic Research* 44 (March–April 1998).

Benton-Hardy, L. R., and J. Lock. "Pregnancy and Early Parenthood: Factors in the Development of Anorexia Nervosa?" *International Journal of Eating Disorders* 24 (September 1998).

Bulik, C.M., et al. "Fertility and Reproduction in Women With Anorexia: A Controlled Study." *Journal of Clinical Psychiatry* 60 (February 1999).

Conti, J., S. Abraham, and A. Taylor. "Eating Behavior and Pregnancy Outcome." *Journal for Psychosomatic Research* 44 (March–April 1998).

Waugh, E., and C. M. Bulik. "Offspring of Women With Eating Disorders." *International Journal of Eating Disorders* 25 (March 1999).

pregnancy and obesity In her studies, HILDE BRUCH found that obesity that develops during or after pregnancy often develops in response to stress. Some women gain weight after each pregnancy, some only after one. Bruch's studies determined that the most frequent causes of stress underlying obesity following pregnancy are disappointment with the marriage, unfulfilled, unrealistic expectations about what the child might do for the mother or frank envy of the care the child receives and resentment about the demands it makes.

Though noting that "much has been written about obesity indicating a desire for pregnancy," Bruch argued against this theory. Although she agreed that some fat women have pregnancy fantasies, she cautioned that those who are not fat do also.

"Occasionally," Bruch added, "a father may become fat after the birth of a child: this occurs in extremely dependent men who, even before the baby is born, feel that they never received quite enough [attention]. They will resort to overeating to combat their anger and jealousy and to compensate themselves for what they feel they are missing."

Physical Effects. Bray wrote that body weight before pregnancy and weight gain during it both affect pregnancy. He cited a study of 3,939 women who delivered babies between 1963 and 1965, in which the "heavy" women (averaging 169 pounds) had significantly higher frequency of toxemia and hypertension and longer duration of labor than "light" women. Because cesarean section was performed on 5.5 percent of the heavy patients but only on 0.7 percent of the light, more obstetrical complications occurred in the heavy group.

Diets to control weight during pregnancy must account for the increased need for protein, iron, folic acid and most other minerals and vitamins. For this reason, during pregnancy weight is best controlled through small decreases in calorie intake, with increased energy expenditure through exercise. VERY LOW CALORIE DIETS are to be avoided during pregnancy unless specifically prescribed by a physician.

Until recently, few studies had been done on pregnancy weight gain and its effect on maternal health. Physiological psychologist Jennifer Lovejoy has been researching the disparity between women's chance of gaining weight and men's (women's is about double) and believes that pregnancy may be a factor. Studies show that the average woman retains two to five pounds after nine months of carrying a baby, far above the normal pace related to aging. Many women end up 20 pounds or more heavier long after childbirth.

Bray, George A. "Effects of Obesity on Health and Happiness." In *Handbook of Eating Disorders*, edited by Kelly D. Brownell and John P. Foreyt. New York: Basic Books, 1986.

Bruch, Hilde. *Eating Disorders: Obesity, Anorexia Nervosa, and the Person Within*. New York: Basic Books, 1973.

Lovejoy, Jennifer C. "The Influence of Sex Hormones on Obesity Across the Female Life Span." *Journal of Women's Health* 7 (December 1998).

Roan, Shari. "A Weighty Problem." *Los Angeles Times*, September 14, 1998.

preloading During experimentation and research testing, the before-regular-meals eating by individuals on restricted diets of some food or quantity of food normally forbidden them—this describes preloading. In tests, subjects ate more after they had preloaded with more food (e.g., two milk shakes) than those who had preloaded with less (e.g., one milk shake). Once their normal restraints on eating were overcome, they ate as if their controls were no longer functioning. Research concluded that people who are on diets, regardless of how much they weigh, are inclined to overeat once they have eaten something they believe contains a large number of calories. Their belief that control has been lost appears to be the decisive factor in this situation, rather than the actual number of calories consumed.

protein-sparing modified fast (PSMF) A diet regimen designed to be safer than formula diets and to produce loss primarily of fat tissue rather than lean body tissue by adding PROTEINS and electrolytes to the FASTING regimen, the PSMF's developers' intent was to minimize or eliminate many of the adverse health consequences of the earlier LIQUID FORMULAS.

The PSMF is recommended for the moderately obese (see OBESITY) when undertaken under close medical supervision. It is not recommended for the mildly obese because the risk from the treatment outweighs the risk from mild obesity; nor is it for the morbidly obese because they are more safely and effectively treated with surgical procedures; nor is it for children and adolescents because there is some loss of lean body mass, which may interfere with growth.

proteins One of the three major types of nutrients (see CARBOHYDRATES and FATS) found in food, proteins constitute about 20 percent of the body's cell mass. They are necessary for the building and repair of all kinds of body tissues, especially of muscles and organs such as the heart, the liver and the kidneys. Skin, hair, ligaments, tendons, muscle and nails are composed of protein. Major sources of protein are animal products such as meat, eggs, fish and milk.

Digestion breaks down protein into its component elements, amino acids, which pass into the blood, some to be used as structural proteins for the building of body tissues, others to be used as enzymes and the rest to be carried to various parts of the body as a reserve. Because they are drawn on directly as a source of energy, there is no noticeable weight gain when high-protein foods are eaten in reasonable amounts. Proteins provide about four CALORIES per gram.

Protein deficiency manifests itself in weakness, poor resistance to disease and swelling of body tissues due to accumulation of fluid in the tissue spaces. When eaten in large amounts, protein-rich foods can cause constipation, kidney dysfunction and heart failure.

Prozac Proprietary name for fluoxetine, Prozac is a long-lasting ANTIDEPRESSANT drug that acts by selectively and effectively blocking the reuptake (reabsorption) of the neurotransmitter SEROTONIN into nerve terminals in the brain. It was introduced in the United States early in 1988 and within a year became one of the most widely prescribed antidepressants in the country.

Experiments on more than 1,000 patients showed that fluoxetine works at least as quickly and effectively as IMIPRAMINE and other tricyclic antidepressants. The main side effects, according to researchers, are nausea and vomiting, insomnia and nervousness. It is less likely than other antidepressants to cause constipation, dry mouth, drowsiness, sexual difficulties or urinary problems. Obese patients given fluoxetine at fairly high doses lost 8 to 10 pounds in two months without dieting, even when the drug caused no nausea or upset stomach.

In more recent years, fluoxetine has also proved effective in the treatment of bulimia. In a University of Illinois at Chicago study of 15 patients suffering from DEPRESSION accompanied by BULIMIA, binge/purge episodes dropped dramatically (93 percent) within the first four weeks on Prozac, compared with a 42 percent drop in a CONTROL GROUP on a placebo. After four weeks of treatment, the fluoxetine group lost an average of four pounds, while the placebo group lost between one and one-and-a-half pounds. Patients reported that CARBOHYDRATE craving diminished considerably. Those who lost the most weight were overweight bulimics. The one subject who was at normal weight lost very little. Fluoxetine helps considerably in controlling bulimic behavior, affecting carbohydrate METABOLISM, decreasing APPETITE and reducing weight.

psychodrama A form of GROUP THERAPY in which patients act out their responses to difficult or conflicted situations from their daily lives, Psychodrama was developed by a psychiatrist, J. L. Moreno (1890–1974) during the 1930s to liberate the "spontaneous" self from the constrictions of Victorian social morality. Today, psychodrama offers adolescents and adults whose "real self" is hiding from hurtful or shameful traumas of the past to reenact these scenes that have led to the disordered behavior of the present. It's a nonconfrontational format intended to make it possible for patients to gain insight into their own conflicted or self-defeating behavior. Psychodrama has been used as treatment for eating disorders.

Veronica O. Bowlan, psychodrama consultant at the Renfrew Center in Philadelphia, explains that psychodrama is not merely role-playing and not acting class:

> In psychodrama, a patient gets a chance to deal with people and events in her past, present, or future. She gets a chance to begin to resolve unsettled or hidden feelings and often learns new ways of handling conflicts in real situations.

> Psychodrama . . . [uses] action rather than talking to help patients deal with difficult feelings. The patient creates and actually steps into a situation to confront the problem and her feelings about it. It is difficult, but it is also very real and powerful . . . [she] demonstrates to each player how the character should behave. She does this throughout the whole drama. This is called role reversal. Reversing roles gives her a chance to see the situation from other perspectives and discover new solutions or ways of interacting.

Baaklini, George. "Psychodrama: A Timely Therapeutic Procedure." *Renfrew Perspective* (fall 1992).

Hudgins, Kate. "Using Psychodrama as a Therapeutic Tool." *Addiction Letter* (October 1990).

psychodynamic approach to obesity The psychodynamic approach to obesity constitutes an understanding of obesity on the belief that overweight people eat in response to stress-engendered emotional states, especially ANXIETY and DEPRESSION, rather than simply to internal HUNGER cues. The stress is due to conditions such as marital or work problems, mother-daughter conflict and PERSONALITY DISORDERS.

The eating response recurs because it works: it relieves emotional distress. Psychodynamic theorists discuss overeating as a means of diminishing anxiety, achieving pleasure, relieving frustration and emotional deprivation, expressing hostility (conscious or unconscious) and so forth (see ORAL FIXATION AND OBESITY).

Opponents of this theory believe that these stress factors are consequences rather than causes of obesity, due largely to diminished SELF-ESTEEM from the discrimination obese people experience today.

psychogenic malnutrition Psychogenic malnutrition is weight loss from psychological causes; the noneating associated with it is incidental. The term covers a wide range of psychiatric disorders including chronic schizophrenia, acute catatonic schizophrenia, mental retardation and schizophrenic disorganization and forms of DEPRESSION. Cases of this type have sometimes been included in anorexia nervosa literature but do not qualify as a true anorexia eating disorder.

psychogenic vomiting Vomiting due to some emotional or psychological reason, but not due to an eating disorder is considered psychogenic; that is, the person is not vomiting because of weight gain but rather due to nausea from some psychological/emotional origin.

psychosomatic medicine A field of medicine begun in the 1930s, Joan Brumberg describes psychosomatic medicine as "the scientific study of emotion and the bodily changes that accompany different emotional states." She continues:

> Psychosomatic medicine involved practitioners from many different specialty areas, not just psychiatry. Followers of the psychosomatic movement shared a common interest in a more integrated approach to etiology and therapy. Body (soma) and mind (psyche) were considered as one.

Brumberg added that anorexia nervosa was particularly suited to psychosomatic research because of "the manner in which bodily changes accompanied neurotic mechanisms," but the attempt to explain it with a simple, single formula was ultimately doomed because of the complexity of the disorder. After World War II, HILDE BRUCH led the way to a broader and more complex view of the significance of food behavior and its relation to individuals' lives.

Brumberg, Joan Jacobs. *Fasting Girls.* New York: Plume Books, 1989.

psychotherapy Psychotherapy is the treatment of mental and emotional disorders by any of various means involving communication between trained therapists and patients, including counseling, psychoanalysis and other types of therapy. Through psychotherapy, patients are helped to understand why they have followed certain behavior patterns and to change those patterns. Psychotherapy aims to help individual suffering from eating disorders achieve a more competent, less painful way of handling their problems. It may involve patients singly or in COUPLES THERAPY, FAMILY THERAPY or GROUP THERAPY.

Individual psychotherapy is generally recommended for all eating-disorder patients and usually forms the foundation for all other treatment. Initially, individuals begin to accept their eating disorders as attempts to solve psychological dilemmas, and they explore attitudes about weight, food and body image. As a feeling of trust is established through the therapists' acknowledgment of the patients' pain, the patients begin to recognize the multiple origins and influences of disorder (social, psychopathologic, genetic, biological, behavioral and familial). Through psychotherapy, individuals can explore concerns, test new behaviors and receive constructive and nonjudgmental commentary. It provides an opportunity for them to develop self-confidence, self-esteem and feelings of power and control. Therapy also helps conquer DEPRESSION, guilt, ANXIETY and STRESS, alleviating the need to turn to, or away from, food to deal with problems. Effective psychotherapy avoids simplistic explanations and solutions. Some anorexics and bulimics will terminate psychotherapy prematurely, unable to relinquish their own control or to see it as a problem.

After researchers concluded that traditional insight-directed psychotherapeutic approaches aimed at personality reorganization had failed to deliver a permanent resolution of the eating-disorders dilemma, others advocated a cognitive-behavioral approach, in which misstatements and misconceptions are challenged in a systematic way. This technique is useful, though it has not proven the most effective approach.

In 1996, Sobel wrote that when treating eating disorders, psychotherapy primarily addresses issues of chaotic eating, hunger, inadequate caloric intake, conditioned response, and profound fear of expressing impulses and feelings, especially those of anger and sadness.

Andersen, Arnold E. "Inpatient and Outpatient Treatment of Anorexia Nervosa." In *Handbook of Eating Disorders,* edited by Kelly D. Brownell and John P. Foreyt. New York: Basic Books, 1986.

Freeman, Barry, and Henderson Dunkeld-Turnbull. "Controlled Trial of Psychotherapy for Bulimia Nervosa." *British Medical Journal* 20 (February 1988).

Siegel, Michele, Judith Brisman, and Margot Weinshel. *Surviving an Eating Disorder.* New York: HarperCollins, 1997.

Sobel, Stephen V. "What's New in the Treatment of Anorexia Nervosa and Bulimia?" *Medscape Women's Health* 1, no. 9 (September 1996).

psychotropic drugs Psychotropic drugs affect psychic (mind) functioning and/or experience and are used sometimes in the treatment of bulimics. These include the phenothiazine derivative tranquilizers (Compazine, Phenergan, Stelazine, Temeral, Thorazine), tricyclic ANTIDEPRESSANTS (Prozac, Zoloft, Elavil, Nardil, Tofranil, Triavil) and other hallucinogenic, sedative, tranquilizing and antipsychotic drugs. Illegal drugs (marijuana, LSD, cocaine, morphine and its derivatives) are all psychotropic drugs.

The use of psychotropic medication is not the primary approach for treating eating disorders because such medication usually accounts for only a temporary reduction in symptoms and thus is generally considered an addition to intensive psychotherapy.

One exception is the case of women who have, one way or another, dealt with issues likely to have been among the most significant causes of their eating disorders but who are unable to control their symptoms. With a medication-related decrease in symptoms, they may be able to gain more from PSYCHOTHERAPY and eventually be able to control the symptoms without medication.

Occasionally, overwhelming reactions to thoughts, feelings or memories long suppressed and replaced in consciousness by symptoms of an eating disorder require the short-term use of medication. Psychotropic medications are also indicated when patients are sufficiently depressed, anxious or thought disordered that they cannot respond to other treatment techniques or when their eating-disorder symptoms remain completely out of control.

puberty The stage of physical development when secondary sex characteristics develop and sexual reproduction becomes possible, puberty usually occurs between the ages of 10 and 12 in girls and between 12 and 14 in boys. However, the onset of puberty has been shown to be more closely related to weight and percentage of BODY FAT than to chronological age. In the United States, the mean weight of girls at menarche (first menstrual cycle) is 105 pounds (and about 22 percent BODY FAT), according to studies. Delayed menarche often occurs with dieting, exercise and extreme thinness and can be as late as age 19 or 20 for athletes and ballet dancers.

Recent research by Sarah Liebowitz at the Rockefeller University in New York has suggested that hormones kicking in at the onset of puberty may be responsible for the craving of high-fat foods that children of that age seem to have. The theory is that the hormones trigger production of a chemical called galanin that stimulates intake of fatty snack foods—which, in a vicious cycle, increases production of even more galanin.

"High Body Fat Brings Early Puberty." *Obesity and Health* (October 1990).

purging A term used to cover the forced expulsion of ingested foods by bulimics, purging has been called a purification rite for bulimics, a means of overcoming self-loathing by gaining self-control. Having regained their self-discipline, they once again feel like "good" persons who are fresh and clean.

Forced VOMITING is the most common method of purging. Other methods of purging unwanted calories are LAXATIVE ABUSE, DIURETIC ABUSE, emetic abuse, FASTING, enemas and excessive exercising (see EXERCISE).

R

religion and eating disorders Because there had been no consensus among researchers on the etiology of the anorexia syndrome, a 1987 Loyola University of Chicago study attempted to examine critically the background from which anorexia develops. Because medical literature places great emphasis on family environmental factors in the development of anorexia, a primary focus of this study was on rituals in the family, particularly of a religious nature.

Conclusions reached were that religion functioned as a reinforcer in developing a personality profile that reflected poor SELF-ESTEEM and that religion was found to be associated with the instillation of guilt feelings. Fear of offending God inhibited the subjects from doing things in their own best interest. It was also found that even though all respondents had left their childhood religions, those who adopted new religions committed themselves to more formalized, structured and controlling belief systems. Consistently, God was portrayed as a controller, a protector and a judge.

Lavallee, Patricia Anne. "Religiosity, Rituals and Patterns in Anorexic and Bulimic Families." Ph. D. diss., Loyola University of Chicago, 1987.

Renfrew Centers The country's first residential facility exclusively devoted to the treatment of women with eating disorders, Renfrew Centers were founded by Samuel E. Menaged, an attorney, and Allen R. Davis, administrator of a private psychiatric clinic. They bought the Renfrew farm in 1984 and secured a license making it a community residential rehabilitation service. The center received $2.9 million in funding from banking and private sources. In June 1985, when the Philadelphia program opened, its philosophy of respect for and empowerment of women and its location in a serene 27-acre environment contrasted sharply with hospital-based, coercive programs offered in psychiatric units or drug and alcohol facilities. In 1990, Renfrew opened a second residential facility in Coconut Creek, South Florida. The Renfrew Center now also has facilities in New York City, northern New Jersey and Long Island. The centers treat patients on both outpatient and residence bases. The largest treatment outcome study ever published on residential treatment for bulimia was conducted at the Renfrew Center.

Gleaves, D. H., G. K. Post, K. P. Eberenz, and W. N. Davis. "A Report of 497 Women Hospitalized for Treatment of Bulimia Nervosa." *Eating Disorders: The Journal of Treatment and Prevention* 1 (1993).

Restraint Scale A test administered by clinicians in the form of a questionnaire, the results of which are used to measure "restrained eating" or chronic dieting, the Restraint Scale was composed originally in 1980 by Janet Polivy and Peter Herman in the attempt to assess the tendency toward COMPULSIVE EATING in chronically dieting college coeds. However, the scope of the testing soon expanded beyond eating behavior itself to encompass attitudes and other indices of chronic dieting. By analyzing results, clinicians are able to assess attitudes and evaluate the resulting behaviors and the fluctuations in weight accompanying them.

Restrained eaters have been shown to differ from unrestrained eaters in a number of respects, displaying greater emotionality, distractibility and salivary responsiveness as well as different eating patterns. In addition, restrained eaters seem to be more likely to be or become bulimic, and patients with anorexia nervosa score significantly above average on the Restraint Scale, particularly if they are also bulimic. A high score on the Restraint Scale may thus indicate a susceptibility or tendency to bulimia, although it is by no means a certain indicator.

Stunkard, A. J., and S. Messick. "The Three-Factor Eating Questionnaire to Measure Dietary Restraint and Hunger." *Journal of Psychosomatic Research* 29 (1985).

restrictor anorexics So-called pure anoretics who restrict their intake of food rather than binge eat or purge, restrictor anorexics, in the nomenclature of the DSM, are termed *anorexia nervosa, restricting type.* (See ANOREXIA NERVOSA.)

rumination Rumination is the voluntary regurgitation of partially digested food into the mouth, where it is subsequently rechewed and reswallowed. The human syndrome is named after a normal digestive process carried out by ruminant animals, such as cattle, sheep and goats, which results in improved digestibility of ingested material. One of the less commonly recognized of the eating disorders, it occurs much more frequently in young infants and mentally retarded children and adults than it does in adults of normal intelligence. However, rumination does plague a number of bulimics. It is often unrecognized by victims or professionals and is often diagnosed as a "digestive problem," secondary to bulimic behaviors.

Rumination in infants typically develops between three and six months of age, although cases developing as late as 12 months have been reported. It is believed to be a psychosomatic illness resulting from a poor mother-infant relationship. Mothers of ruminating infants are often characterized as having difficulty in enjoying their babies and in sensing what gives the baby satisfaction, resulting in the infant's turning to self-stimulating behavior. The appearance of infants during rumination has been described as "withdrawn and self-absorbed," as though they were deriving gratification from the process.

Because rumination can lead to growth failure, weight loss to the point of emaciation, electrolyte imbalances and dehydration, it is considered a serious medical condition. Because of the electrolyte imbalance, ruminating children can die early in life from cardiac and other complications. The condition is often overlooked initially as the primary cause of weight loss because rumination usually occurs when infants are left alone and the behavior is not observed. Once established, it is difficult to interrupt. Treatments attempted with minor success have included behavioral, medical and surgical. The most effective treatment has been shown to be increased social stimulation and reestablishment of a positive interaction between the mother and infant.

Rumination in mentally normal adults is increasingly being recognized as a distinct clinical syndrome. There appear to be two types of adults ruminators: those in whom the behavior develops during childhood and apparently persists without severe negative consequences and those in whom rumination is associated with bulimia nervosa.

In one study of patients with bulimia nervosa, a small but significant proportion were found to ruminate. Because this behavior is often performed in secret, diagnosis, especially in bulimics, can be very difficult and is frequently missed.

Comparisons of ruminating bulimics with nonruminating bulimics have found a higher incidence of history of anorexia nervosa and previous psychiatric treatment for an eating disorder among the ruminators. Most of the patients have reported the activity as being "soothing," regardless of whether they felt the practice was shameful or innocuous.

Bulimic ruminators display a greater tendency to spit out, rather than reswallow, the regurgitated food in an attempt to reduce the amount of food absorbed. The medical consequences of rumination in bulimics can be very similar to those in bulimics who induce VOMITING, which adds to the difficulty of making a correct diagnosis. The most serious consequence is probably electrolyte depletion. The presence of digestive acids, mixed with undigested food, in the mouth can also affect the mucosal membranes and the teeth. A ruminator can also develop esophageal ulcers as a result of the passage up and down of hydrochloric acid. In the chronic ruminator, the salivary glands become quite enlarged. There is a tendency in adult rumination for weight loss because food is not properly digested and the nutrient value is reduced.

Rumination occurs throughout the day, not specifically after meals. Patients have reported ruminating from five or six times a day to as many as 30 times a day. One who ruminated all the time consumed dozens of mints and used toothpaste to hide the smell. The process is not unconscious at all; ruminators can bring the undigested food into the mouth at will.

Treatment of rumination in adults can be very difficult, owing to the apparent pleasure derived from it. Patients have described a sense of relief during the reswallowing. For those with bulimia nervosa, treatment resulting in reestablishment of control over eating has led to cessation of rumination. In nonbulimics, behavioral treatment directed at training them to relax before and after meals has largely proven unsatisfactory, mostly because there is less incentive than for bulimics to stop the behavior. In two reported cases of pharmacologic treatment, administration of paregoric prior to eating completely inhibited after-meal rumination; and premeal administration of dopamine blocking agents reduced after-meal rumination. In other cases, paregoric at first had a PLACEBO effect, with patients feeling a beneficial impact, but it soon wore off. More successful has been a combination of COGNITIVE THERAPY and ANTIDEPRESSANTS. Appropriately controlled trials are needed to establish the best therapy.

Fairburn, C. G., and P. G. Cooper. "Rumination in Bulimia Nervosa." *British Medical Journal* 288, 1984.

Larocca, Felix E. F., and Mary Anne Della-Fera. "Rumination: Its Significance in Adults with Bulimia Nervosa." *Psychosomatics* 27, March 1986.

Malcolm, A., et al. "Rumination Syndrome." *Mayo Clinic Proceedings* 72, July 1997.

Russell, Gerald F. M. (1928–) Director of Eating Disorders at Hayes Grove Priory Hospital, Kent, England. Dr. Russell in 1979 published the first extensive description of an "ominous new variant of anorexia nervosa," which he named BULIMIA NERVOSA. At the time, Dr. Russell was a professor in the Academic Department of Psychiatry at Royal Free Hospital in London.

Russell's principal works include "Anorexia Nervosa: Its Identity as an Illness and Its Treatment," in *Modern Trends in Psychological Medicine,* edited by John Harding Price. London: Butterworths, 1970; "Anorexia Nervosa and Bulimia Nervosa." In *Handbook of Psychiatry.* Vol. 4. *The Neuroses and Personality Disorders,* edited by G. F. M. Russell and L. A. Hersov (Cambridge: Cambridge University Press, 1983); and "Bulimia Nervosa: An Ominous Variant of Anorexia Nervosa," *Psychological Medicine* 9 (1979).

S

satiety Satiety is a state of fullness and satisfaction (see APPETITE). Factors that affect how much a person eats include how pleasant the food is to the taste, emotional state (stress turns off hunger in animals, but humans may eat more or less; see STRESS AND EATING DISORDERS), hormones and general state of health.

After eating, digestion breaks down food for immediate energy needs (carbohydrate), tissue repair (protein) and energy reserve (fat). Digestion is controlled by the hypothalamus, which determines how we utilize food and energy. The hypothalamus controls the pituitary gland, which regulates feeding behavior. The venteromedial hypothalamus is said to be the locus of the feeling of satiety—if it is injured, a person becomes hyperphagic (eats excessively) and obese. If the lateral hypothalamus is destroyed, a person becomes aphagic (noneating) and eventually starves to death. (See HYPOTHALAMIC DISEASE.)

On a reducing diet, hunger stress might be alleviated by the use of certain menus and even occasionally an APPETITE SUPPRESSANT drug to increase the satiating effect of the food that has been eaten. This would help reduce the desire to snack between meals or take second helpings.

A number of digestive hormones have been thought to be satiety hormones, and the best known of these is CHOLECYSTOKININ (CCK), though its locus of action remains controversial. Receptors in the vagus nerve or in the central nervous system may be involved. Cholecystokinin inhibitors increase food intake, suggesting that cholecystokinin has a role in inducing satiety.

seasonal affective disorder *Seasonal affective disorder* is the common term for the specifier *with seasonal pattern* when applied to the pattern of major depressive episodes. Some 10 million people have a seasonal affective disorder (SAD). According to DSM-IV, in most cases, the episodes begin in fall or winter and remit in spring. Less commonly, there may be recurrent summer depressive episodes. SAD episodes are often characterized by sluggishness, excessively long periods of sleep, overeating, weight gain and a craving for carbohydrates. SAD appears to be more prevalent at higher latitudes, among younger persons and among women, who comprise 60 percent to 90 percent of persons with seasonal pattern.

Recent findings suggest that the severity of bulimia nervosa peaks during fall and winter months and that persons with this disorder respond to treatment with bright artificial light. However, the rates of eating disorders among patients treated for winter depression (SAD) are unknown.

Gruber, N. P., and S. C. Dilsaver. "Bulimia and Anorexia Nervosa in Winter Depression: Lifetime Rates in a Clinical Sample." *Journal of Psychiatry and Neuroscience* 21 (January 1996).

secondary amenorrhea Cessation of menstruation after menarche (the first menstrual period of a girl in PUBERTY), secondary amenorrhea is a condition most common in anorexics but not uncommon among bulimics, particularly those who rely heavily on FASTING and/or extreme DIETING as means of PURGING. In many instances it is attributed to undernourishment. In addition, the menstrual cycle can be interrupted by environmental stress, a primary factor in bulimia.

See also AMENORRHEA.

self-esteem Self-esteem is belief in one's own value, one's self-respect. Low self-esteem is often a symptom of eating disorders. People with eating disorders feel inadequate, and this adversely affects their recovery. Self-esteem is also considered a factor in adolescent obesity.

self-help groups Therapy groups that rely on their members to supply one another with support, assistance and positive influence so that individual members do not have to try to help themselves in isolation are called self-help groups.

The ideal self-help (or mutual-aid) group does not involve professionals. In practice, however, the most stable groups do involve them. Although an association with professionals appears to infringe on the self-help premise of "equal-status" relationships, when groups are formed without such assistance, they tend eventually to deteriorate into unproductive complaint sessions, which may erode the members' motivation. Some authors also suggest that the poor interpersonal and leadership skills of many anorexics and bulimics prevent long-term commitment to such groups. Professional therapists can assist by acting as organizers, teachers of social skills, role models and consultants and can provide a structure for meetings without infringing on the primary purpose of groups, mutual support. Groups that maintain connections with professionals have the potential to train group leaders capable of facilitating constructive group interaction. These "lay" leaders may be parents of anorexics or bulimics who are motivated to help other parents or individuals who have themselves recovered, or who are recovering, from eating disorders.

Families of members also benefit from these groups. The setting reduces social isolation and provides a noncritical environment for exploring issues. Through shared experiences, parents can learn how to cope with their children's problems and their own feelings. In groups that mix parents and children of different families, the greater emotional distance can sometimes enable the older generation to hear and appreciate better what the younger generation has to say. For previously unresponsive therapy patients, the contact with people who have "been there" and found themselves capable of changing has proven particularly beneficial.

Self-help groups are not a substitute for other forms of treatment. They differ significantly from individual or group therapy, whose purpose is to free patients from disabling forms of psychological disorder by developing insight into and understanding of underlying causes, eventually enabling changes in dysfunctional behavior. But one valuable function groups often perform is to refer individuals to qualified professional treatment. Some groups are parts of multimodal treatment programs. Self-help groups sometimes are also the preferred resource of anorexics and their families for financial reasons or by personal choice, especially if they fear professionals or have had previous unsuccessful encounters with them.

Because self-help groups for eating disorders have originated so recently, no standardized nationwide procedures have been developed. Effective guidelines based on the successful experience of existing groups, however, are beginning to emerge. According to recent social science literature on self-help, the ideal mutual-aid group provides members with information (factual knowledge and referrals to appropriate professionals); opportunity to share and learn from one another's experience; mutual support; positive association (members can identify with group goals); collective willpower; and benefit from the exchange itself.

See also ANOREXIA NERVOSA; BULIMIA NERVOSA; OBESITY; GROUP THERAPY; PSYCHOTHERAPY.

self-monitoring The process of keeping a careful record of one's own body weight, food intake and its caloric value, physical activity and, in some cases, the circumstances (time, place, occasion, company) of eating, self-monitoring is a key element in almost all BEHAVIOR MODIFICATION programs and typically the first behavior change requirement. In obesity treatment, it is frequently prescribed before any attempts to diet or increase exercise are made. Originally intended strictly as an information-gathering tool, it has proven to have other value.

Monitoring eating habits affects eating behavior in a number of ways. First, the very act of recording can force awareness of previously unconscious patterns of behavior; for example, because snacking usually becomes a routine, automatic behavior, most people express surprise at the amount of food—and calories—they discover they eat in a day. This awareness can be a first and necessary step in their efforts to control how much they eat. It can also reveal behaviors likely to have defeated previous attempts to lose weight or keep it off. Second, self-monitoring provides specific information that allows eating-disordered persons to evaluate their progress and then reward or punish accordingly. Third, records of eating behavior can provide information useful to therapists in assisting the obese to make behavior changes.

Therapists suggest that self-monitoring is most effective and successful when patients have convenient forms for recording the information, when behavior is recorded soon or immediately after it occurs and when feelings, degree of HUNGER and concurrent problems are also noted.

self-mutilation Self-mutilation is the act of deliberately injuring oneself. Mutilation of one's own or another's body has always been a part of human existence and continues to be a normal part of some cultures even today. Many cultures have long used mutilation of the body in religious or other social rituals, such as circumcision (of both sexes), tattooing or scarring the skin during rites of passage into adulthood or the binding of feet to make women more attractive. These forms of mutilation or self-mutilation are not meant to be harmful; on the contrary, they often signify strength or rebirth.

In our culture, self-mutilation generally is not an attempt to commit SUICIDE but a way of dealing with anxieties and stress. Many self-mutilators find bleeding to be comforting and scarring a welcome sign of healing.

The mentally retarded may do things that result in injury to themselves, and psychotics sometimes perform drastic acts such as poking out their eyes or cutting off extremities. The most common cases of mutilation are more subtle in nature. Typically they involve cutting or burning parts of the body or interfering with the healing of wounds.

Medical literature suggests that self-mutilators have a high incidence of eating disorders. Out of four studies mentioned by Armando R. Favazza, associate chairman of the Department of Psychiatry at the School of Medicine, University of Missouri–Columbia, the percentages of self-mutilators who also had a history of an eating disorder (anorexia nervosa, bulimia or overweight) ranged from 57 to 93 percent. In a study by Paul Garfinkel in 1989, only 9.2 percent of the bulimics in the study practiced self-mutilation; however, in another study, 38 percent of the female eating-disorder patients also practiced self-mutilation. In a third study, reported in the September 1990 *American Journal of Psychiatry,* female eating-disorder patients demonstrated significantly higher levels of dissociative psychopathology than non-eating-disordered subjects. This appeared to be specifically related to a propensity for self-mutilation and suicidal behavior.

Favazza reported on some of his own cases of self-mutilators who also suffered from eating disorders. One patient developed a fear of becoming overweight after being treated on an outpatient basis for self-mutilation at age 16. After this treatment her mutilating behaviors decreased; however, at 19, when she was hospitalized for her eating disorder, the self-mutilating behaviors intensified. After one year in treatment, both behaviors stopped, but when events in her life became stressful, she relapsed once again into the eating disorder. For another of his patients with a history of alcohol abuse, eating disorder and self-mutilation, the three behaviors were "interchangeable ways of hurting myself."

According to Favazza, an impulse-control problem seems to be the basis for self-mutilation, eating disorders and substance abuse; he feels that a good number of those with one of these problems may also be affected by another.

Although psychotherapeutic treatment is currently available for self-mutilators, researchers are now speculating that a deficiency of SEROTONIN, a neurotransmitter that influences HUNGER, SATIETY, sexual drive and pain response, among other feelings, may be a biological contributor to self-mutilation.

Jewell, Regina. "Self-mutilation and Its Kinship to Eating Disorders." *BASH Magazine*, November 1989.

Yaryura-Tobias, J. A., et al. "Self-Mutilation, Anorexia, and Dysmenorrhea in Obsessive Compulsive Disorder." *International Journal of Eating Disorders* 17 (January 1995).

serotonin One of a family of NEUROTRANSMITTERS that mediate the passing of impulses through the nervous system, the chemical serotonin is produced in the brain when an impulse passes between two nerve endings. Most is then reabsorbed by the nerves.

A link between eating disorders and serotonin is assumed because eating CARBOHYDRATES stimulates the production of serotonin in the brain. It paves the way for other neurotransmitters that stimulate an appetite for protein and fat. It is thought that bulimics, who suffer from diminished serotonin activity, become depressed as their serotonin level drops. As a result they develop a CRAVING for foods that trigger production of the substance, as if they were using pasta and sugar as a "natural" antidepressant (see ANTIDEPRESSANTS). However, any existing serotonin imbalance may also be caused by chronic dieting, especially restriction of carbohydrates. Furthermore, there is evidence that dieting changes serotonergic functioning in women but not men, which may partially explain why there is a much higher incidence of bulimia among women than men.

Serotonin can also make you sleepy. Karen Collins, a Washington, D.C. registered dietitian, reported on the MSNBC.com that eating large amounts of carbohydrate foods, such as sweets, potatoes and grain products, increases brain levels of serotonin and sleepiness, but that protein eaten along with the carbohydrates causes the serotonin levels to stay low.

Fairburn, Christopher, Zafra Cooper, and Peter Cooper. "The Clinical Features and Maintenance of Bulimia Nervosa." In *Handbook of Eating Disorders*, edited by Kelly D. Brownell and John P. Foreyt. New York: Basic Books, 1986.

Goodwin, G. M., C. G. Fairburn, and P. J. Cowin. "Dieting Changes Serotonergic Function in Women, Not Men. Implications for the Etiology of Anorexia Nervosa?" *Psychological Medicine* 17 (1987).

Goodwin, G. M., et al. "Plasma Concentrations of Tryptophan and Dieting." *British Medical Journal* 300, June 9, 1990.

set-point theory There is persuasive evidence that animals and humans naturally maintain, and thus will always return to, a constant weight range, just as the body naturally returns to its own temperature level following illness or external influence. This weight level is referred to as the body's set point. However, the term set-*point* is probably an inaccurate term because it is not a specific point, but rather a range of possible weights that the body attempts to maintain.

In support of the set-point theory, studies have shown that once "starved" volunteers are given free access to food, they eat ravenously until their weight returns to its normal level, when appetite and caloric intake level off at prediet amounts. Similarly, after experimental forced feeding to increase weight as much as 25 percent, weight rapidly returns to normal levels when volunteers are once again allowed to eat whatever they want, with no attempt to control weight in either direction.

It is this set point, proponents say, that explains why dieters invariably return to their prediet weight once they cease to restrict food intake. An individual's set point can vary as much as 10 to 20 pounds over time. It is believed that a combination of factors, including METABOLISM and the number of FAT CELLS, work together to "set" a level of fat (weight) that's "normal" for that person. If weight drops below the set point, HUNGER increases and the body burns fewer CALORIES until weight once again stabilizes.

It is believed, but not proven, that the set point can sometimes be changed by EXERCISE, certain drugs such as nicotine, hormonal changes and aging.

Hellmich, Nanci. "Aging Americans Settle Up in Size." *USA Today*, November 15, 1999.

sexual abuse and eating disorders There is an increasing awareness that many survivors of sexual abuse develop eating disorders. Root and Fallon reported in *Bulimia: A Systems Approach to Treatment* that 60 percent of 172 bulimics studied had been sexually and/or otherwise physically victimized, and other authors have indicated an even higher rate. Studies at the RENFREW CENTERS also revealed the high correlation between sexual abuse and eating disorders—61 of a sample of 100 women had been sexually abused before the age of 18. Of these, 24 were victims of incest, 47 were molested by acquaintances and 18 by strangers. Realizing that this population had a need for specific treatment, the Renfrew Center of Florida, in June 1992, opened a program for survivors of abuse.

Jane Shure, a consulting therapist at Renfrew, writes that "the development of an eating disorder such as bulimia or anorexia is a logical response to the emotional experiences and messages received throughout the abused child's formative years. As the young child moves into adolescence and young adulthood, she turns to food as a means of comfort and a tool for avoiding feelings. Fasting, or bingeing and then purging, both help create an illusion of being in control—while also reinforcing her shame and feeding the desperate need to isolate [herself]. (See BINGE EATING; FASTING; PURGING.)

Findings at the Johns Hopkins Eating and Weight Disorders Clinic showed that 50 percent or more of bulimic and anorexic women have histories of sexual abuse, including rape and incest.

Using data from 190 university women, a 1996 study found that women with histories of assaults from within the family were more likely to suffer a serious eating problem (47 percent) than women who had no history of sexual assault (21 percent) and women who reported only assaults from outside the family (36 percent).

However, not all researchers support the connection between sexual abuse and eating disorders. Pope and Hudson, for example, reviewed the scientific literature on childhood sexual abuse as a risk factor for the development of bulimia nervosa. They concluded that "controlled studies generally did not find that bulimic patients show a significantly higher prevalence of childhood sexual abuse than control groups. Furthermore, neither controlled nor uncontrolled studies of bulimia nervosa found higher rates of childhood sexual abuse than were found in studies of the general population that used comparable methods. Therefore, current evidence does not support the hypothesis that childhood sexual abuse is a risk factor for bulimia nervosa."

Waller found that bulimics were substantially more likely to report a history of unwanted sexual experience than anorexics. He suggested that sexual abuse may not cause eating disorders but may determine the nature of those disorders when they have been prompted by other factors.

Perhaps a more important question is not whether or not sexual abuse is a risk factor for eating disorders, but rather in what way is it important when it is present. Gleaves and Eberenz examined this question among a group of hospitalized eating-disordered individuals and found that, although sexual abuse was unrelated to severity of eating disorder symptoms, it was highly related to additional problems such as suicide attempts, alcohol problems and self-injurious behaviors.

Baldo, T. D., et al. "Effects of Intrafamilial Sexual Assault on Eating Behaviors." *Psychological Reports* 79 (October 1996).

Bulik, Cynthia M., Patrick F. Sullivan, and Marcia Rorty. "Childhood Sexual Abuse in Women with Bulimia." *Journal of Clinical Psychiatry* 50 (December 1989).

Gleaves, D. H., and K. P. Eberenz. "Eating Disorders and Additional Psychopathology in Women: The role of prior sexual abuse." *Journal of Child Sexual Abuse* 2 (1993).

Palmer, R. L., et al. "Childhood Sexual Experiences with Adults Reported by Women with Eating Disorders: An Extended Series." *British Journal of Psychiatry* 156 (May 1990).

Pope, Harrison G., Jr., and James I. Hudson. "Is Childhood Sexual Abuse a Risk Factor for Bulimia Nervosa?" *American Journal of Psychiatry* 149 (April 1992).

Waller, Glenn. "Sexual Abuse as a Factor in Eating Disorders." *British Journal of Psychiatry* 159 (November 1991).

sexuality and eating disorders Abed has suggested that eating disorder syndromes, together with the phenomenon of the pursuit of thinness, are manifestations of female intrasexual competition. The contention is that eating disorders originate in the human female's psychological adaptation of concern about physical attractiveness, which is an important component of female "mate attraction" and "mate retention" strategies. Abed argues that the present-day environment of Western countries presents a range of conditions that have led to the overactivation or the disruption of the archaic female sexual strategy of maximizing "mate value." The predictions theorized by Abed need to be tested.

Abed, R. T. "The Sexual Competition Hypothesis for Eating Disorders." *British Journal of Medical Psychology* 71, December 1998.

Abraham, S. "Sexuality and Reproduction in Bulimia Nervosa Patients Over 10 Years." *Journal of Psychosomatic Research* 44, March–April 1998.

sialodenosis Sialodenosis is the swelling of the salivary glands, most evident in the parotid glands and frequently seen in bulimics. "Puffy cheeks" may be an indication of this problem.

simple overeating The most common form of eating disorder, simple overeating is what results when people do not reduce their food intake in response to the natural lowering of energy output that accompanies aging.

For overeaters, the desire to eat almost always exceeds their need for food, and when they allow their APPETITE free rein, they become fat. Overeaters who attempt to deal with their problem resist focusing their attention on their appetite. They worry instead about their bodies, which they see as disfigured with excess fat. They are often dieting or looking for a simple and easy cure that will cause the fat to melt away.

Simplesse A FAT SUBSTITUTE developed by NutraSweet, Simplesse can replace fat and thus reduce calories in such foods as frozen desserts, mayonnaise, salad dressing and margarine. One of dozens of fat substitutes being developed by food manufacturers, Simplesse is composed of proteins from milk and egg whites, which are heated and whipped to create tiny spheres one-tenth the size of a grain of powdered sugar. On the tongue, Simplesse particles taste and feel like cream. The first product made with Simplesse to be marketed to the U.S. public was Simple Pleasures, an ice "cream" with half the calories of the real thing and virtually no fat.

sitomania (sitophobia) *Sitomania* and *sitophobia* are interchangeable terms included as diagnostic categories in U.S. medical dictionaries during the mid-1850s to describe a "phase of insanity" characterized by "intense dread of food." Sitophobics were not classified among the FASTING GIRLS of that period. They claimed no special powers, and no public pronouncements were made about the duration of the fasting or the patients' miraculous inspiration. Sitophobic girls came from well-educated and well-situated middle-class families. No organic explanation could be found for their not eating. In *Fasting Girls,* Joan Jacobs Brumberg refers to sitomania as a "prehistory of anorexia nervosa."

size discrimination Size discrimination consists of systematic restrictions in employment, housing, child adoption and other areas based on weight rather than ability, training or other qualifications.

In 1989, University of Vermont researchers reported the results of a survey they conducted on employment, medical and housing discrimination against fat people. The survey included 367 women and 78 men. It found that more than 40 percent of fat men and 60 percent of fat women claimed to have been refused a job because of their weight. In contrast, almost none of the nonfat respondents indicated that this had ever occurred. More than 30 percent of fat men and women indicated that they had been denied promotions or raises, and more than 25 percent said that they had been denied benefits (such as health and life insurance) because of their weight. Nearly 70 percent of fat men and women had been questioned about their weight on the job or urged to lose weight; and this was also true of about 30 percent of moderately fat people and 10 percent of nonfat people. In general, fat people were employed in jobs that had lower prestige.

Some employment discrimination cases have been won by fat plaintiffs using state disability laws, defining their obesity as a perceived disability. The Trump Shuttle airline reportedly scrapped size requirements for its flight attendants after considering the costly legal battles waged by other airlines. Pan Am, for instance, settled a suit by 116 female flight attendants by paying $2.35 million.

In 1999, Mark Roehling of Western Michigan University's Haworth College of Business examined studies on employee discrimination and concluded that weight discrimination is more common than discrimination based on other factors, including race and gender. He noted that only one state, Michigan, has a law against weight discrimination.

"Results of the NAAFA Survey on Employment Discrimination." *NAAFA Newsletter*, April 1989.

skin-fold measurement The thickness of a fold of skin at a selected body site, usually the upper arm (triceps) or the upper abdomen, skin-fold measurements are used to calculate body fat to evaluate nutritional status.

Triceps skin-fold measurements are based on the assumption that 50 percent of the fat is subcutaneous (under the skin). The person making the measurement pinches up a full fold of skin and subcutaneous tissue with the thumb and forefinger of the left hand at a distance one centimeter above the site at which the measurement is to be taken. The fold is pulled away from the underlying muscle. The pressure on the fold is exerted by the calipers and not the fingers. The dial of the calipers is read to the nearest 0.5 millimeter after releasing the handle and applying pressure to the skin fold. Skin-fold measurements are then translated into percentage of body fat by means of standard equations.

When carefully used, skin-fold measurements provide a good indication of body fatness. (See BODY FAT.) They are most accurate when applied to healthy subjects who are not either grossly obese or severely underweight. Measurements are more accurate when extremes in temperature are avoided. Extreme heat can cause skin-fold swelling. Edema, which in severe cases can cause a great increase in body weight, can cause errors in skin-fold measurements. Recent weight loss may also have an effect on tissue tension or the pattern of subcutaneous fat thickness.

smoking cessation and weight gain Cigarette smokers have a lower average body weight than nonsmokers, and the fear of weight gain is a barrier to quitting in some smokers, particularly in women. Studies suggest that women gain an average of 20 pounds and men 17 pounds following smoking cessation. In a Canadian study of undergraduate college students, dieters who were former smokers reported considerably more weight gain than nondieters. A Japanese study found that although heavy smokers may experience large weight gain and weigh more than nonsmokers in the early years following smoking cessation, they then lose weight until they are at the same level as the nonsmokers. However, light and moderate smokers gain weight up to the nonsmoker level once they stop smoking, but not any amounts beyond that level. In a double-blind trial, fluoxetine appeared to forestall weight gain following cessation of smoking, allowing time for the weight-conscious smoker to focus on quitting smoking rather than on preventing weight gain. Although the overall prevalence of smoking in the general population has been diminishing over the past few years, the prevalence of first-time smoking and smoking behavior in adolescent girls and young women is growing. Part of the reason, researchers say, is the use of smoking as a weight control method.

According to a 1999 Swedish study, the use of nicotine gum combined with a low-calorie diet is a good way to stop smoking without gaining weight.

Borelli, B., et al. "Weight Suppression and Weight Rebound in Ex-smokers Treated With Fluoxetine." *Journal of Consulting and Clinical Psychology* 67 (February 1999).

Charnow, J. "Weight Gain After Smoking Cessation Underestimated." *MDX Health Digest* 39, no. 20 (1998).

Froom, P., et al. "Smoking Cessation and Weight Gain." *MDX Health Digest* 46, no. 6 (1998).

Jarry, J. L., et al. "Weight Gain After Smoking Cessation in Women: The Impact on Dieting Status." *International Journal of Eating Disorders* 24 (July 1998).

social factors in obesity In industrialized societies, obesity is more prevalent in lower social classes, whereas the reverse pattern has been observed elsewhere, as in rural India. Stunkard wrote that social mobility has also accompanied changes in the incidence of obesity; in the United States, upward mobility has been associated with decreasing obesity, and downward mobility is associated with increasing obesity. In New York City, incidence of obesity has been found to be seven times higher in the lowest than in the highest social class. There also is a tendency for slim women to move up the social scale and overweight women to move down.

The proliferation of cars and labor-saving devices is blamed for much of today's rise in obesity. A sedentary lifestyle means that APPETITE is not a trustworthy guide to energy needs. Weinsier and colleagues determined that because of the difficulties in maintaining low-fat diets in the presence of today's fast foods and social feasts, the current trend toward increasing body weight is not likely to be reversed solely through dieting. Activity levels will have to increase.

See also OBESITY.

Stunkard, Albert J. "The Control of Obesity: Social and Community Perspectives." In *Handbook of Eating Disorders,* edited by Kelly D. Brownell and John P. Foreyt. New York: Basic Books, 1986.

The Solution A diet program called the Solution is based on the book *The Solution: Never Diet Again* (Regan Books, 1998) by obesity researcher Laurel Mellin. Since the book's release, 150 groups using this method have sprung up across the country, all led by registered dietitians and psychologists. The Solution avoids the health risks of drugs and restrictive dieting and thus far has shown lasting weight loss.

spot reducing Exercising a particular group of muscles such as those of the stomach or upper arms to lose weight, tone muscles or reduce fat in that area is called spot reducing.

Exercising specific muscles does tighten and increase the tone of these muscles but does not preferentially mobilize fat from storage cells overlying these muscles. AEROBIC EXERCISE is required for mobilization of fat; the sequence of mobilization from various areas of the body varies from person to person.

starch blockers Substances derived from concentrated protein from certain beans that inhibit digestion of starch by preventing complete METABOLISM of CARBOHYDRATES, starch blockers are marketed as aids in weight reduction.

Any weight loss that starch blockers may effect is due to the malnutrition this process causes, along with flatulence and gastric upset. In 1984, starch blockers were taken off the market pending Food and Drug Administration approval. Those currently available are effective only in preventing breakdown of complex carbohydrates and have no effect on the digestion of the simple sugars abundant in the U.S. diet.

"Automatic Weight Loss with Cal-Ban? Send for Your Refund Now!" *Consumer Reports Health Letter,* June 1990.

starvation syndrome Studies have shown that starvation influences behavior and reasoning, from preoccupation with food to mood swings to social isolation. Garfinkel and Kaplan wrote that all the symptoms described in studies of starving people are also prominent in anorexia nervosa. "That they result from starvation per se and not from a pathophysiological process unique to anorexia nervosa has allowed greater diagnostic specificity and more emphasis on weight gain as a critical aspect of treatment."

Berg, Frances S. "The Starvation Syndrome." *Healthy Weight Network,* September 1998.
Garfinkel, Paul E., and Allan S. Kaplan. "Anorexia Nervosa: Diagnostic Conceptualizations." In *Handbook of Eating Disorders,* edited by Kelly D. Brownell and John P. Foreyt. New York: Basic Books, 1986.

steatopygia Characterized by abnormal fatness of the buttocks, steatopygia is seen to an extreme in certain parts of Africa. Location of this excess fat accumulation in the buttocks apparently represents an evolutionary adaptation to a very hot climate. If this fat were spread throughout the subcutaneous tissue, normal cooling of the skin would be severely limited.

Stein-Leventhal syndrome A disorder in women characterized by irregular menses, mild obesity and hirsutism, Stein-Leventhal syndrome usually begins during the years of puberty and worsens with time. Chronic anovulation, and therefore infertility, is present as a result of inappropriate feedback signals to the hypothalamic-pituitary unit. Also known as polycystic ovary syndrome or PCO, this disorder is benign (not life threatening), and there is no ideal therapy for it. Treatment to induce ovulation is administered when pregnancy is desired.

stimulus control A BEHAVIOR MODIFICATION technique, also called cue elimination, stimulus control attempts to alter the circumstances that may trigger the impulse to eat, while also including measures used in traditional weight reduction programs. Every effort, for instance, is made to limit the amount of high-calorie food kept in the house and to limit accessibility to the food that is kept. Foods that require preparation replace those that require none. Spare change is kept to a minimum to decrease the likelihood of impulse buying of candy or snacks. Eating is confined to scheduled mealtimes and places. (See EATING HABITS MONITORING.)

At the same time, new stimuli for eating are established; for example, the obese adult might restrict all eating to special table settings or unusually colored place mats and napkins—anything to make the eating process special and intentional (as distinct from habitual, almost subconscious snacking). Emphasis is put on the eating process rather than the amount of food eaten.

Brownell, Kelly D., and Thomas A. Wadden. "Behavior Therapy for Obesity: Modem Approaches and Better Results." In *Handbook of Eating Disorders,* edited by Kelly D. Brownell and John P. Foreyt. New York: Basic Books, 1986.

Fairbum, C. G. "Cognitive-Behavioral Treatment for Bulimia." In *Handbook of Psychotherapy for Anorexia Nervosa and Bulimia,* edited by D. M. Garner and P. E. Garfinkel. New York: Guilford Press, 1985.

Wheeler, M. E., and K. W. Hess. "Treatment of Juvenile Obesity by Successive Approximation Control of Eating." *Journal of Behavior Therapy and Experimental Psychiatry* 7 (1976).

stomach stapling A general term, *stomach stapling,* is used for about 20 surgical operations that create artificially smaller stomachs out of portions of the original stomachs. Usually the stomach is closed off with a staple gun, although other means are sometimes used, such as the insertion of plastic mesh. Some involve gastric bypass, in which the intestine is severed and reattached to a hole punched in the stomach pouch. These operations cause weight loss by limiting food intake; as soon as a few mouthfuls are eaten, the person feels nauseated and must stop eating to avoid vomiting.

When these procedures were first developed, the stomach was reduced from its original capacity of more than a quart to five ounces. Currently, a two-ounce capacity is most common; one-half ounce is not uncommon.

Ernsberger, Paul. *Report on Weight-Loss Surgery.* Bellerose, N.Y.: National Association to Advance Fat Acceptance (NAAFA), 1986.

Stop the Insanity A weight-loss program led by Susan Powter, who became a celebrity while promoting the program on infomercials and television talk shows, Stop the Insanity's program's thesis is that diets don't work, that you can eat a lot of food if you stick to low-fat foods, and that you must exercise regularly. Powter advocates replacing scales and monitoring weight with calipers and measuring body-fat percentage. (Calipers are provided with the program materials.) The program costs about $80 and includes audio tapes, videotapes, booklets, exercise techniques and motivational tips.

stress and eating disorders Some eating-disorder patients, particularly those who ruminate, use their eating-disordered behaviors as a way to improve stress or anxiety. It is thought that infants may use RUMINATION to decrease the stress of poor maternal bonding. A British study concluded that women with eating disorders are less effective in coping with stress than women without eating disorders.

The precise role that stress plays in the development of eating disorders remains unclear, however. One theory is that biological changes within the body that occur during times of stress may promote the development of eating disorders. Another is that psychological changes accompanying life stresses may affect the response to such stresses.

Stress may influence the development of eating disorders because of the effect it can have on various biochemical systems within the body, especially those that govern APPETITE. Changes may occur within the hypothalamic-pituitary-adrenal axis within the endorphin system. Because the body is a complex system of biochemical processes, there may be changes in one or all of these systems as a result of stress. Therefore, the exact relationship between stress and eating disorders remains unknown. It is evident, however, that stress requires a response of some type from the organism. As Thomas P. Donohoe, of the University of Nottingham, England, concludes in his paper, "Stress-induced Anorexia" (1984), "Psychosocial stress may combine with dieting behavior to produce changes in hypothalamic function or other systems to generate or shape the symptoms of anorexia nervosa."

Although the precise role of stress and DIETING in the development of eating disorders remains unknown, that they can be precipitating factors is not in doubt. Concerns about body image or physical changes affecting peer-group approval can often be sources of stress. Social emphasis on thinness may also be accentuated in peer groups, regardless of age, encouraging further self-consciousness and dieting behaviors. Issues of social or financial independence may become chronic strains for older persons. Such stresses may promote dieting to regain a sense of control but may lead to the development of an eating disorder.

Donohoe, T. P. "Stress-induced Anorexia: Implications for Anorexia Nervosa." *Life Sciences* 34, 1984.

Fischman, Ben. "Unsweetened Stress." *Psychology Today,* March 1989.

Levine, M. D., and M. D. Marcus. "Eating Behavior Following Stress in Women With and Without Bulimic Systems." *Annals of Behavior Medicine* 19 (Spring 1997).

Rutter, M. "Meyerian Psychobiology, Personality Development, and the Role of Life Experiences." *American Journal of Psychiatry* 143, no. 9 (1986).

Schmidt, U. H., et al. "Events and the Onset of Eating Disorders: Correcting an Age-Old Myth." *International Journal of Eating Disorders* 25 (January 1999).

Schotte, David, Joseph Cools, and Richard McNally. "Film-induced Negative Affect Triggers Overeating in Restrained Eaters." *Journal of Abnormal Psychology* 99, no. 3 (August 1990).

Troop, N. A., and J. L. Treasure. "Psychosocial Factors in the Onset of Eating Disorders: Responses to Life Events and Difficulties." *British Journal of Medical Psychology* 70 (December 1997).

Troop, N. A., et al. "Stress, Coping, and Crisis Support in Eating Disorders." *International Journal of Eating Disorders* 24 (September 1998).

sucrose polyester (SPE) See OLESTRA.

sugar A sweet-tasting simple CARBOHYDRATE containing carbon and hydrogen usually in the ratio of 1:2, the food we call sugar is refined from sugarcane, but sugars are found universally in plants and animal tissues. Americans consume about 133 pounds of sugar a year from all sources; that accounts for 20 to 25 percent of all calories, about 500 to 600 calories per day per person. Glucose, the main sugar in the blood and a basic fuel for the body, is essential to the functioning of all cells, particularly brain cells. Contrary to popular belief, there are no nutritional differences among sugars. Our bodies use all types of sugars in the same way.

Sugar is not the leading cause of obesity. Eating more calories than one uses is the basic problem, and for most people most excess calories come from FAT, not sugar. So concluded two studies in the *American Journal of Clinical Nutrition,* which found that lean people tend to eat more sugar and less fat than obese people. Not only does fat have more calories than sugar (about 36 versus 16 calories per teaspoon), but studies have also suggested that dietary fat may be more efficiently converted to body fat than carbohydrates (sugars) are.

People often blame sugary foods for weight gain, forgetting that the cakes, ice cream, chocolate and cookies they're eating derive most of their calories from fat, not sugar. Many a "sweet tooth" may actually be a "fat tooth."

Studies have failed to show that artificial sweeteners keep people from gaining weight, much less help them lose significant amounts. One problem is that instead of eating artificially sweetened foods *in place of* high-calorie ones, many people simply add them to their diet. Moreover, artificial sweeteners do not suppress appetite—they may even increase it.

Sugar can lead to tooth decay; however, so can all forms of carbohydrates if decay-producing bacteria are also present. Between-meal sugary snacks play a bigger role in dental caries than sugar eaten during a meal, according to studies.

Sugar is *not* a cause of diabetes. It—along with other simple carbohydrates, total caloric intake or stress—can contribute to a rise in blood glucose levels in persons who already have diabetes.

"The Healthy Eater's Guide to Sugar." *University of California, Berkeley Wellness Letter,* December 1989.

Mahan, L. Kathleen, and Sylvia Escott-Stump (editors). *Krause's Food, Nutrition, and Diet Therapy.* Philadelphia: W. B. Saunders, 1999.

Williams, Sue Rodwell. *Basic Nutrition and Diet Therapy.* St. Louis: Times Mirror/Mosby College Publishing, 1994.

suicide Suicide has been estimated to comprise half the deaths in cases of anorexia nervosa. Suicidal behavior (attempts and threats) is also common with bulimia; several researchers report that approximately one-third of their samples have attempted suicide. Others report lower but still significant rates. In one study of 142 bulimic women, researchers found that 49 percent of their sample had suicidal thoughts and 20 percent had attempted suicide. According to Fairburn, Cooper and Cooper, "few are a true suicide risk."

Root, Fallon and Friedrich wrote in *Bulimia: A Systems Approach to Treatment* that "it is surprising that suicidal behavior in the bulimic population has not been studied more extensively. Irritability, depression, mood swings, and anxiety are commonly observed and reported in the bulimic. While these affective states do not necessarily predict suicidal behavior, they have been correlated with increased suicidal ideation and threats."

In a more recent study of 495 eating disordered patients, 13 percent of the patients reported at least one suicide attempt and 29 percent reported current suicidal thoughts. Of those who had attempted suicide, 26 percent reported multiple attempts.

(See ANXIETY, BULIMIA NERVOSA and DEPRESSION.)

Fairburn, Christopher G., Zafra Cooper, and Peter J. Cooper. "The Clinical Features and Maintenance of Bulimia Nervosa," In *Handbook of Eating Disorders,* edited by Kelly D. Brownell and John P. Foreyt. New York: Basic Books, 1986.

Favaro, A., and P. Santonastaso. "Suicidality in Eating Disorders: Clinical and Psychological Correlates." *Acta Psychiatrica Scandinavica* 95 (June 1997).

Reto, C., M. P. P. Root, and P. Fallon. "Incidence of Suicide in a Bulimic Population." Paper presented to the Washington State Psychological Association, Vancouver, B.C., 1985.

sulpiride Sulpiride is an antipsychotic medication experimented with in treating anorexia. In a 1984 study, there was a slight trend favoring the drug compared with a PLACEBO, but no statistically significant effect was demonstrated either on weight gain or on patient attitudes or behavior.

See also ANTIDEPRESSANT.

superobesity Extreme morbid OBESITY, Superobesity affects less than one-half of 1 percent of the population. Superobesity appears to shorten life expectancy by nearly five years. The superobese often find themselves the objects of unwanted public attention.

Superobese people have received more clinical attention in recent years since reducing by starvation or LIQUID FORMULAS has become popular. Though they are capable of losing enormous amounts, they are likely to regain their weight, bringing their hypercellular ADIPOSE TISSUES back into metabolic balance (see SET-POINT THEORY). HILDE BRUCH noted that "some of these superobese people accept themselves with more equanimity than the many people who struggle with minor weight deviations." (See HUDSON, WALTER.)

superstitious (or magical) thinking Superstitious thinking is based on a belief that there is a cause-and-effect relationship between unrelated events, a belief common among anorexic patients, according to Garfinkel and Garner in *Handbook of Psychotherapy for Anorexia Nervosa and Bulimia.* They found that anorexics often assume that every last calisthenic in their exercise regimen must be completed or they will gain weight: "One patient developed an elaborate set of exercise rituals in which various situations required her to perform specific rigorous exercise routines. Passing post boxes or street lamps had to be followed by jogging for one block."

As with superstitious behavior in general, the rituals are designed to avoid or mitigate either specific or, more often, obscure but ominous consequences. This behavior is so powerfully controlled by the belief in bizarre internal relationships and contingencies that it is hardly affected even by extremely punishing external consequences. Like other avoidance behavior, superstitious rituals are resistant to critical examination because the beliefs governing them insulate the believer from acknowledging contradictory information and experience. (See ANOREXIA NERVOSA.)

support groups A term sometimes used interchangeably with SELF-HELP GROUPS, generally, support groups are free of charge and members may enter or leave at any time. Support groups are considered an adjunct to therapy, not a substitute for professional treatment. They are useful because they provide a social network, emotional support, self-help techniques and information.

T

taste The bodily sense that distinguishes flavors, taste is dependent on sense organs located on the surface of the tongue. These organs, called taste buds, when appropriately stimulated, produce one or a combination of the four fundamental taste sensations: sweet, bitter, sour and salty.

Both anorexic and bulimic women tested for perception of taste quality and intensity exhibited impaired sensitivity in estimating the magnitude of higher concentrations of all four different taste qualities, with bitter and sour tastes most severely affected. Bulimics' cravings for sweets have been suggested as due to an impaired sense of taste. One mechanism for this change in taste sensitivity may be the saliva because saliva is important for taste perception and because endocrinological changes that occur in eating disorders influence the composition of saliva. No data, however, support this hypothesis.

Results of testing by a Yale University research team headed by Judith Rodin provided evidence of a taste disturbance in bulimia nervosa, most likely caused by the acid in vomit damaging palate receptors. Rodin suggested that, because of this taste disturbance, bulimics may be less responsive to the taste of vomit as the disorder progresses, which could prolong its existence. Rodin stressed that this research does not reveal whether bulimics' taste disturbances are consequences of, or predisposing factors to, bulimia nervosa, but she suspects they are the result of bulimia nervosa.

Jirik-Babb, P., and J. L. Katz. "Impairment of Taste Perception in Anorexia Nervosa and Bulimia." *International Journal of Eating Disorders* 7 (1988).

Rodin, Judith, et al. "Bulimia and Taste: Possible Interactions." *Journal of Abnormal Psychology* 99, no. 1, February 1990.

Rosenbaum, Joshua. Taster's Choice. *Avenue,* March 1990.

"Taste Matters." *Food Insight,* International Food Information Council, July/August 1999.

TCM This term for Traditional Chinese Medicine is used by some therapists to treat eating disorders, along with Western medicine. TCM works to find balance energetically within the entire system and organs. According to therapists who use TCM, compulsive eaters are most receptive to this treatment.

tea (See DIETER'S TEAS)

Tenuate An appetite suppressant that is chemically related to amphetamine, Tenuate's active ingredient is diethylpropion. When used in a program that includes a low-fat diet and regular exercise, it can increase the diet/exercise weight loss by an additional 10 percent. On average, patients lose about 15 pounds over three months. Possible side effects of Tenuate include nervousness, insomnia, irritability, sweating, tension, dry mouth, nausea, constipation and headaches.

therapy Any treatment designed to mitigate or eliminate disease or disorder, physical or psychological is considered to be therapy. Among the therapies often used in treating eating-disordered persons are individual PSYCHOTHERAPY, FAMILY THERAPY, GROUP THERAPY and various physical treatments. Which type of therapy or combination of therapies to use depends on the age, the needs and the living situation of the person seeking treatment.

In individual psychotherapy, patients meet with therapists alone, usually at least once a week for 45 minutes to an hour at a time. Patients in therapy work to understand the role that eating or PURGING has served in their lives and to find replacements for destructive behaviors while developing healthier coping mechanisms.

In family therapy, sessions include not just eating-disordered persons but members of their families. These may include parents and siblings, spouses and even grandparents or other relatives. In family therapy, the eating disorder is seen as a "red flag," signaling that whole families are troubled, not just the persons with the eating disorders.

A therapy group usually consists of five to 12 people who meet with a therapist weekly. The group therapy approach is particularly helpful in countering feelings of isolation, of being all alone with the problem. Groups can provide feedback and support for those attempting to change their eating patterns. They are also safe places for members to learn new ways of relating, to express feelings and to develop trusting relationships of the kind whose absence led in the first place to their self-destructive relationship to food.

thermodynamic approach to obesity From the perspective of thermodynamics, obesity is understood in terms of energy balance. Because the law of conservation of energy must be preserved, obesity is the outcome of energy (food) intake in excess of energy (heat) output. HILDE BRUCH described this as a limited approach because it does not consider the underlying reasons for this disturbed energy balance, such as possible endocrine and biochemical factors. The reasons for variations in energy needs and the underlying mechanisms remain a matter of controversy.

thermogenic drugs Drugs that enhance resting metabolic activity, these compounds increase energy expenditure, which is important because weight loss is associated with metabolic readjustment to reduce energy output (see OBESITY). Thus, metabolic enhancers ensure that energy expenditure is maintained when food intake is reduced. (See also SIBUTRAMINE.)

Carruba, M. "Advances in Pharmacotherapy for Obesity." *International Journal of Obesity and Related Metabolic Disorders* 22, suppl. (August 1998).

thymoleptic medications Medications effective in the treatment of major DEPRESSION or bipolar disorder, these ANTIDEPRESSANTS have been used in treating bulimia on the theory that it may be closely related to mood disorders—the family of psychiatric illnesses that includes depression and manic-depressive illness.

thyroid disease (hypothyroidism) A deficiency of thyroid gland activity, resulting in underproduction of the hormone thyroxine, hypothyroidism lists among its consequences a lowered BASAL METABOLIC RATE and weight gain.

Probably nothing has been blamed more often as the cause of obesity than hypothyroidism, but studies show that thyroid function in obese people is usually within normal limits. Thyroid disease is not diagnosed unless there is strong laboratory evidence of reduced thyroid function accompanied by findings of classic physical symptoms and a medical history that includes a long-standing goiter, thyroiditis or thyroid surgery. Weight gain develops insidiously rather than suddenly. Associated features include some coarsening of scalp hair, dryness of skin, yellowing of palms, generalized obesity, some thinning of the eyebrows and sluggish and delayed reflexes. Hypothyroid patients frequently complain of constipation. Menstrual periods are usually characterized by excessive bleeding; a history of dysfunctional bleeding may be the earliest clue to thyroid disease. In cases in which thyroid disease is the true cause of obesity, weight control is achieved in over 90 percent of these cases through treatment with thyroxine (see THYROID HORMONE).

Frawley, Thomas F. "Obesity and the Endocrine System." *Psychiatric Clinics of North America* 7, no. 2 (June 1984).

thyroid hormone (thyroxine) Prescribed for patients suffering from hypothyroidism (see THYROID DISEASE), whose thyroid glands produce it in insufficient amounts, thyroxine raises the basal metabolic rate (see METABOLISM), causing more calories to be burned.

It is also the metabolic medication most commonly prescribed and marketed as a weight reduction agent, even to people whose thyroid glands are in good working order. But for overweight people without thyroid disease, thyroxine is of no value. Thyroid hormones are especially dangerous for people with heart disease.

According to some authors, use of this thyroid hormone increases breakdown of muscle protein rather than fat. In addition, the body quickly adapts to the administration of extra thyroid hormone by reducing its natural production of this hormone, thus returning metabolism to its normal rate. Excess thyroid hormone causes anxiety, irritability, sweating, rapid heartbeat and other possible side effects.

TOPS (Take Off Pounds Sensibly) TOPS is a nonprofit support organization for overweight people founded in 1948 that incorporates some of the principles of behavior therapy into its program. There are almost 300,000 members in nearly 12,000 chapters throughout the United States, Canada and other countries. It is patterned after Alcoholics Anonymous and employs group dynamics, competition and recognition (for those who have achieved greatest weight loss) to aid the overweight. There are weekly meetings with weigh-ins; programs vary, but all in some way provide members with motivation and reinforcement. TOPS is medically oriented and asks members to obtain their individual weight goals and dietary regimens from their personal physicians. The organization has had an active research program for several years, headquartered at the Medical College of Wisconsin in Milwaukee. Areas of study have included the relative importance of heredity and environment in the development of obesity, psychosocial differences between those successful and those unsuccessful in losing weight, the effect of obesity on pregnancy and the relationship of overweight to infertility and various diseases.

total parenteral nutrition (TPN) See HYPERALIMENTATION.

Traffic Light Diet A simplified diet developed for children, the Traffic Light Diet divides food into three colors, the same as the ones in traffic lights, green, yellow and red. Green foods contain fewer than 20 calories per serving. Yellow foods have 20 calories per average serving. Red foods are those whose caloric value exceeds those of yellow foods and thus have lower nutrient density.

Epstein, Leonard H. "Treatment of Childhood Obesity." In *Handbook of Eating Disorders,* edited by Kelly D. Brownell and John P. Foreyt. Basic Books, 1986.

trans fat Popular name for trans fatty acid, also known as hydrogenated fat, trans fat can raise blood levels of LDL, the "bad" cholesterol, increasing the risk of heart disease. Trans-fatty acids are found in some margarines, vegetable shortening, crackers, cookies, doughnuts, fast food french fries and snack foods. They are used by the food industry to increase shelf life and flavor. In November 1999, the Food and Drug Administration proposed that consumer labels list the amount of trans-fatty acids in a serving.

Triax Metabolic Accelerator The Food and Drug Administration warned consumers in November 1999 not to buy or consume Triax Metabolic Accelerator, calling it a potentially dangerous hormonal drug masquerading as a dietary supplement. FDA also urged Triax users to see a doctor if they have symptoms of thyroid disease, including fatigue, profound weight loss, diarrhea, anxiety, nervousness or insomnia. The product—which contains the ingredient tiratricol, another name for the thyroid hormone TRIAC—is promoted in health food stores and on the Internet as a way to lose weight by increasing metabolism. Triax's distributor insisted the product is safe and threatened to sue the FDA.

trichophagia The (compulsive) habit of eating hair or wool and considered to be a variant of PICA, trichophagia could also be considered a perilous disorder because trichobezoars (hairballs) can form and obstruction of the bowel may occur, requiring surgical intervention.

trichotillomania (trichologia) A compulsion or irresistible urge to pull out one's own hair, trichotillomania has been described only scantily in the psychiatric literature. Recent reviews agree that the degree of incidence of the disorder has not been established and that most of the medical and psychological literature consists primarily of single-case reports.

tummy tuck A tummy tuck is the commonly used name for an ABDOMINOPLASTY.

Turner's syndrome Turner's syndrome results from defective gonad development, characterized by retarded growth, sterility, heart defects, webbing of the neck, low posterior hairline and other deformities. It is associated with absence or structural abnormality of the X chromosome.

The association of Turner's syndrome and anorexia nervosa was first described in 1963. Since then the coexistence of these two conditions has been the subject of speculation and various interpretations. Because of the mention of low mood in several of the reported cases involving both syndromes, the association of Turner's syndrome and a major mood disorder with secondary anorexia nervosa has been considered. It has been suggested that in these cases, the anorexia nervosa may not result from social influences during puberty but from the genetic influence of Turner's syndrome, which may also predispose the patient to DEPRESSION. Some support for this possibility comes from suggestions that mood disorders and eating disorders may be related. (See MOOD DISORDERS AND EATING DISORDERS.)

V

vibrator belts Vibrator belts are gadgets sold as a means of eliminating localized fat deposits. Their premise is based on the idea that localized stimulation breaks down fat cells, releasing fat stores into the bloodstream so that they can be effectively eliminated from the body. The localized vibration also stimulates blood circulation in the treated area, thus purportedly enhancing the transport of released fat. There is no scientific evidence to support this concept.

See also FRAUDULENT PRODUCTS.

vitamin deficiency This insufficiency of vitamins in the diet is a form of malnutrition that can result from malabsorption of fat by the intestines of bulimics (caused by abuse of laxatives) or from self-starvation by anorexics. Vitamin deficiency can also result from taking drugs that have side effects of reducing absorption of vitamins in the intestines. When physicians prescribe these drugs, they will frequently also prescribe vitamin supplements to correct the situation.

vomiting Generally, vomiting is the forcible ejection of contents of the stomach through the mouth. Self-induced vomiting is the most dramatic, quickest and most common method employed by bulimics and anorexics to eliminate unwanted CALORIES. They believe they can do so before the calories "take effect," but research has actually demonstrated that a sizeable proportion of calories are absorbed even when vomiting occurs almost immediately after eating. Vomiting also provides instant relief for the painfully overstuffed stomachs of bulimics. They justify it as a means of getting rid of what is regarded as protrusion of the stomach.

To induce vomiting, many patients use "starters" such as Q-tips; they are effective and have been described as less "disgusting" than fingers. Drinking large amounts of liquids makes the vomiting easier. Eventually, most patients can vomit at will.

Patients have reported self-induced vomiting as frequently as 18 times a day or more. Vomiting has led to severe tearing and bleeding in and around the esophagus, hiatal hernias and severely infected salivary glands, not to mention serious electrolyte disturbances. It also can lead to loss of control over the vomit reflex; some severe patients get to the point that they vomit spontaneously even when they don't want to.

According to Neuman and Halvorson in *Anorexia Nervosa and Bulimia,* there is a subgroup of anorexics consisting of individuals who resort to vomiting regardless of whether they also restrict their food intake or binge. Other authors have theorized that vomiting may be the driving force in bulimia nervosa rather than BINGE EATING. They feel that binge eating might not occur if the person could not vomit afterward, citing cases in which once bulimic individuals begin to vomit, they binge eat more frequently. These patients also discover that it is easier to vomit after eating a lot and therefore prolong their binges. Some patients report that the only reason they binge eat is to make it physically easier to vomit.

W

weight phobia The fear of gaining weight, the term *weight phobia* was coined by Arthur H. Crisp to describe the anorexic's attitude toward being of a normal body weight.

Weight Watchers A commercial corporation that markets a line of packaged, reduced-calorie "diet" foods, meant to be used according to a company-sponsored diet and BEHAVIOR MODIFICATION plan, Weight Watchers also sponsors fee-collecting support groups. The company was purchased in 1978 by H. J. Heinz, which took control of both the diet program and a prepackaged food line.

Wellbutrin See BUPROPION SR.

winter depression See SEASONAL AFFECTIVE DISORDER.

Xenical® This is the trade name of orlistat, an obesity drug approved in 1999. (See CHAPTER 5.)

Y

yo-yo dieting A habitual cycle of weight loss by dieting followed by weight regain, yo-yo dieting is an inability to maintain weight loss. Studies have shown that yo-yo dieting increases body fatness and may ultimately result in an inability to lose weight even on a very low caloric intake.

People who become caught up in the yo-yo cycle take progressively longer each time to shed pounds and then gain them back progressively faster. Kelly Brownell, a psychologist then at the University of Pennsylvania, found in 1986–87 that yo-yo dieting increased the activity of lipoprotein lipase, an enzyme that promotes the storage of body fat, and because fat tissue is metabolically less active than muscle, with each diet cycle the daily caloric needs dropped and weight was gained on fewer calories. Dr. Brownell concluded that yo-yo dieting increases the body's efficiency in using food for fuel and may ultimately make weight loss impossible.

In agreement with this is David A. Booth, a psychologist at the University of Birmingham, England, who says that yo-yo dieting "may have physiological and psychological consequences which would make weight loss more difficult when it became medically more important." A constantly repeated yo-yo dieting cycle has been shown to be more of a health risk than remaining at a stable weight, even if high, particularly for those who are genetically predisposed toward obesity.

In a 1989 report in the *American Journal of Clinical Nutrition,* Djoeke van Dale and Wim H. M. Saris of the University of Limburg, The Netherlands, compared body composition (fat to lean ratio), resting metabolism rate and conversion of fats into fatty acids among those with a history of yo-yo dieting with those of dieters without such a history. After 14 weeks, significant differences in weight loss and fat loss were revealed between dieting-only and diet-and-exercise groups, but not between yo-yo and non–yo-yo dieters. Resting metabolic rate decreased in all groups, but there was a significantly smaller decline after 14 weeks for the diet-exercise groups. No effects of frequent dieting or exercise on basal and fat-burning activity were observed.

Evidence continues to mount that yo-yo dieting makes subsequent weight loss more difficult. In the Van Dale and Saris study, researchers examined the weight loss patterns of obese patients participating in a university weight loss program for the second time. The dieters had all lost weight on the program but had regained at least 20 percent—more typically 120 percent—of their lost weight in the intervening years. Though they were placed on the same weight loss regimen, and compliance was monitored by a battery of laboratory tests, the dieters lost significantly less weight the second time. The researchers speculate that chronic dieting leads to a slowdown in METABOLISM, which sets the stage for weight gain and makes future attempts at weight loss more difficult.

More recently, Dr. Brownell, now at Yale University, led a research team that studied and analyzed data collected from 3,200 participants in the Framingham (Massachusetts) Heart Study over a period of 32 years. The much-heralded results of the study were reported in the June 27, 1991 *New England Journal of Medicine.* Among the conclusions: "Persons whose body weight fluctuates often or greatly have a higher risk of coronary heart disease and death than do persons with relatively stable body weights." Controversy remained because the study did not address the issue to whether weight fluctuations are more dangerous than obesity.

Despite claims that weight cycling may be harmful and that staying at one weight is better even if one is obese, the National Institutes of Health (NIH) issued a report that "no convincing evidence supports these claims." The report goes on to say that most studies have shown that weight cycling does not affect one's metabolic rate, but it cautions that people generally experience a slowing of the metabolism as they age. The report does say that further research on the effect of yo-yo dieting (or weight cycling) is needed.

"Weight Cycling." NIH Publication Number 95-3901, March 1995.

Z

zinc deficiency Zinc is necessary in the body in small amounts; too little leads to hair loss, brittle nails and anemia. A shortage of zinc, the result of malnutrition or starvation, can greatly alter taste perception, so some clinicians have suggested it may play a role in the bizarre food combinations eaten by starving anorexics. But C. J. M. van Binsbergen et al. reported in the *European Journal of Clinical Nutrition* in 1988 that no significant difference was found in the concentration of zinc in plasma between 20 female anorexics and 20 lean to normal-weight female control subjects.

Zoloft An antidepressant, Zoloft is one in a family of selective serotonin reuptake inhibitors (SSRIs). Researchers at McLean Hospital in Belmont, Massachusetts, announced the results of a 1999 trial detailing how Zoloft was effective in the short-term treatment of binge-eating disorder.

Zyban (See BUPROPION SR.)

PART III

Finding Help and Information on the Internet

Where to Go for Help

FINDING HELP AND INFORMATION ON THE INTERNET

Searching the vast World Wide Web looking for information or sources can be intimidating. Even when you are familiar with the Web, you have to be wary about wrong information, especially when it will directly affect your health. But along with the myths, invalid theories and actual scams perpetrated on the Web, you will find mountains of scientific fact, valid studies, current news and helpful sites full of accurate information and motivation.

Following are steps you can take to better separate the good and reliable from the bad or even dangerous:

- Look for reliable sources you are familiar with or have read about in newspapers, magazines and medical journals—sites sponsored by medical schools, government agencies, professional medical organizations and national associations.
- Look for sites that list an editorial board or medical advisory board that reviews content.
- Look for sites that list the date the site was last updated and/or post the date a news item or article was put on the site.
- Look for sites and content that refer to specific studies, giving authors, journal names and dates. Content backed solely by one individual's personal story and anecdotes is not scientific evidence.
- If the site makes claims unsupported by noted scientific evidence, search the Internet for reputable health professional organizations devoted to that disease or disorder to see if they validate those claims. If not, use their email, their feedback tools or your telephone to ask what their medical experts think about these claims.
- Avoid sites that promise cures, put down other sites or insist that you buy a special product.
- Never follow any medical advice, even if it comes from an on-line medical professional, without checking with your doctor, registered dietitian or other health professional first to see if it's appropriate for your particular circumstances.
- Most likely to offer reliable information are sites displaying the HON code symbol. This means that the site conforms to the Health on the Net Foundation's Code of Conduct. You can search for reputable health sites through the HON site at http://www.hon.ch.

Sources: Mayo Clinic Women's HealthSource (1-800-351-8963); "The Mouse that Roared," *Food Insight* May/June 1999 (International Food Insight Council).

General Health Information Sites that Include Obesity and/or Eating Disorders Content

A Doctor In Your House™
http://www.adoctorinyourhouse.com/index.html

American Academy of Cosmetic Surgery
http://www.cosmeticsurgery.org/

American Heart Association
http://www.americanheart.org/

American Psychological Association
http://www.apa.org/

CBS HealthWatch by Medscape
http://healthwatch.medscape.com/

Doctor's Guide To the Internet
http://www.docguide.com/

Global Medical Search Engine
http://www.allhealthnet.com/

Government Healthfinder
http://www.healthfinder.gov/

Health Central.com
http://www.healthcentral.com/home/home.cfm

Health Web
http://healthweb.org/

HealthScout Network
http://www.healthscout.com/

Health World Online
http://www.healthy.net/index.html

Internet Grateful Med and Medline®
http://igm.nlm.nih.gov/

Internet Mental Health
http://www.mentalhealth.com/main.html

Johns Hopkins Health Information
http://www.intelihealth.com/IH/ihtIH

Mayo Health Oasis (of the Mayo Clinic)
http://www.mayohealth.org

The Med Guide
http://www.themedguide.com/

Medical World Search
http://www.mwsearch.com/

Medem Health News and Medical Research
http://www.medem.com/

Medscape Psychiatry & Mental Health
http://www.medscape.com/Home/Topics/psychiatry/psychiatry.html

National Heart, Lung, and Blood Institute
http://www.nhlbi.nih.gov/

National Institutes of Health
http://www.nih.gov

National Institute of Mental Health Search Page
http://www.nimh.nih.gov/search/Search_Form.cfm

National Library of Medicine's LOCATORplus
http://www.nlm.nih.gov/locatorplus/

The NECI Scientific Literature Digital Library
http://researchindex.com/

The Nemours Foundation, KidsHealth.org
http://KidsHealth.org/index2.html

NetWellness
http://www.netwellness.org/

On Health
http://www.onhealth.com/ch1/index.asp

WebMD™ Health
http://my.webmd.com/index

Wellness on the Web
http://www.wellweb.com/

Your Health
http://www.yourhealth.com/

General Food and Nutrition Sites

American Dietetic Association
http://www.eatright.org

Center for Science in the Public Interest
http://www.cspinet.org/

International Food Information Council Foundation
http://ificinfo.health.org

Rating Guide to Nutrition Websites
http://navigator.tufts.edu/profess/cspi.html

Tufts University Nutrition Commentary
http://www.commentator.tufts.edu/

Tufts University Nutrition Navigator
http://navigator.tufts.edu

U.S. Food and Drug Administration
http://www.fda.gov/

Specific Weight-Control, Obesity and Eating-Disorders Sites

Activism and Size News
http://www.dimensionsmagazine.com/activism/

After the Diet™ Online
http://www.afterthediet.com/

American Obesity Association
http://www.obesity.org/

American Society of Bariatric Physicians
http://www.asbp.org/bariatrics/bariatrician.htm

Anorexia Nervosa and Related Eating Disorders, Inc. (ANRED)
http://www.anred.com/index.html

Ask NOAH About: Eating Disorders
http://www.noah.cuny.edu/wellconn/eatdisorders.html

Barbara's Obesity Meds and Research News
http://www.obesity-news.com/

British Weight Management Clinic
http://www.weymouthclinic.co.uk/

Clinical Psychology Resources
http://www.psychologie.uni-bonn.de/kap/links_20.htm

Color Therapy for Anorexia and Depression
http://www.positivehealth.com/permit/Articles/Light%20and%20Colour/demarco35.htm

Concerned Counseling, Eating Disorders Website
http://www.concernedcounseling.com/eatingdisorders/eatingdisordersindex.html

Diet Watch
http://www.dietwatch.com/index.asp?show=yes

Doctor's Guide to Obesity Information & Resources
http://www.pslgroup.com/OBESITY.HTM

Dr. Koop Fitness Center
http://www.drkoop.com/wellness/fitness/

Eating Disorders Resources (books, tapes, treatment facilities, organizations and more)
http://www.gurze.com/

Eating Disorders Shared Awareness
http://www.eating-disorder.com/

Healthy Weight Network
http://www.healthyweightnetwork.com/

HUGS International: The center for information and resources about nondieting
http://www.hugs.com/

International Journal of Obesity
http://www.stockton-press.co.uk/ijo/index.html

Journal of Psychotherapy Practice and Research
http://jppr.psychiatryonline.org/cgi/collection/eating_disorders

La Montagne Treatment Center
http://www.lamontagne.org/

Males and Eating Disorders
http://www.primenet.com/~danslos/males/home.html

Mayo Clinic: Weight Control—What Works and Why
http://www.mayohealth.org/mayo/9406/htm/main.htm

National Association to Advance Fat Acceptance
http://www.naafa.org/

The National Eating Disorder Information Centre (Canada)
http://www.nedic.on.ca/default.html

Nutrition Counseling Service
http://www.power-nutrition.com/

Place for Health, Nutrition, Wellness, Weight Loss
http://www.phys.com/

Radiance Magazine On-line
http://www.radiancemagazine.com/radiance_magazine.htm

The Renfrew Center
http://www.renfrew.org/index.html

Shape Up America!
http://www.shapeup.org/

The Science of Obesity and Weight Control
http://www.loop.com/~bkrentzman/

The Solution
http://www.weightsolution.com/

Southwest Bariatric Nutrition Center
http://www.weight-control.com/index.html

TOPS Club Inc.
http://www.cedarnet.org/tops/

Understanding Adult Obesity
http://www.niddk.nih.gov/health/nutrit/pubs/unders.htm

Understanding Eating Disorders
http://www.ndmda.org/eating.htm

Weight Loss Diet Tips and Diet Screensaver
http://www.ValuHealth.com/

Web Sites Exposing Health-Related Frauds

Better Business Bureau—Weight Loss Promotions
http://www.bosbbb.org/lit/0147.htm

FAT CITY Broadsheet: "All the News that's not fit to eat"
http://www.dietfraud.com/

Guide to Health Fraud, Quackery
http://www.quackwatch.com/

WHERE TO GO FOR HELP

National Organizations

The American Anorexia Bulimia Association (AABA)
(formerly the American Anorexia Nervosa Association)
165 W. 46 Street, Suite 1108
New York NY 10036
Phone: (212) 575-6200
Web: http://www.aabainc.org/home.html

AABA is a nonprofit organization dedicated to the prevention and treatment of eating disorders. Through education, advocacy and research, AABA serves as a national authority on eating disorders and related concerns. AABA promotes social attitudes that enhance healthy body image and works to overcome the idealization of thinness that contributes to disordered eating. AABA has chapters in Long Island, Westchester, New Jersey and Pennsylvania. (See Regional and State Organizations below.)

Anorexia Nervosa and Related Eating Disorders Inc. (ANRED)
P.O. Box 5102
Eugene OR 97405
Phone: (503) 344-1144
Web: http://anred.com/

ANRED is a nonprofit organization that provides information about anorexia nervosa, bulimia nervosa, binge-eating disorder, compulsive exercising and other less well-known food and weight disorders. Material includes details about recovery and prevention.

Center for Science in the Public Interest
1875 Connecticut Avenue NW, Suite 300
Washington DC 20009
Phone: (202) 332-9110
Fax: (202) 265-4954
http://www.cspinet.org/

The Center for Science in the Public Interest (CSPI) is a nonprofit education and advocacy organization that focuses on improving the safety and nutritional quality of our food supply and on reducing the carnage caused by alcoholic beverages. CSPI seeks to promote health through educating the public about nutrition and alcohol; it represents citizens' interests before legislative, regulatory and judicial bodies; and it works to ensure that advances in science are used for the public's good.

Council on Size and Weight Discrimination
P.O. Box 305
Mt. Marion NY 12456
Phone: (914) 679-1209

Eating Disorders Awareness and Prevention, Inc. (EDAP)
603 Stewart Street, Suite 803
Seattle WA 98101
Phone: (206) 382-3587
Fax: (206) 292-9890

Information and referral hotline: (800) 931-2237
Web: http://www.edap.org/
EDAP is a nonprofit organization dedicated to increasing the awareness and prevention of eating disorders through education and community activism. Founded in 1987, EDAP has grown to become one of our nation's largest nonprofit organizations dedicated solely to the prevention and awareness of eating disorders. EDAP is governed by a Board of Trustees composed of health care professionals and citizen leaders from across the country.

National Association to Advance Fat Acceptance (NAAFA)
(formerly the National Association to Aid Fat Americans Inc.)
P.O. Box 188620
Sacramento CA 95818
Phone: (916) 558-6880
Fax: (916) 558-6881
Web: http://www.naafa.org/
Founded in 1969, the National Association to Advance Fat Acceptance is a nonprofit human rights organization dedicated to improving the quality of life for fat people. NAAFA works to eliminate discrimination based on body size and provide fat people with the tools for self-empowerment through public education, advocacy and member support.

National Eating Disorders Organization (NEDO)
(formerly the National Anorexic Aid Society)
6655 South Yale Avenue
Tulsa OK 74136
Phone: (918) 481-4044
Fax: (918) 481-4076
Web: http://www.kidsource.com/nedo/index.html
NEDO was founded in 1977 by Patricia Howe Tilton to help people with eating disorders find support, education and treatment. In October 1995, NEDO became affiliated with Tulsa's Laureate Psychiatric Clinic and Hospital, a not-for-profit psychiatric comprehensive mental health care facility. NEDO's philosophy is that eating disorders are primarily multidimensional in development—developed and sustained by biological, social, psychological and familial factors.

Overeaters Anonymous
6075 Zenith Court NE
Rio Rancho NM 87124
Phone: (505) 891-2664
Web: http://www.overeaters.org/
Overeaters Anonymous is a fellowship of individuals who, through shared experience, strength and hope, are recovering from compulsive overeating. The OA recovery program is identical with that of Alcoholics Anonymous, using AA's 12 steps and 12 traditions.

TOPS®
4575 South Fifth Street
P.O. Box 07360
Milwaukee WI 53207-0360
Phone: (414) 482-4620
Web: http://www.tops.org/
TOPS® (Take Off Pounds Sensibly) is the popular name for TOPS Club, Inc., an international nonprofit weight-loss support group. TOPS provides members with information, motivation and fellowship in attaining and maintaining their physi-

cian-prescribed weight goals. TOPS has almost 275,000 members in 11,000 chapters in the United States, Canada and numerous other countries throughout the world. Membership includes women, men and children. The oldest major weight-control group, TOPS was founded in 1948 in Milwaukee by Esther S. Manz, a homemaker.

Weight Watchers International, Inc.
175 Crossways Park West
Woodbury NY 11797
Phone: (516) 390-1657
Fax: (516) 390-1632
Web: http://www.weight-watchers.com/
Weight Watchers maintains the global philosophy that healthful weight management involves a comprehensive program that includes a food plan, an activity plan and behavior modification, provided in an environment of group support.

Regional and State Organizations

MASSACHUSETTS

Massachusetts Eating Disorder Association, Inc. (MEDA)
92 Pearl Street
Newton MA 02458
Phone: (617) 558-1881
Web: http://www.medainc.org/
The Massachusetts Eating Disorder Association, Inc. was founded in 1994 by Executive Director Rebecca Manley to meet the need for services in the field of eating disorders. The agency consists of a professional staff of licensed clinicians, physicians, nutritionists, psychiatrists, master's level counselors and a support staff of volunteers and interns. MEDA is wholly dedicated to the prevention and treatment of eating disorders and serves as a support network and resource center for individuals recovering from a variety of eating disorders.

NEW JERSEY

NJ AA/BA
721 Executive Drive
Princeton, NJ 08540
Phone: (609) 252-0202
Fax (609) 252-0184
Information line: (800) 522-2230
NJ AA/BA sponsors a number of support groups throughout the state that meet on a regular basis.

NEW YORK

Eating Disorder Council of Long Island (EDCLI)
82-14 262nd Street
Floral Park NY 11004
Phone: (718) 962-2778
The EDCLI is a nonprofit organization devoted to prevention, education and support: prevention of eating disorders, education about eating disorders and support to sufferers of eating disorders, their families and their friends. The EDCLI runs several professionally led support groups in the Nassau County, Suffolk County and Queens County areas. There are no set fees to attend; donations are accepted. The EDCLI is an active local chapter of the American Anorexia Bulimia Association (see National Organizations).

PENNSYLVANIA

American Anorexia Bulimia Association
Pennsylvania Chapter
P.O. Box 68
Wyncote PA 19095-0068
Phone: (215) 221-1864
Offers information and referrals to therapists and support groups in Pennsylvania. Separate support group meetings are held for people with eating disorders and for family and friends. Both meetings are held on the same date and at the same time. All support group meetings are held at Children's Hospital of Philadelphia at 34th Street and Civic Center Boulevard.

Medical Resources

American Academy of Cosmetic Surgery
401 North Michigan Avenue
Chicago IL 60611-4267
Phone: (312) 527-6713
Fax: (312) 644-1815
Web: http://www.cosmeticsurgery.org/
The American Academy of Cosmetic Surgery brings together all medical specialties devoted to the dissemination of knowledge, technical skill and expertise in the practice of cosmetic surgery. Its goal is to ensure uniform excellence in the care of our patients.

American Board of Medical Specialties
1007 Church Street, Suite 404
Evanston IL 60201
Phone: (847) 491-9091 or (800) 776-2378
Fax: (847) 328-3596
Web: http://www.abms.org/
The American Board of Medical Specialties (ABMS) is the umbrella organization for the 24 approved medical specialty boards in the United States. Established in 1933, the ABMS serves to coordinate the activities of its member boards and to provide information to the public, the government, the profession and its members concerning issues involving specialization and certification in medicine.

American Dietetic Association
216 West Jackson Boulevard, Suite 800
Chicago IL 60606
Phone: (312) 899-0040
Web: http://www.eatright.org/
The American Dietetic Association is the world's largest organization of food and nutrition professionals. With nearly 70,000 members, ADA serves the public by promoting nutrition, health and well-being.

American Psychiatric Association
1400 K Street NW
Washington DC 20005
Phone: (202) 682-6000
Web: http://www.psych.org
The American Psychiatric Association is a medical specialty society recognized worldwide. Its 40,500 U.S. and international physicians specialize in the diagnosis and treatment of mental and emotional illnesses and substance-use disorders.

American Society for Bariatric Surgery
140 NW 75th Drive, Suite C
Gainesville FL 32607
Phone: (352) 331-4900
Fax: (352) 331-4975
Web: http://www.asbs.org/
Founded in 1983, the society offers educational and support programs for surgeons and allied health professionals. The purposes of the society are to advance the art and science of bariatric surgery by continued encouragement of its members to pursue investigations in both the clinic and the laboratory; to interchange ideas, information and experience pertaining to bariatric surgery; to promote guidelines for ethical patient selection and care; to develop educational programs for physicians, paramedical persons and lay people; and to promote outcome studies and quality assurance.

American Society of Bariatric Physicians
5600 South Quebec, Suite 109A
Englewood CO 80111
Phone: (303) 779-4833
Fax: (303) 779-4834
Web: http://www.asbp.org/
The American Society of Bariatric Physicians (ASBP) is a national professional medical society of more than 1,400 licensed physicians (doctors of medicine [M.D.] and osteopathy [D.O.]) who offer specialized programs in the medical treatment of obesity (bariatrics) and its associated conditions. Formed in 1950, ASBP has been instrumental in offering practical information that doctors can use in their bariatric practices and that members of the general public can use in locating a bariatric physician.

American Society of Plastic and Reconstructive Surgeons
444 E. Algonquin Road
Arlington Heights IL 60005
Phone: (847) 228-9900 or (800) 635-0635
Web: http://www.plasticsurgery.org/

Treatment Centers

ALABAMA

UAB Nutrition Clinic
University of Alabama Hospital
222 Webb Building
1675 University Boulevard
UAB Station
Birmingham AL 35294
(205) 934-5112

ARIZONA

Mirasol, Inc.
Arizona Center for Eating Disorder Recovery
5366 N. Camino de la Culebra
Tucson AZ 85735
(520) 615-9311
(888) 520-1700

Remuda Ranch
One East Apache
Wickenburg AZ 85390
(800) 445-1900

CALIFORNIA

Behavioral Medicine Clinic
Department of Psychiatry—Behavioral Medicine
Stanford University Medical Center
Stanford CA 94305
(650) 723-6811

Eating Disorders Resource and Referral Service
P.O. Box 34524
San Diego CA 92103
(619) 236-0300

Oak Knoll Family Therapy Center
12307 Oak Knoll Road
Poway CA 92064
(619) 748-4323

Physicians' Weight Reduction Centers
14104 Magnolia Boulevard
Sherman Oaks CA 91423
(818) 501-3881

The Radar Programs
12099 Washington Boulevard, Suite 204
Los Angeles CA 90066
(800) 841-1515

CONNECTICUT

ANAD of Connecticut Self-Help Group
Wheeler Clinic
91 Northwest Drive
Plainville CT 06062
(860) 793-3500

Wilkins Center for Eating Disorders
#7 Riversville Road
Greenwich CT 06831
(203) 531-1909

FLORIDA

ERE Association
7325 SW 63 Avenue, Suite 101
South Miami FL 33143
(305) 284-1143

The Renfrew Center of South Florida
7700 Renfrew Lane
Coconut Creek FL 33073
(954) 698-9007

Willough at Naples
9001 Tamiami Trail East
Naples FL 34113
(941) 775-4500
(800) 722-0100

ILLINOIS

Eating Disorders Program
Northwestern Memorial Hospital
250 E. Superior Street
Chicago IL 60611
(312) 908-2000

KANSAS

Eating Disorders Program
The Menninger Clinic
5800 SW 6th Street
Topeka KS 66601
(785) 350-5000
(800) 288-0317

MASSACHUSETTS

Adolescent Clinic
Children's Hospital
300 Longwood Avenue, Suite 325
Boston MA 02115
(617) 355-6000

Behavior Therapy Unit
McLean Hospital
115 Mill Street
Belmont MA 02178
(617) 855-2500 ext. 2994

Eating Disorders Unit
Massachusetts General Hospital
55 Fruit Street
Boston MA 02114
(617) 726-2000

Kingsmont Camp
Box 100
West Stockbridge MA 01266
(914) 777-3705

MICHIGAN

Eating Disorders Support Group
Orchard Hills Psychiatric Center
42450 West Twelve-Mile Road #305
Novi MI 48377
(248) 349-7337

MINNESOTA

Department of Psychiatry
University of Minnesota Hospital and Clinic
Harvard Street at East River Road
Minneapolis MN 55455
(612) 626-6188

Psychiatry Department
Mayo Clinic
Baldwin Building, 4th Floor
200 First Street SW
Rochester MN 55905
(507) 284-2933

MISSOURI

La Montagne
P.O. Box 300
Crystal City MO 63019
(636) 931-3883

NEW JERSEY

Weight Watchers Center
49 Midland Avenue
Paramus NJ

NEW YORK

Camp Camelot for Girls
949 Northfield Road
Woodmere NY 11598
(516) 374-1366

Center for the Study of Anorexia and Bulimia
1 West 91st Street #1
New York NY 10024
(212) 595-3449

Four Winds Hospital
800 Cross River Road
Katonah NY 10536
(914) 763-8151

The Fredda Kray Weight Wayside Cottage
1039 Post Road
Scarsdale NY 10583
(914) 723-2997

Pediatrics Department
Mt. Sinai Medical Center
One Gustave L. Levy Place
New York NY 10029
(212) 423-0900

Schneider Children's Hospital
26901 76th Avenue #158
New Hyde Park NY 11040
(718) 470-3000

Weight Watchers Center
115 Rockland Center
Nanuet NY 10954
(800) 221-2112

Weight Watchers Center
Cross County Mall
6M Upper Mall Walk
Yonkers NY 10704
(800) 221-2112

OHIO

North Community Counseling—The Bridge
4897 Karl Road
Columbus OH 43229
(614) 846-2588

Section of Child and Adolescent Psychiatry
Cleveland Clinic Hospital
9500 Euclid Avenue
Cleveland OH 44195
(216) 444-2200

PENNSYLVANIA

AABA of Philadelphia
Philadelphia Child Guidance Clinic
34th and Civic Center Boulevard
Philadelphia PA 19104
(215) 590-1000

Eating Disorder Unit (COPE)
Western Psychiatric Institute and Clinic
3811 O'Hara Street
Pittsburgh PA 15213
(412) 624-2100

Juvenile Weight Control Program
Hahnemann University Hospital
Broad & Vine Streets
Philadelphia PA 19102
(215) 762-7000

Prader-Willi Clinic
Rehabilitation Institute of Pittsburgh
6301 Northumberland Street
Pittsburgh PA 15217
(412) 521-9000

The Renfrew Center
475 Spring Lane
Philadelphia PA 19128
(215) 482-5353

TEXAS

Department of Psychiatry
Baylor College of Medicine
Houston Medical Center
1200 Moursund Avenue
Houston TX 77030
(713) 798-4856

WASHINGTON

Prader-Willi Clinic
Center on Human Development & Disability
Mail Drop WJ-10
University of Washington
Seattle WA 98195
(206) 685-1242

BIBLIOGRAPHY

Andersen, Arnold E. *Males With Eating Disorders.* New York: Brunner/Mazel, 1990.

Andersen, Arnold E., Leigh Cohn, and Thomas Holbrook. *Making Weight: Healing Men's Conflicts With Food, Weight and Shape.* Carlsbad, Calif.: Gürze Books, 1999.

Berg, Frances M. *Afraid To Eat: Children and Teens in Weight Crisis.* Hettinger, N.D.: Healthy Weight Journal, 1997.

Bode, Janet. *Food Fight: A Guide to Eating Disorders for Preteens and Their Parents.* New York: Simon & Schuster, 1997. (Paperback edition, New York: Aladdin Paperbacks; 1998.)

Bordo, Susan. *Unbearable Weight: Feminism, Western Culture and the Body.* Berkeley, Calif.: University of California Press, 1995.

Brownell, Kelly D., and Christopher G. Fairburn, eds. *Eating Disorders and Obesity: A Comprehensive Handbook.* New York: Guilford Press, 1995.

Brownell, Kelly D., and John Foreyt. *Handbook of Eating Disorders: Physiology, Psychology, and Treatment of Obesity, Anorexia, and Bulimia.* New York: Basic Books, 1986.

Bruch, Hilde. *Eating Disorders: Obesity, Anorexia Nervosa, and the Person Within.* New York: Basic Books, 1985.

———. *The Golden Cage: The Enigma of Anorexia Nervosa.* New York: Random House, 1979.

Brumberg, Joan Jacob. *Fasting Girls: The Emergence of Anorexia Nervosa as a Modern Disease.* New York: Plume Books, 1989.

Cash, Thomas F. *Body Image Workbook: An 8-Step Program for Learning to Like Your Looks.* Oakland: New Harbinger Publications, 1997.

Ciliska, Donna. *Beyond Dieting: Psychoeducational Interventions for Chronically Obese Women: A Non-Dieting Approach.* New York: Brunner/Mazel, 1990.

Cohen, Mary Anne. *French Toast for Breakfast. Declaring Peace with Emotional Eating.* Carlsbad, Calif.: Gürze Books, 1995.

Cooke, Kaz. *Real Gorgeous: The Truth About Body and Beauty.* New York: W.W. Norton & Co., 1996.

Costin, Carolyn. *The Eating Disorder Sourcebook: A Comprehensive Guide to the Causes, Treatments and Prevention of Eating Disorders, 2nd Edition.* Los Angeles: Lowell House, 1999.

D'Amico, Peter. *Eat Right For Your Type.* New York: Putnam Publishing Group, 1997.

Fairburn, Christopher. *Overcoming Binge Eating.* New York: Guilford Press, 1995.

Fraser, Laura. *Losing It: America's Obsession With Weight and the Industry that Feeds on It.* New York: Dutton Books, 1997.

Hall, Lindsey. *Full Lives: Women Who Have Freed Themselves from Food & Weight Obsession.* Carlsbad, Calif.: Gürze Books, 1993.

Hall, Lindsey, and Leigh Cohen. *Bulimia: A Guide to Recovery,* 5th Edition. Carlsbad, Calif.: Gürze Books, 1999.

Hays, Kate F. *Working It Out: Using Exercise in Psychotherapy.* Washington, D.C.: American Psychological Association, 1999.

Kano, Susan. *Making Peace With Food.* New York: HarperCollins, 1989.

Kinoy, Barbara. *Eating Disorders: New Directions in Treatment and Recovery.* New York:

Columbia University Press, 1994.

Lemberg, Peter, ed. *Controlling Eating Disorders with Facts, Advice, and Resources.* Phoenix: Oryx Press, 1992.

Macht, Joel. *Poor Eaters: Helping Children Who Refuse to Eat.* New York: Plenum Press, 1990.

Maine, Margo. *Father Hunger: Fathers, Daughters and Food.* Carlsbad, Calif.: Gürze Books, 1991.

McFarland, Barbara. *Brief Therapy and Eating Disorders: A Practical Guide to Solution-Focused Work With Clients.* San Francisco: Jossey-Bass Publishers, 1995.

Medoff, Jillian. *Hunger Point: A Novel.* New York: Harper Mass Market Paperbacks, 1998.

Mellin, Laurel. *The Solution: Never Diet Again.* New York: Regan Books, 1998.

Montignac, Michel. *Eat Yourself Slim.* Frederick, Md.: Erica House Book Publishers, 1999.

Pipher, Mary. *Hunger Pains: The Modern Woman's Tragic Quest for Thinness.* New York: Ballantine Books, 1997.

Satter, Ellyn. *How to Get Your Kid to Eat, but Not Too Much.* Menlo Park, Calif.: Bull Publishing Co., 1987.

———. *Child of Mine: Feeding With Love and Good Sense,* Menlo Park, Calif.: Bull Publishing Co., 1991.

Schwartz, Mark F., and Leigh Cohn. (Editors). *Sexual Abuse and Eating Disorders.* New York: Brunner/Mazel, 1996.

Siegel, Michelle, Judith Brisman, and Margot Weinshel. *Surviving an Eating Disorder: New Perspectives and Strategies for Family and Friends.* New York: HarperCollins, 1997.

Thompson, Becky. *A Hunger so Wide and so Deep.* Minneapolis: University of Minnesota Press, 1996.

Thompson, Ron A., and Roberta Trattner Sherman. *Helping Athletes With Eating Disorders.* Champaign, Ill.: Human Kinetics Publishing, 1993.

Vandereycken, Walter, ed., and Greta Noordenbos. *The Prevention of Eating Disorders (Studies in Eating Disorders: An International Series).* New York: New York University Press, 1998.

Waterhouse, Debra. *Like Mother, Like Daughter: How Women Are Influenced by Their Mother's Relationship With Food—And How to Break the Pattern.* New York: Hyperion, 1998.

Werne, Joellen. *Treating Eating Disorders.* San Francisco: Jossey-Bass Publishers, 1996.

Wiseman, Nigel, and Feng Ye. *A Practical Dictionary of Chinese Medicine.* Brookline, Mass.: Paradigm Publications, 1998.

Zahang, Yu Huan and Ken Rose. *Who Can Ride the Dragon? An Exploration of the Cultural Roots of Traditional Chinese Medicine.* Brookline, Mass.: Paradigm Publications, 1999.

Zerbe, Kathryn J. *The Body Betrayed: A Deeper Understanding of Women, Eating Disorders, and Treatment.* Carlsbad, Calif.: Gürzě Books, 1995.

INDEX

F

G

R